Doers & Dowagers

Felicia Warburg Roosevelt

Doers &
Dowagers

Doubleday & Company, Inc.
Garden City, New York
1975

Library of Congress Cataloging in Publication Data

Roosevelt, Felicia Warburg.
  Doers & dowagers.

  1. Women—United States—Biography. I. Title.
CT3260.R58   920.72
ISBN 0-385-06527-2
Library of Congress Catalog Card Number 74-12708

For my family, past and present
With love

Preface

IN AN ERA when speed and mechanization have almost ploughed
human beings under, the young woman of today is often torn
between tradition and self-liberation, unlike the woman of three
generations ago.

American women in the 1970s share much in common besides
their sexuality. Among the so-called leisure classes, the lack of
individual initiative and serious integrity is a threat to our marriages and our family dedication. The old adages—"the ties that
bind," "till death do us part"—are simply not valid any more.
Being a "square," a "conservative" or a "traditionalist" is buck-
ing a woman's movement that not only strips us of our feminin-
ity but also of our female roles. A liberated woman's place may
not always be to stay at home but it certainly is to make one; and
if marriage is to survive at all, the successful partnerships, I think,
are those where the woman is inwardly independent yet subtly
dependent.

All of the women I have chosen have lived through at least
seven decades, and represent, some more, some less, the strengths
and purposefulness of which the females of succeeding generations can take note.

Both of my grandmothers inspired me to turn to this generation of seasoned ladies who have traveled the route of experience.
Buffeted by the whole gamut of human emotions, the surge of
progress, and now from the vantage point of age, they lure us
to follow them. Rich or poor, they have achieved. They have
given and shared with strangers and family, and each story is
quite unique, quite special. They have all learned—and most not
from books, but by living—what their own limits are and what

now makes them emotionally comfortable. Tolerance and love
stoke their existence and reach to their and our youth.

I know the words that have so recently fallen out of use—respect, esteem; I know that they are not just words but principles
and guidelines to give our lives a framework. Tradition and
family *esprit* I know personally. They can sustain you in moments of crisis more than medicine and the escape tools of liquor
and drugs. The elders will tell you, these doers and dowagers,
for they have made their own way and survived. Dignity suits
them, and if I were to aspire to any state of being in my future
years, it would be to emulate this admirable quality. For these
women have ridden the roller coaster of decades. Of the twenty
women, one died during the writing of this book, fourteen are
widows, three are divorced, and two are still married. Five have
been married more than twice, and all but two have borne children. Mrs. Luce, Mrs. Buckley, Mrs. Kennedy, Mrs. Post, Mrs.
Hull, and Mrs. Roth, through their husbands, have enjoyed the
benefits of great wealth. So, although they are women, they are
quite a disparate group.

Why I chose these particular women is a question I will have
to answer. Obviously there are thousands of others, some well-
known, others much less so. The list is admittedly incomplete
and I do not make any pretenses in drawing conclusions from
these women's lives. My selection is strictly personal, selfish perhaps, in that all of the ladies personify, in a small measure, qualities that I particularly admire. How they have handled segments
of their lives were questions I enjoyed asking of them, and I was
well rewarded by their answers.

For twenty-six years I have piloted my own course, free from
parental decision. I have only a few more years than that before
I will reach seventy, and with good health perhaps I will live
longer than that.

What can I do in the ensuing years to be as vital and as interesting as the women on these pages are? is a question I ask myself. Perhaps, too, other women will be stimulated by these life
stories and realize that the rich years of a woman's life can continue far into her eighties and nineties. We all, as in a recipe, have
the ingredients within us to personalize the final product, to em-
phasize, as with herbs, key qualities in ourselves. How we choose

to put them all together and in what direction we tend to strive give us our individuality. But whether we are ambitious enough to achieve in self-appointed careers and can manage the complicated roles of wife and mother, we have accepted responsibility. What life seems to require of us is to be mature enough to deal with the emotional blows without being felled by them and to be able to answer to ourselves. Being women, circumstances have forced us at different times in our lives to cope without the benefit of male counsel. It seems to me that my generation of women was brought up, inaccurately, to believe that marriage was a romantic and idealistic state that eligible females over twenty-one entered into as a natural adjunct to graduating from college, and, like ice cream and cake, you and your intended rode into the sunset with nary a backward glance.

Unfortunately, I, as well as many of my contemporaries, both male and female, were unrealistic in their selections and immature, and "in air" attitudes and marriages began failing with the advent of the first argument. Maturity came upon us after the divorce, not as it should have, before the wedding.

Having benefited from spending many hours with these older women, I wonder now whether in many ways they haven't enjoyed greater fulfillment as women living in a society of stricter mores, accepting the roles their husbands dealt them. True, the matriarchs and dowagers have all come into their own as people after their husband's death. But not one complained that they resented what young women of today would consider an inequitable relationship where the male is dominant.

My purpose in playing back the lives of a few special American women over seventy was to look for clues that might give younger women insight into their own lives. These pages indicate only my impressions of twenty women who have left their mark. They all seem to have emerged with individual strength and dedication. Their energies are perhaps even more vital today, possibly because they have been through yesterday and have sorted out their priorities. These priorities may not be yours or mine, but they have elements of fundamental truths. In my own living museum, each of these women is a special treasure.

Contents

Dowagers

"Dowager," by definition, implies a woman who has inherited money from her husband. The word also has come to mean a woman of certain social standing who has achieved because of age, position and status among her peers. It is this connotation I allude to in the following chapters, for certainly money alone cannot buy the prestige of these elders.

Mrs. Tucker, Mrs. Post, Mrs. Sibley and Mrs. Roth are products of eminently successful fathers. Mrs. Hull and Mrs. Woodward were born into Society and made fortuitous marriages among their own set, and as widows of wealthy husbands they are well-endowed. In the 1900s each of these women was part of America's aristocracy. They were raised and groomed by their parents under a set of standards that seems obsolete to us today. Education was far less important to Society families than the postured and traditional rounds of debuts and parties; manners, charm and dancing ability helped to land a husband who could hopefully perpetuate class and blood lines.

Of the six women, Mrs. Tucker and Mrs. Roth, from already well-known families, brought husbands of lesser social background into their own charmed circle. Mrs. Post married three out of four socially acceptable husbands, as did Mrs. Hull with both her husbands, Vincent Astor and Lytle Hull. Mrs. Sibley did not have to go far afield to find her spouse.

All in their eighties (Mrs. Post, now deceased, was eighty-six), these monarchs of yesteryear are feminine thoroughbreds. Brought up only to be wives and mothers, they are particularly remarkable to me because they played their expected roles while their husbands were alive. It was only as widows that they fulfilled themselves in completely new lives. Mrs. Sibley continues, with seemingly more zest and energy, to carry on the interests she and her husband worked on together. Rochester, New York, has its lilacs and Mrs. Sibley to be ever proud of.

All majestic women who rose above the restrictions of their times and the narrow-minded views of their families, they have survived eight decades and have found satisfaction and inner peace.

Mrs. Marjorie Post

I WAS UNABLE to see Mrs. Post at the time I wrote this book, since she was confined to her bed in Palm Beach because of illness which brought about her death, in the fall of 1973, at the age of eighty-six. However, members of her family were helpful to me in piecing together the highlights of the remarkable life of a *grande dame*.

Marjorie Post personified, because of her grandiose life style and social position, the true dowager. In fact, if America ever had a respected Queen of Society, Mrs. Post would have won the title handily, although she made it on her own with a great sense of determination.

In Springfield, Illinois, where Marjorie is reputed to have been born in 1888 to Ella and Charles Post, there was no hint of the kind of prosperity the family would enjoy, nor the success Marjorie would enjoy as a member of High Society.

Her father, C. W. Post, was an itinerant farm-tool salesman born in Fort Worth, Texas, in 1855. Known as Charlie to his family in the early days, as fame caught up with him intimates referred to him as C.W. To support his wife and daughter, Post spent many months a year on the road selling tools. It was a rough life of one-night stands and poor eating, and he constantly complained of digestive trouble. He had also suffered nervous breakdowns. In 1892, when he was thirty-seven and Marjorie was four, he decided to seek a cure for his illness, and he took his daughter and wife to Battle Creek Clinic in Michigan. He had heard of the famous sanitarium there run by Dr. John Harvey Kellogg and his brother, W. K. Kellogg, and arriving penniless and in poor health, he hoped to be cured by treatment at this health center.

He immediately got a job working in the kitchen of the center, and in exchange for the employment he was allowed to eat the health foods for nothing. At the end of four months he had $69.75 in his pocket. But he had a dream which he confided to his wife and Marjorie.

If Dr. Kellogg could make a powdered drink and sell it with great success to his patients, why couldn't Post adapt the same idea and sell it under his own name. The idea intrigued him, so he bought a grinder and some wheat and, with a mixture of glutenous bran, roasted wheatberries and New Orleans molasses, invented a satisfactory substitute for pure coffee, which he could never drink. He called it Postum.

The year was 1895 and Marjorie went to public school in the afternoons in Battle Creek; but to help her father, from the age of eight on, she licked labels for his packages of Postum, and together they would walk all over Battle Creek with brown paper sacks begging store owners to sell Postum on consignment at fifteen cents a package. In two years, Post sold five thousand dollars' worth of Postum. In short order, he marketed Grapenuts and Post Toasties, and much later these products became part of the giant General Foods Corporation.

C. W. Post became a millionaire at the age of forty-four. He obviously made a strong impression on his only child and Marjorie admired the traits that brought him success. He was a perfectionist, and his advertising slogan, "There's a reason," emphasized his logical business type of mind. But he always found time in Battle Creek, and later in Fort Worth, to take Marjorie with him to visit factories of competitors of Postum, and he tried to teach her about the business end of the company. He taught her how to hunt and trap moles and skin them and how to shoot and clean game. He, more than her mother, paid a great deal of attention to her grooming and was always reminding her to stand erect and cultivate personal charm.

Having made a success in Battle Creek, Post dreamed of buying land in his native Texas. In the early 1900s, Marjorie traveled with her father and mother by train to Wichita Falls, and then by horsedrawn wagon and mule team to Fort Worth. It was a long and arduous trip, but well worth the rigors, for outside of Colorado City, near the Texas panhandle, they visited a ranch called "Curry Comb," comprising 112,000 acres. Post bought the ranch, and a few weeks later he bought 50,000 adjoining acres. The cost was $6,000. Before the year was out, he bought three more ranches, bringing his total holdings up to 250,000 acres. In 1907 he built Post City and set up an entire farming, business, and residential community. Unfortunately, the oil that he dreamed might be on his land was only discovered after his death. But some of the land and about 30,000 producing wells and refineries comprise part of the wealth that Marjorie inherited.

Of her teen-age years little is known and the story is sketchy. At some point she lived in Washington, D.C., and went to Mount Vernon Seminary. While there, her father and mother's marriage broke up. Marjorie's mother did not care to keep up with the pace of C. W. Post's expanding career, so they were divorced in 1903. On November 7, 1904, Marjorie's father married Lelia Yang, who had worked for him in a secretarial capacity. Marjorie was never fond of her stepmother, but her affection for her father never dimmed, nor did Post's remarriage change his feelings about his only daughter. They remained in close touch for the next ten years.

The facts about Marjorie Post's life are documented from 1905 on. She met Edward Close, an eligible bachelor, and they fell in love. To Old Society in New York, Marjorie Post was *nouveau riche* and certainly not readily acceptable to the Old Guard to whom Edward Close's family belonged. Marjorie certainly had money and personal charm, but no lengthy pedigree which could identify her forebears. There is a story told that on the day of the wedding rehearsal, as Marjorie took a practice walk down the church aisle, she overheard some friends of her fiancé turn to each other and comment on the fact that she was just a simple western girl with no background. From that moment on, Marjorie vowed that someday people like that would eat their words, and she decided to dedicate herself to achieving the social acceptance she felt had been denied her.

She married Edward Bennett Close at the Grace Episcopal Church in New York in 1905, and thus began the first of four marriages and her introduction into Society, with a large financial boost from her ever-loving father who, typically, wrote her a letter which was delivered on the train that carried her and her husband on their honeymoon.

DEAR LITTLE SWEETHEART:

Well, the small toddler who has been over the road so long with Daddy is now a grown woman. It naturally brings a tinge of sadness to realize that the little girl of the past with whom I had so many good times has faded into the past, but I am more than comforted with the splendid young woman. Daddy feels well repaid for every effort he has made for you, my sweet daughter, and now I feel very sure you are going to be happily married and I find myself liking Ed as I would a boy of my own. Always remember that Daddy is somewhere around on call and that he loves you always, my sweet daughter.

Yours,
DADDY[1]

Mr. Post gave Marjorie a very generous wedding present: an enormous house called "The Boulders" in Greenwich, Connecticut, with extensive grounds, the first of many houses she was to live in. Marjorie helped with the landscaping, planning and decorating, but it was her father, more than her husband, who undertook to see that it came up to his high standards. He assigned a housekeeper to her for the first six months of her marriage, and she had to manage the staff, inside and out, which he had selected. For the first year, he insisted that she keep careful accounts, run the staff and show him her accounting at the end of the year. When she gave the figures to her father, she was off six cents. To her great shock, he made her go over the books until she located the mistake and the balance was correct. A suite of rooms was even kept for him at "The Boulders," which he could use whenever he chose. He was always in touch with his daughter, giving fatherly advice on financial matters and admonishing her about wasting money.

"Do not have the men haul away these extra rocks until you make up your mind where to put them, hauling them around

[1] Reprint from C. W. Post, the Hour and the Man by Nettie Leitch Major.

more than once can be an expensive proposition and a complete waste of money."

He also had a few stern words about her riding sidesaddle. "Fashionable or not, no daughter of mine can ride sidesaddle and endanger her neck. There is only one way to ride a horse and that is astride in the western fashion where you can be in command of your position and horse, and that is the final word I intend to say on that subject."

Ed Close enlisted in World War I and Marjorie charitably gave two thousand beds to a hospital in Savenay, France. She did Red Cross work, brought up her two daughters, Eleanor and Adelaide, and even joined a delegation to Washington in 1917 to discuss woman suffrage with Woodrow Wilson. Still at "The Boulders," she found commuting to New York to visit the Post plant difficult, so she took an apartment at 373 Park Avenue. It turned out to be not big enough, so in 1915 the Closes bought the Burden House at 2 East Ninety-second Street.

When her father died in 1914, after a nervous breakdown, Marjorie Post, at the age of twenty-six, became the owner of the Postum Cereal Company. Although she had been trained to understand the business, she had no real interest in running it, and upon her divorce in 1919 from Ed Close, she married Edward F. Hutton of the brokerage firm of E. F. Hutton & Company, New York. Hutton, a businessman like her father, took a leave of absence from his company and became Chairman of the Board of Postum Cereal Company in 1923. Marjorie was entering phase two of her marital career. Hutton was an able businessman of the American elite. While he worked, she began to acquire collections and possessions.

In December 1923, a daughter, Nedenia, was born to the Huttons. It was in the twenties that the Huttons spread their wings socially and began acquiring the symbols that wealth makes possible. A shooting preserve in South Carolina, a country house in Roslyn, Long Island, a camp in the Adirondacks, a winter home in Palm Beach and quite a few large yachts: first, a powerboat named *Lady Baltimore;* then the *Huzzar*, a bigger boat; then the three-masted schooner *Huzzar IV;* and finally the *Huzzar V*, which took five years to build in Kiel, Germany. *Huzzar V*—with six staterooms, each with electric fireplaces,

Louis XVI mantelpieces, and Lowestoft and Dresden porcelains cemented to the tables—could accommodate four hundred guests.

During this period the Postum Cereal Company, Ltd., began acquiring a number of well-known brand names—Jell-O, Swan's Down Cake Flour, Minute Tapioca, Log Cabin Syrup, Walter Baker's Chocolate, Maxwell House Coffee, Calumet Baking Powder, Hellmann's Mayonnaise. In 1929, with the acquisition of Frosted Foods and its equipment and patents held by Clarence Birdseye, a new company was formed called General Foods Corporation.

Marjorie, with the help of Lord Duveen, began her art collection during World War I. She and her husband sold the Ninety-second Street house property to a realtor who erected a large apartment building, and they maintained elegant quarters in it. There was a separate entrance for the Huttons maintained by a special doorman, and a private elevator which took the family straight up to their apartment on the fourteenth floor. There was a ballroom, a garden, and a playroom on the roof for Adelaide and Eleanor Close to entertain their friends in. The first Palm Beach property, called "Hogarcite," proved too small for the growing family, so Marjorie bought some property and spent four years building her now famous Mar-A-Lago, which upon her death was to be given to the United States Government as a winter White House. She retained life tenancy. It is valued for taxes at $4,291,584. Mrs. Post has set up funds for its future maintenance. The house was built by Marion Wyeth in 1927, and a Viennese architect was commissioned to do the inner decor and stone designs. A Viennese sculptor, Franz Barwig, did the façades, stone carvings and some interiors. The style is Hispano-Moresque with upper and lower cloisters. The house is made up of many suites, each beautifully appointed, one Venetian, another Portuguese; Mrs. Post's suite is in the period of Louis XIV. For many years, Mrs. Post enjoyed the *Huzzar V*, but after her divorce from Hutton in 1935, she wanted to change the name because of its close association with her ex-husband, so she rechristened it *Sea Cloud*. During World War II she gave it to the U. S. Government to use for the duration, at a cost of a dollar a year. The ship was returned to Mrs. Post after the war, but it had to be entirely rerigged and furnished, since it had been used as a fighting ship. It was the largest privately owned clipper ship and it has since been sold. Even during the Depression years it was maintained by Mrs. Post so as not to put any more people out of work. Never actively engaging in charity work as such, Mrs. Post instead gave money to establish food kitchens in New York, operated by the Salvation Army, from 1929–35. Because of economic conditions, she felt strongly that all people in her employ be kept on so as to assure them jobs in the Depression years.

After she divorced Hutton, she married an adviser to President Roosevelt, the Honorable Joseph Davies, who left his wife for her. It was at this period that Marjorie became a member of the International Set. She had given a substantial amount of money to Roosevelt's campaign, and as a result Davies was named Ambassador to Russia. It was here that Marjorie's entertainment skills were brought to the fore. She loved the role of Ambassadress, even to the point of refurbishing the U. S. Embassy in Moscow to her own taste and adding extravagant touches to the dull Russian food, like sending to Belgium for endive and lettuce, and to Poland and Finland for fresh vegetables and fruit. It was here, too, that Mrs. Davies began acquiring a rare collection of Russian *objets d'art* which would later be sent to her house in Washington. From Russia, the Davieses were sent to Belgium after three years in Moscow, but they soon returned to Washington, since a government order stipulated that no embassy family could return to European assignments (World War II).

The last piece of property Marjorie Merriweather Post bought was in Washington, D.C., near Rock Creek Park. There she built her famous Hillwood mansion. It was meant to be home for the Davieses, but they were divorced in 1957, and in 1958 she married a Pittsburgh industrialist, Herbert A. May. Hillwood housed her famous collection. Since her death the house has become part of the Smithsonian Institution. It is a veritable museum and a great tribute to her taste and discrimination. The Louis XVI drawing room exhibits the finest examples of furniture and porcelain of that period. On one wall is the famous portrait of Empress Eugénie by Winterhalter. Sèvres service in *doré vitrines* flank the fireplace. The sofas and chairs are done in tapestry from the Gobelin looms. The wall tapestries are Beauvais from designs of François Boucher, a Savonnerie rug, large *Famille Rose* urns and lapis lazuli insets in the table are but some of the valuable *objets d'art* collected from all over Europe. The entire suite was made for Louis XVI and Marie Antoinette as a gift for Prince Henry of Prussia. There are formal French gardens, pools and a Japanese rock garden.

Mrs. May was quietly divorced from her fourth husband, leaving one to ponder why a woman who seemingly had everything that wealth and society can provide was never happily married. Edward Hutton perhaps came closest to her expectation of a husband, perhaps because he had many of the intellectual qualities coupled with business acumen that Marjorie so admired in her father. Whatever the reasons for her marriage failures, she attained the personal success she had for years sought to achieve, and Society claimed her as their own.

Always an elegant and statuesque woman, *soignée* Mrs. Post was meticulous to the end in her personal grooming, carrying out the early teachings of her father. She always wore white gloves and was often glimpsed swimming with these, plus a complete bathing costume and white socks. No curl in her hair was ever out of place; detail and order were determinedly carried out. When it was time to leave the Palm Beach house for another of her residences, the furniture was carefully covered and each object was assigned a number corresponding to the antique table it sat on, so that when Mrs. Post was ready to return the following winter the staff knew just where all the treasures belonged.

She also took great pride in setting a beautiful table. Before every lunch and dinner she would decide on a different color scheme, and then from her enormous collection of crystal, glassware, porcelain service and linen, she would create an artistic setting according to her mood. The food, worthy of the finest restaurants, was an extra fillip.

Mrs. Post enjoyed her houses. They were not merely possessions to be filled with expensive bibelots. Each residence was the scene of family get-togethers and dances, a form of entertainment the hostess preferred, since she herself was very fond of every form of dance. The most graceful of waltzers, the most enthusiastic of square dancers, she mixed all ages at her gay parties.

For a complete change of scene, away from the Palm Beach "swells," the balls and the constant resort entertaining, Mrs. Post preferred the casual life at the camp she bought in 1921 on Upper St. Regis Lake in the Adirondacks. The word "camp" implies rural, simple living. Certainly it lacked the formal framework of her other estates, but by most standards, with its large staff and great comforts, it was an idealized version of backwoods living.

Her children and grandchildren preferred the more natural setting of Mrs. Post's "camp," where they could wear informal attire and enjoy sports on the lake.

Arriving at camp by Mrs. Post's motorboat, guests and family would get off on the shore and reach the main building by means of an escalator which rose eighty feet to the front door. The large living room was filled with American handicrafts, and animal skins covered the floor. Scattered here and there were wooden cigar-store Indians. The dining-room walls were covered in New York State's native birch bark. All the rooms had huge fireplaces, and the outbuildings comprised numerous guest cabins all complete unto themselves with bathrooms, sitting rooms, bedrooms and screened porches. A variety of activities lured the more athletic types and the younger children: water skiing, swimming and boating, fishing, and nearby, golf. In the evenings Mrs. Post had a projection room where she would show first-run movies, and the living room was the scene of regularly scheduled informal dances.

Mrs. Post's luxurious life style and vast expenditures, unequaled almost anywhere, suggest a frivolous, luxury-loving woman. True, she lived in the grand style and certainly one that few people then or now could afford. But she also was a generous and thoughtful woman.

For her lifelong contributions to the Boy Scouts she was given a special pin. She originated Music for Young America, a project sponsored by the National Symphony Orchestra. These were free concerts underwritten by Mrs. Post and given in Washington, D.C., every Easter vacation for children visiting the Capital from all over the country. Her first Hillwood estate, bought in the 1920s in Roslyn, Long Island, was given by her in 1954 to Long Island University and was renamed Post College as a memorial to her beloved father. She also commissioned a book to be written about him and chose the author, Nette Leitch Major, who wrote *C. W. Post, the Hour and the Man*. It was privately printed at Mrs. Post's expense for friends of the family.

Her two daughters by Edward Close, Adelaide and Eleanor, were both married three times and gave her a total of four grandchildren and eleven great-grandchildren. Adelaide Riggs enjoys the country life with dogs and horses and is a sportswoman. Her sister, Eleanor Barzin, is interested in the arts. Their half-sister, Nedenia (known as Deenie), whose father was Edward Hutton, has had two marriages. By her first husband she had two sons and a daughter. One son, David Rombaugh, was tragically killed at twenty-two in a motorboat accident, just three days before his grandmother died. Deenie has a young daughter, Heather, by her second husband, actor Cliff Robertson, and she herself, using the name Dina Merrill, has had a successful career as an actress on television and in the movies. It is hard to believe that such a beautiful woman, who loves tennis and golf and is a devoted mother, was brought up and remains completely natural and unspoiled, despite great wealth and the background in which she grew up. But she credits her mother, who in her wise ways was very strict and brooked no nonsense from her children, even after they were grown and married. Marjorie Post always maintained old-fashioned discipline, and Deenie told me that when she was visiting her mother a few winters ago in Palm Beach she was invited to a friend's house for dinner. Mrs. Post steadfastly refused to let her go alone, insisting that the butler accompany her across a narrow street because it was dark.

There are few women of our era who have lived the glamorous life as fully as Mrs. Post. Owner of her own clipper ship, private railroad car and plane (called *The Merriweather*), she led totally different lives with four husbands and emerged as a proud figurehead, spending millions of her vast fortune which, as a child, she could never have dreamed possible. Society fully accepted Marjorie Post, who yearned sixty years before to be part of the elite. But somehow even the greatest dowager, with enormous resources to dispense, never gave up what her father's greatest inheritance gave her, his strengths of logic and reasoning. These qualities, plus her father's imagination, saw her through her various careers and kept her mentally energetic and supremely organized. Marjorie Close Hutton Davies May was in the beginning as she wanted to be known at her death—Marjorie Merriweather Post.

Mrs. Lytle Hull

HELEN HUNTINGTON HULL is a thoroughbred pureblood who is as classical as the music she has loved since she was a child. At eighty-two, nothing for her has really changed. The gracious life, as a member of a social Hudson River family, is still hers, and the grand manner still persists. From childhood to a celebrated marriage to a man from her same background, albeit, abundantly wealthy, she was and is, despite several husbands later, often referred to as The Mrs. Astor. Now her proudest achievement and still abiding interest is as active Chairman of the Board of New York City's Musician's Emergency Fund, and because of this she is often called by friends and admirers the First Lady of Music. Her magnificent estate near Rhinebeck on the Hudson, where she has lived for so many years, is the scene where musicians, patricians and friends are entertained in a setting not easily forgotten. Not just because the hostess is a great lady and a perfectionist, but the ambiance of opulence in the physical setting overlooking the river is matched only by the splendor of the gloved staff and its dedication to serving you in a manner that hardly exists elsewhere today. The aristocratic life has almost vanished in America, but here on the shores of the Hudson Helen Hull has, and will continue for the rest of her life to draw, serenity from the graciousness of her style of life.

The property in Staatsburg, Dutchess County, was where Helen grew up. Here she lived with her mother and father and grandparents. The land had originally belonged to her great-grandparents on her mother's side. Mr. Huntington, Helen's father, was an architect, who worked in New York during the week and returned to the country on weekends. Her parents' relationship was similar to others of that generation.

"Mother adored Father and everything he said was perfect and everything he did was perfect. He really brought up me and my brother and sister very strictly," Helen said. The children never ate with their parents and, instead, with their governess had earlier meals in the dining room. Only when they were sixteen did their father allow them to have dinner with him and his wife, the former Helen Dinsmore. (Her bearing, her perfectly tailored clothes, her beautifully coiffed gray hair with two little bows, bear to this day a classical stamp.)

The Huntingtons were Society, and Helen says that Society then meant knowing the "so-called Right People." It had nothing to do with having money. People in Society knew who people's parents were and where they came from, and the group was insulated from the realities of life. "When I was a child I took it all for granted. My father stressed manners: Be polite to your elders, don't speak until you're spoken to, always show respect. Of course, there never was any question of disobedience. For instance, I accepted the fact that no stage person would ever be asked to our house as a friend. It would have been unthinkable. My father had slaves on his plantation in South Carolina, but he treated Negroes with great gentleness. Thinking back, it was never a question of looking down on anybody, but we just knew we were superior, I suppose."

Schooling was incidental. Helen went for the first time to the Master's School at Dobbs Ferry at thirteen. Up until then, two governesses tutored her, and once a week, on Wednesdays, she would be taken into New York for dancing school in the afternoon and opera that evening. She came back on Thursday mornings. But she had to work Saturdays to make up for the Wednesday trip to New York. Helen graduated from the Master's School at seventeen. "I never thought of going on to college because very few girls did in those days. It was never even thought of. I think I knew three or four girls from school who were accepted at college and I looked at them with awe, to think that first of all they had brains enough, and secondly, that they wanted to. I never would have had the desire."

The idea fostered by her family was that Helen would live at home until she found a suitable husband to marry. In the meantime the coming-out party was the usual method of exposing Social young ladies to suitable young men.

Helen's party was at the old Sherry's in New York and included about two hundred guests. "In my day, since college was unheard of, the debutante parties went for a whole season, from November to March. Every night I went to a different dance, except on weekends, and at each party the family maid had to sit and wait for me to bring me home. Sometimes it was two or four in the morning. Wasn't that terrible? But just once I defied my parents and went tea dancing at the Hotel Plaza with a young man . . . unchaperoned. That's the worst thing I ever did. And I never told the family. Just think of that."

Helen loved dancing particularly and she had many beaux. Vincent Astor was one of the many boys she had met during her teens in the country. Picnics and walks and a drive in the carriage were the activities and social life. Vincent Astor and Helen Huntington began seeing each other often, and they got married in 1914, when she was twenty-one. Astor was certainly Social and moneyed, but the Huntingtons were not exactly approving. "They didn't think it was a good idea," is all she will say. They proved to be right.

Although they were married for twenty-five years, there were no children. Vincent Astor was a strong and demanding man and Helen did whatever he wanted. "Always, always."

"I was very amenable, but I think that came from my upbringing. Gradually, as I grew older, I grew more independent."

The Astors had no children, led an opulent life and had an enormous yacht called *Nourmahal*. They were very much a part of Society in New York and Rhinebeck, where they had a large house on the Hudson.

"I seemed to be busy all the time and quickly became interested in music, which Vincent was not. He hated opera. That wasn't what made the difference, but after twenty-five years I got a divorce. Vincent remarried before I did, and Lytle Hull, a man I had known for years, and I married a year later. But I learned long ago, having had two husbands, that there is only one way to lead a happy married life. I disapprove to this day of the idea that husbands and wives have to do the same thing in the evening. It's just too silly! If Lytle wanted to go to the club, or read at home, and I wanted to go to a concert, we each did, as you now say, 'our own thing.' Why should one partner suffer because the other likes to dance, say, or play bridge? Why doesn't one of them just go home, or stay home, rather than make their spouse miserable, and have fights all the way home? When I was married to Vincent he didn't like dancing. I did, so I'd stay at parties right through the evening, and he'd leave." With Mr. Hull, who didn't care for concerts, Helen would often go without him. Music took up more of her time during their marriage. She became very active with the New York Philharmonic Symphony, first on the Women's Committee and later as its Director. "I'm now the oldest Director, having served for over forty years on the Board. But back in 1931, I heard of an organization that has really now taken over most of my life, The Musician's Emergency Fund. What fascinated me was that they took a personal interest in an artist's life, like giving funds to allow a singer to buy a dress for an important public appearance. I liked this way of giving because you can see directly the results of your help. So, having expressed an interest, they naturally grabbed me and I became a member of the Lay Board and now I am Chairman." She is also a founder of Lincoln Center for the Performing Arts, Vice-president of the New York City Center, and has been interested for years in the Hospitalized Veterans Service.

As the widow of Lytle Hull, since 1958, and an ardent supporter of musical causes in New York City she now typifies an aristocratic breed of woman and, at eighty-two, is still active because it gives her pleasure and because she feels a keen sense of responsibility to help struggling artists.

Her love affair with music began on those Wednesdays in New York as a child, but she has always been the observer and organizer, never the publicity seeker or ego tripper in the charity business. The only time she appeared publicly on her own behalf was in her one and only concert debut, playing twin pianos with Major John Adams Warner of Albany, who was Superintendent of State Police. The occasion was the opening of the winter season of the Dutchess County Philharmonic Orchestra in 1949.

"Oh, I was so terribly nervous," she said. "It was terrible. I

scarcely touched the piano, I was so frightened." Mrs. Franklin
D. Roosevelt and other prominent Hudson River residents were
in the audience. But her listeners in recent years are the friends
she invites up to Staatsburg on weekends, when someone usually
joins her at one of her two pianos. Many are years younger than
she.

"I have few friends of my own age left. My men friends are
all much younger. I couldn't bear to go out with a man my own
age. They're usually dull old men. My companions are fifteen or
twenty years younger than I and love music and ballet (but I'm
terribly conservative—Bach and Mozart are still my favorites).
We go to these events in the evening. I never go out with women
and I don't like dinner parties much. Those boring ones where
first you talk to the man on the right, then to the one on your left,
and then someone comes and finds you after dinner. It's all too
stiff. I'd much rather go out and meet new people even though
physically it's hard for me to get around much due to a disease
called labyrinthitis, which makes me dizzy and unbalanced physically."

As a Dutchess County dowager and with a treasure of a butler,
named Stanley, who runs her house and orders the meals, while
unseen hands arrange fresh bouquets of flowers in all the rooms,
all from her own garden, Mrs. Hull has the freedom now to
choose and make her own schedule, but still prefers to look out
over the Hudson and play court to a series of aging dogs who
loll on the manicured lawns, or make guests open the door for
them when they want to come in, even in the middle of a formal
luncheon.

Without a doubt this great lady living amongst the beautiful
porcelains and antique furniture, all of which she chose and
bought years ago, is far from the Social power base, which she
purposely shuns. When I discussed power with her, the word
seemed as remote as Women's Lib or the Jet Set, because her
sheltered world precludes new movements and life style changes.
In female terms she thinks of Indira Gandhi and Golda Meir as
being powerful. Alice Longworth, to Helen Hull, is not really
powerful, because "Power is manipulating something. Alice has a
vivid personality and I think she was a bit wild as a young

woman, but she has an amusing mind and I've always liked her enormously, but she certainly is not in a position of influence."

Mrs. Hull, born to Society and her constant role as New York's First Lady of Music, is a Renaissance woman. She is proud not only in bearing but as a descendant of a great traditional Hudson River family. She expects no rewards for her volunteer work and instead derives from her love of the country the simple pleasure of a guest's admiration of nature and old-fashioned estate life. Beautifully and meticulously attired on the arm of her butler and overlooking a sweep of the Hudson, she is truly genteel. She has filled her life with an interest and, despite wealth, has enriched her personal scope in the musical world. At eighty-one, she still worries about the financial situation of the arts, and being a true dowager, her self-made niche in her realm unfortunately will not pass on to a successor. Her society is dead and the quiet, refined support she has lent to artists will pass with her. The mansion on the river, the private, yet totally human lady, so classically correct in taste and manner (and with a mind of her own) has a special soul that could never be imitated. Great self-discipline is evident in her demeanor, and from her strict parents she developed character which has never abandoned her.

There is a tinge of sadness underlying the lady living out her years in her beloved Hudson Valley. The gentle life that once was the glory of the country aristocracy is now a moment caught in time when you leave the imposing house, the graceful tree-lined driveway.

I think Mrs. Hull realizes the impossibility of continuing in the 1970s the graceful existence she once knew. She certainly is at the end of a tradition but is proudly living out the fragile splendor of teacups and treasures and greenhouses and great music. Her greatest joy now is to share the grandeur of the past with younger weekend guests who aren't too young to appreciate the luxury of a delicious life.

Mrs. William Woodward

ELSIE WOODWARD is having more fun at ninety-three than she ever had at any point in her life. In fact, her current life style is quite shocking to what is left of Old Guard society in New York, which doesn't really bother her one bit.

There was a time, however, when she did worry, for Elsie was brought up by her proper Social family, the Duncan Cryders, to lead the expected life of a nice young lady and to settle down with a rich and Socially acceptable husband. Being a dutiful daughter she played out that role, raised children with not overly great enthusiasm, and was Mrs. William Woodward, wife of a man whose great interest was in his racing stable. William Woodward died twenty-one years ago, leaving Elsie a widow at seventy, but his death, rather than leaving her saddened and lonely, served to free her from the restrictions of an uninteresting, staid life style she never really enjoyed. At last she is a free spirit, responsible to no one and kicking up her heels at nightly New York parties with the Jet Setters and the storied people, and despite her age and relative unsuitability to these groups, each derives mutual enjoyment from the other.

Naturally, her early years and later married life are total non-sequiturs to her present life. She lives in the Waldorf Towers in one of the smaller one-bedroom apartments, tastefully furnished but completely lacking in any personal touch. Nothing of her past or present life intrudes into the period-decorated rooms except a large painting of a horse by the Nineteenth-Century English painter John Frederick Herring, part of a larger collection put together in earlier days by her husband. Since his death she has built a wing at the Baltimore Museum of Art, where

the remainder of the Herrings hang, and there too she built a little
library which has a case containing William Woodward's racing
trophies. Billy Baldwin, Society's favorite decorator, helped her,
and this is her memorial to her husband.

She lives alone now except for one maid who comes in the
morning after she's fixed her own breakfast, and another who
comes in the afternoons and cooks if she is staying home, which
isn't often because she is out partying most nights.

"I had a big apartment before, but then my old butler had to
retire," she said, sitting primly on the sofa. "He'd been with me
for forty years. Ah, then I began to think, now I'm getting old,
I don't want to bother about anything, and living in a hotel is so
much easier."

She asks nothing from anyone but to lead her own life, developing in the last twenty years a social gregariousness which
even astounds her family. It was as if her past Woodward life
was over and, with her husband's death in 1952, she felt a
blessed release. Elsie Woodward is a woman whom *real* Society
produced but who usually felt out of "sync" with each period
she aged through. Now she has what she always has longed for
but was not available before—personal freedom.

"Honey, I don't know why you want to talk about my life.
You know, I've never done anything. Just aged," she said, peering
through dark glasses. She says, apologetically, that she can't see
the way she used to, but that's because—unbelievably—she had
20–20 vision until ten years ago. She also says she's deaf and her
legs hurt her and if she walks a lot she gets dizzy, so she com-
plains to the doctors; and when she asks them for remedies and
they tell her there is nothing they can do, she becomes irritated.
She just hasn't come around to accepting the infirmities of old
age, since she has had the good fortune to have never been sick
or hospitalized. She admits that at ninety-three she is just making the most of a life that she feels has gone on too long. "I just
loathe old people, old men, old women. There are too many in
the world and they're all being kept alive as long as possible. I
think death is a release. I don't know why people are so afraid to
die. I'm ready to get out. I'm the oldest living woman and it's
perfectly ghastly." Or so she would like you to believe.

But her childhood years would be quite unbelievable to today's

generation, for Elsie, Edith and Ethel Cryder, triplets born in
1882, lived a sheltered, pampered existence in an exclusive, conventional society. The Cryder triplets apparently were so much
alike in looks and weight that the only way to distinguish them
was by their different hair ribbons, one red, one light blue, and
the other white. They wore these throughout their childhood,
although they enjoyed fooling people by switching colors. Elsie's
parents, the Duncan Cryders, didn't have much money, but
much more importantly, they were part of New York Society,
particularly Mrs. Cryder, who was born an Ogden and came
from Boston. Duncan Cryder, it appears, was a gentleman, but his
credentials were not quite Social, coming, as he did, from White-
stone, New York, a town on Long Island that didn't merit too
much attention from Social thoroughbreds. When the triplets
were small the Cryders took them to Europe until they were fifteen, presumably to get some culture, and Elsie says sadly, "We
learned absolutely nothing.

"Mother was a wonderful woman but she was thirty when
she met Father. He, too, married late in life. He had been in the
tea business in China until his partner absconded with the company's funds and left him broke. He and mother came back from
China after their first child, Anita, was born there. When they
settled in New York Anita became sick and died, and we were
born, and fifteen months later a boy arrived. So there they
were, with Father doing a little trading on the stock exchange,
four children and an income of one thousand dollars a year. It
was a hard struggle for Mother to make ends meet, and as if
that wasn't enough, our brother was killed in a streetcar accident
at seventeen. Father never really recovered from the shock."

The newpapers and Society chroniclers tried to make much of
the comings and goings of Society triplets. Little did they know
that the three girls seldom went out at the same time. Not because, as the press tried to indicate, they were publicity shy or
that Society frowned on such public displays; the real reason was
that they usually had only enough money for two dresses, so one
triplet always had to stay at home. Even when they came out at
a debutante cotillion their dresses were frugally made from one
bolt of material, all exactly alike. Similarly in Europe, their father,
who liked bicycles, used to take the triplets through the country-

side. He had his own bicycle and another one built for two. The sister who was feeling least well rode with him. Money was tight.

Elsie has all but erased the past, but she does remember going to a country castle in England with Edith and Ethel, and a lot of people began to congregate and stare at the three of them. "We all thought people were astonished because we were triplets when, in fact, we found out that they were thoroughly surprised that all Americans weren't black."

Society in New York imposed certain standards, one of which was that young ladies were brought up to find as suitable and as rich a husband as possible. Naturally, the Cryders expected their daughters to follow this pattern. Schooling didn't matter, and of course, as Elsie reminded me, "thinking of going into business was shocking. You would no longer be in Society. A friend of mine, named Kitty, who was very much of a lady decided to go into the hat business. My dear, you might have thought she had committed the ultimate sin. Even a man had to be in an established business like banking, or he would be ostracized. You did what was expected and you followed the rules of Society, which was—in New York, anyway—ruled by two reigning queens: Old Mrs. Astor and Old Mrs. Belmont. If they didn't like you, you were out of it Socially, and if you weren't invited to Mrs. Astor's? Why, you just were nobody!" Shaking her head, she muttered, "It was such a stupid Society."

Two of the Cryder girls, however, fulfilled their parents' dream by marrying men with money. Edith was first; she married Lothrop Ames from Boston. Much later she married Roger Cutler. Ethel, though, was the reprobate; she married a charming Englishman without a dime who took her to live in a London attic, where he left her when she came down with pneumonia. When she returned to New York she remarried. Elsie's marriage, the only one that lasted fifty years, made her a wealthy woman but not necessarily a happy one.

According to friends, Bill Woodward was not only rich but a most charming man from a southern family in Maryland. His father's successful cotton business made it possible for William to spend part of his youth in England as a private secretary to a Mr. Choate. Elsie remembers meeting the attractive twenty-four-year-old Woodward at a horse show. She was then eighteen, and the Cryder family was scrimping along on meager finances.

"I'll never forget meeting William," she said. "I noticed him sitting behind me in a box, but I couldn't turn around and really look at him because my dress didn't have enough material, as usual, and the lace didn't meet in the back. It was really love at first sight, and I eventually met him and he asked me to marry him. It was nice that he had a certain amount of money, because I had nothing. One thing I'll never get over is not having money in my youth."

William Woodward certainly could keep Elsie in a style to which she was not accustomed. His income was ten thousand dollars a year, which was big money in those days. William Woodward had made his money as President of the Hanover Bank, so the young couple lived well. But when they were first married, they went to live with Mrs. Woodward, Sr., which was a great disappointment to Elsie, who had hoped to have her own house. "The house was on West Fifty-first Street, and this West Side neighborhood was considered very chic in the early 1900s." But Elsie's life was run by her mother-in-law. "It was rather defeating for me," she said sadly, "because whenever we gave a dinner party, there was my mother-in-law receiving instead of me, and always in formal black velvet dresses and pearls. There was never any question who ruled the roost, so our social life was really restricted." Edith Bancroft, now dead, the Woodward's first daughter, was born in that house. When their second daughter, Libby, was on the way they moved to 9 East Fifty-sixth Street; there, two more daughters, Sarah (now Sewall) and Ethel (now De Croisset), and a son, William, Jr., were all born. Ten years later, in 1918, William Woodward built a beautiful house at 9 East Eighty-sixth Street, where he and his wife lived for twenty years and which she sold only after his death.

William Woodward was urged by his family to go into banking at the Hanover. "He was very conscientious," his wife said, "about people's money, and he went through two panics. I think the responsibility nearly killed him. Today bankers aren't that dedicated. They're promoters." From banking he went into horse racing. Horse racing was not quite as respectable as banking, so he raced under a friend's name, P. A. Clarke, for a number of years before starting his famous Bel Air stud farm, for which he will always be remembered.

But what is interesting, so far as Elsie's life is concerned, was her role as wife and mother. No different, of course, than her contemporaries, for women were mothers and wives, and that was it. She had very little to say about anything, and unfortunately was not interested in the children. William Woodward was a strong man and Elsie tried hard—to be interested in the family, to be interested in her husband's banking career, to be interested in his racing career. She tried very hard.

The five children were brought up by the governess, who started with the two eldest and worked her way down as the other children arrived. As Edith and Libby got older, their big treat was graduation from the upstairs nursery to meals with their parents. William Woodward worked all day and, in the gentlemanly tradition of the day, would then go to his club, the Knickerbocker, and arrived home around 7 P.M. Elsie knew that she was expected to be interested in her husband's friends, whom she considered pretty stuffy. Bankers were a conservative bunch, and most of the fun they had was clearly not at home.

"Father did adore Mother and he'd give her anything, but he wasn't going to lead a frivolous life, or what he considered frivolous—people of the theater or the arts," Libby said.

Woodward, tired of banking, went into the racing business and later started his now famous Bel Air stud farm. Bel Air stables in Maryland—on 2,200 acres at its peak—had all the great horses, including Sir Galahad and Damascus, two of racing's great studs. Racing and breeding became a full-time occupation for Woodward. Elsie had a book and tried gallantly to learn the names of the horses and attended the races with the children at Saratoga for a few weeks every summer. But in later years she preferred Newport, where there were more people and a gayer life. Still, Bel Air was where they spent spring and fall, among the horsey set.

One gets the impression that Elsie tolerated her life and sublimated her real desires and feelings until after her husband's death. During all the years prior to this, she was a stoic woman, not given to showing warmth and affection. Her children recall life as being very formal when they were little, kissing their mother goodnight while she was getting dressed and, if they were lucky, watching her do her hair, which the maid helped her arrange. The servants in the Maryland house were black, and many nights one or more of the children would spend the night in the cook's bed. Thunderstorms would send them scurrying to her protective arms; the only thing that gave the children courage was that the cook was more scared than they. A child's perception is often extraordinary, and since their parents' bedroom door was always closed, they never went to them in need. But Annie, the cook, with her long hanging tooth, was their solace and gave them deep affection. The children somehow never questioned why it wasn't so with their parents. One just didn't. They were brought up to toe the mark, and it seemed to be made clear just what the mark was. The girls weren't allowed to go out with boys until they were sixteen, even though the boys were older, and as the girls grew older the governess always had to accompany them on drives and to the movies. Questions were answered with a definite yes or no. Never maybe. "Girls aren't allowed to do that," was a familiar retort.

Elsie's greatest tragedy was the accidental shooting of their only son, Billy, twenty years ago when he was just thirty-five. All her hopes for her son to take over the racing stables from his father were destroyed overnight. Elsie's friends noted a decided change in her whole outlook after that. She never again wanted to talk about Billy, even within the family. She somehow developed a facility to eradicate thoughts at will. Not religious, she nevertheless believes in God, and she believes that if she conducts herself now in a special way she will be ready to meet her husband and her son in the next world.

She was seventy years old when her husband died after a long illness. "I knew it was best for him to die. We talked it over unemotionally about what would happen to me," Elsie said, "and he said, 'I leave you everything and I want you to give up all your committee meetings and everything and devote yourself to taking care of the estate.' And I have followed his wishes. I have money and nobody has to support me." Her son Billy's tragic death followed his father's by two years. She had kept the Eighty-sixth Street house for years, thinking that Billy might

want it. When he was shot she wanted to move out. Too much of
the past was there. She sold the old mansion and gave the pro-
ceeds to her surviving children. "I sold it to a very fine man, a
Jewish judge." Most of her possessions—a marvelous collection
of Chinese export porcelain, furniture, a Coromandel screen—
were disposed of. Many of her family, (all girls) would have
liked to keep such lovely pieces, but she brushed them all off saying, "You've no room, my dear. I'm going to sell them." To the
horror of many she has sold her glassware and the Coromandel
screen, the latter for $10,000, which in this inflated antique
market the family felt could have gone for four times as much.
If Elsie didn't want her family to have her treasures, they in turn
were piqued that she made such a poor decision.

But it pleased her to make a clean sweep of the stuffy past
decades, the parties which bored her so when she was younger.
"My dear, such a dull Society then. You'd have a dinner and
everyone would rise to their feet and leave at ten." And the
summers in Newport: "You'd drive around Ocean Drive and
then you'd go to the beach and some poor boy had to wait with
your carriage and hold the horses. I loathed those picnics. The
whole thing was so formal." All slid into the past.

Life has changed totally for this ninety-one-year-old dowager.
She doesn't mind being alone and even tells her children that
she feels lucky to have her freedom—a complete reaction to the
stiffness of her former life. Her great interest now is in meeting
new, always *new*, people. She confides, with a certain touch of
satisfaction, "The trouble is that I know too many people in
different groups. I love bridge—absolute relaxation for the aged.
I love the theater. I love meeting new men who are attractive and
intelligent."

She is truly remarkable, enjoying the company of people who
are successful and creative. At Jet Set parties, invariably Elsie
Woodward will be included. She's as fascinated by Andy War-
hol as by Arthur Schlesinger, Jr. She draws people out and gets
them to talk about themselves, a trait she has recently discovered.
She's developed into a listener, but more than that, she is highly
flattered by people's attentions.

"Oh, Andy [Warhol] bought me such a present. I wish you
could see it. It's a bracelet—one of those plastic kinds that you

see all the colored girls wearing. It was fun. But, you know, I
never mix my friends; Andy and his group just wouldn't get
along with my bridge-playing friends. Why, my old group just
doesn't understand and can't even converse with my new painters
and writers and TV stars. I've changed my whole life, you see.
In my day you married and led your husband's life. You never
had a choice."

She believes marriage as an institution is finished anyway. "If
a girl wants her own life and her own career, how can she give
the attention a man demands? The woman has to give up something."

Women like Clare Luce, though, intrigue her. "She was so
ravishing when I first met her. After her daughter's death she became very frail-looking but she always carried on. Audiences,
and particularly men, were intrigued by her great beauty. She
was absolutely wonderful. She has that amazing combination of a
man's brain and a feminine exterior, plus a very strong character."

Family life and taking an interest in her grandchildren doesn't
seem to be a part of Elsie Woodward's life. She hates holidays
and has never encouraged family gatherings. Friends question
whether this disinterest is selfish or whether she feels that she
would be intruding by interjecting herself. She doesn't give of
herself in any maternal way. She's loosened her social straitjacket
and she is a familiar figure in restaurants and at cultural events.
Money has made a rather shy, impecunious woman, the last of
the Cryder triplets, totally independent. Widowhood released
the last responsibilities of a woman yearning to break out. Lack
of education, hobbies, and a specific drive make her seem to
be marking time as a dowager socialite trying to be part of a
younger, do-it-yourself group. But she is never without invitations, and as she says, "I have money and no one has to support
me."

The interesting point of Mrs. Woodward's long life is that she
is at last free of Society's expectations. She has found it is too
late to go back to her old kind of social conformation, and besides, she doesn't want to. Wisely, she knows the only thing left
is to meet people who are doing things, and most of her new
friends would never be found in her old bible, the Social Regis-

ter. She's having fun and she finds life interesting after so many years of being a dutiful wife kept in the background, a dutiful daughter-in-law, the proper mother to her children, all subjugated roles Society required of her. The futility of behaving according to class rules and regulations she realized shortly after her son's death when, unlike many of her contemporaries, it occurred to her that she had been short-changed as an individual. Fortunately, she has the time now to "do her own thing." Few of her background have had the courage.

Mrs. Harper Sibley

ROCHESTER, NEW YORK, has many claims to fame, and the Sibley family has been interested in many aspects of the city's civic activities. Carrying on most notably the family tradition is Mrs. Harper Sibley. She may be eighty-seven, she may be a widow and mother of five, but packed into a five-foot body is an amazingly interested and energetic woman, and there is almost no one in Rochester who is not familiar with this number-one citizen.

No idle socialite she, although she might well have remained only a line in the Social Register, having spent twenty traditional years as a socialite. Instead, she has developed into a national church leader and an active exponent of minority groups. She is an American churchwoman who has brought her expertise to bear in male-dominated spheres, and as a woman commands the respect of her family, her community and her country. Her list of accomplishments is staggering, and her ebullient spirit and bubbly warmth have carried her to the heights of her interests. One of the last of the great matriarchs, who celebrated her eighty-fifth birthday with fifty members of her family for a sit-down dinner in her dining room, Mrs. Sibley has no plans to cut down on the demanding schedule she follows, and obviously it agrees with her.

I flew up to Rochester one afternoon to meet her and spent two and a half hours chatting and five hours at airports and in the air, due to terrible weather. She had already been to a public lunch honoring General Lucius Clay and was to attend an English-speaking Union dinner that evening. Both events she had very kindly invited me to attend with her but I had previously declined, a fortunate decision in view of developing weather con-

ditions between Rochester and New York which kept me involved with American Airlines until 9 P.M. that night.

I arrived at the Sibley mansion, via a hidden driveway off a
commercial avenue, at three o'clock in the afternoon. The Sibley
house was a large structure, an imposing sculpture of bygone
architecture and filled with a garniture of family portraits, stuffed
animal heads, dark furniture and the smell of lilacs.

Mrs. Sibley, mother of five (her daughter Elizabeth died suddenly at fifty-eight the summer of 1974), grandmother of
twenty-two, and great-grandmother of twenty-four, greeted
me in the old-fashioned hall and we gravitated toward the large
living room. There were vases of lilacs on various tables fixed
by her spinster companion, Marie, a former school athletic in-
structor. "Rochester is known as the lilac city," my hostess informed me as she and I sat on a sofa in front of a table that was
going to be set for tea at 4 P.M. "Would you like some tea?" she
asked. "I always have it at four o'clock." Never having been
known to turn down food, I answered in the affirmative and was
gloriously surprised with old-fashioned cinnamon toast and thin
little lettuce and mayonnaise sandwiches. Between mouthfuls,
Mrs. Sibley and I talked informally, and this little dynamo
proved to be a fascinating memory bank.

Mountain Station, New Jersey, was Georgianna Farr's birth-
place, although she lists West Orange on official documents because it is better known. Her father, T. H. Powers Farr, was a
great polo player and worked in New York as a stockbroker.
His family came from Philadelphia, where they had owned a
big drug company. Her mother's side of the family had many
distinguished members. Georgianna's great-great-granduncle,
Benjamin Rush, signed the Declaration of Independence and was
the first scientific doctor in the United States. Her great-great-
great-grandfather, William Rush, was the first American sculptor.

Georgianna was one of five children. Her three brothers went
to Groton School, where one of them was in the same class as
Harper Sibley. Her brother Barkley Farr was one of Kermit
Roosevelt's best friends, "and my own close friend was Corrine
Alsop the daughter of Teddy Roosevelt's sister Corrine. Married
to Douglas Robinson, they were next-door neighbors," Mrs. Sibley told me. "This is why we knew the Theodore Roosevelts

and Eleanor. She would visit the Robinsons at Christmas and vacations because Corrine Roosevelt Robinson was her aunt."

Georgianna first went to the Dearborn Morgan coeducational school in Orange, New Jersey, but her mother felt that at fourteen she was becoming too involved with boys and would do better at an all-girls school, so she sent her to Miss Beard's, also in Orange, and then at fifteen to Miss Spence's private school for girls in New York.

Mrs. Sibley says her family was not wealthy but that she had every advantage, which is certainly evident. Brought up by a French governess and heavily chaperoned, Georgianna moved in the social circles of Orange and New York City. School was out in May and the Farrs went to their country house in New Jersey, where they stayed until October, when school began in New York and they returned to their house on West Thirty-seventh Street. Often they would go to the Jersey seashore in the summer at Bayhead, and from the time Georgianna was fourteen they would spend part of the summer in Northeast Harbor, Maine, still a fashionable resort for Social families.

The Farrs were a happy couple and Georgianna was admiring of her father and mother. "Father and I rode a great deal together. He was the gayest of the gay. Mother was much more of an intellectual and more self-contained. She had strong ideas and was really part of the Puritan tradition, but she had tremendous stamina." This trait her daughter happily inherited. "Father was gay, even during the Depression," his daughter continued. "When most men on Wall Street were feeling low, he was fun and outgoing. But I was brought up very strictly and my parents believed in a strong moral code. I was never even allowed to hold a boy's hand, and I did just once and as a punishment I wasn't allowed to go on a special picnic I had been looking forward to. I was also expected to be respectful and have good manners, and of course we were never allowed to drink or smoke. This was all part of our tradition and we never thought to challenge it. We naturally accepted our parents' judgments and decisions."

Mrs. Sibley felt that her mother and father had a wonderful marriage and they really loved one another. The family atmosphere and home environment were happy. Divorce, of course, was unthinkable. In fact, the Farrs never had a divorced person in their house, nor did their daughter. The first divorcee was Mrs. Sibley's daughter Georgianna, and later her son Harper, Jr., but until that generation divorce was not even discussed.

Mrs. Sibley puts a lot of stock in her early religious training. "We were strong Episcopalians and we went to church every Sunday. Father sang in the choir, and when he was going to do a tenor solo we all used to worry so that we couldn't eat breakfast. But there is no doubt that my great religious interest stemmed from those early days. It has given meaning to my life and has been a very thrilling vocation."

But Georgianna Farr wasn't all serious. She loved parties and dancing and boys. After she graduated from Spence in 1905 she enjoyed the social life. Dancing school, Miss Robinson's classes, was "the" expected thing for nice young ladies, and many of the dances were held in the great private houses in New York. Gladys Vanderbilt, Harriet Alexander, the Fulton Cuttings were where these young ladies danced in grand ballrooms and had supper on little gilt chairs. All the houses had ballrooms and usually a gold piano, and at Christmas the parties included boys, and summer and picnics were bisexual events that all the prominent daughters looked forward to. Friends' coming-out parties were each season's great events. "Just sixty-five girls came out my year," Mrs. Sibley said. "I came out at a tea because of the death of my grandmother. I had to wear black or white for a year because of the practice of observing mourning." But she still attended the parties and the Junior assemblies.

The Depression did not really have any great effect on the Farrs. "Well, we just didn't have as many maids or buy as many clothes," Mrs. Sibley confirmed, "but life went on."

There was never a question of going to college or getting a job in Mrs. Sibley's set. It never occurred to her that there was any other role for a woman to play than to look forward to marriage and motherhood. Preferably, one's husband-to-be would be from the same rung of society. And so it was that Georgianna Farr met Harper Sibley first at fourteen when both their families were summering at Northeast Harbor. He was sixteen and their relationship was casual and friendly in the beginning. "Oh," Mrs. Sibley said with authority, "one was hardly in love at fourteen. But by sixteen, yes, I was very crazy about him. But just in the summer. In the winter, girls being much more sophisticated than their male counterparts, I'd go to parties with older boys, of say twenty. But Harper and I kept seeing each other in Maine and he invited me often on his family's yacht. It was a transformed lake steamer and was a great big boat. Hardly beautiful, but Harper's mother liked to be comfortable. Mr. Hiram Sibley, his father, loved yachting and she went along, but she wasn't the sporting type at all."

Georgianna Farr led the gay Society life immersed in the heady parties of 1905. That was a year she has never forgotten, and it was not for two years that she was to succumb to the charms of Harper Sibley. First the giddy party whirl had to be dealt with.

"It all began, the coming-out season, with the Tuxedo Ball in October," Mrs. Sibley recalled. "I stayed with my friend Harriet Alexander and her parents in Tuxedo Park, New York, and every day there was a lunch and tea and a dinner. I even had certain dresses that were convertible. I had two waists, one with a high neck for the teas and then a low-necked bodice for the dinner parties."

Families provided their debutante daughters with a horse and carriage to go from one event to another. Some were simpler than others. Georgianna had one brougham with two horses and one man on the box, and she was either accompanied by her own maid or her father, who loved parties and was a great hit, according to his daughter, because he'd dance with all the wallflowers. The coachman remained in the Farr family for about fifty years and Georgianna remembers apologizing to him after she was married. She had always felt guilty about keeping him up so late at night. "Years later," she confessed, "I apologized to Garret and told him I was so ashamed because I never left any ball until they played 'Goodnight Ladies,' which was usually about 3 A.M. My maid would wait with the other maids in the little dressing rooms until I left. But poor Garret had to sit on the box of the carriage, no matter what the weather and with no heat or radio. Why, he must have often frozen but he told me he really hadn't minded. 'It was all right,' he said. 'You see, the servants would bring all the coachmen hot coffee and we'd walk the horses.'" Mrs. Sibley took pains to point out that the horses had blankets to keep them warm, but in those days the well-being of coachmen and staff was never a concern of their employers.

A typical example of a spoiled young lady, Mrs. Sibley pointed out, was her good friend Margaret Roosevelt, of the Oyster Bay Roosevelts. She had a carriage called a victoria, a very grand model, and she had two men on the box. She would invite Georgianna to ride in it, which was a great treat. One time Georgianna turned to her friend Margaret and said, "Don't you thank God every time [and in repeating this she said very sincerely, "and I used the Lord's name with great reverence"] you get into this beautiful carriage. And she answered, 'Well no. My grandmother had it. My mother had it. I just grew up expecting it.'"

The small figure beside me was still shocked by this remark, and shaking her short gray hair, said, "Really, isn't that remark and philosophy unbelievable?" In the light of life nowadays, it is unthinkable. I'm sure in the privileged classes of the early 1900s, it was quite acceptable.

At twenty, Georgianna began to take Harper Sibley more seriously. The summer's freedom and outdoor living which they enjoyed, the picnics, boating and mountain climbing brought them closer together. Sibley was at Harvard and graduated in 1907. He proposed to Georgianna when she was twenty, and she coyly admitted being disappointed that he hadn't asked her on a romantic occasion like commencement in Harvard Yard. Instead, it was a dusty road on a Sunday morning going to church. "He wanted to be a lawyer, which I thought was wonderful, and decided to go to New York Law School rather than Harvard because he could be through in two years."

Georgianna did not tell her family immediately of her marriage plans, although both the Sibleys and the Farrs were devoted to the young couple. "When we got engaged, Teddy Roosevelt was President," Mrs. Sibley said. "The Theodore Roosevelts always had the most superb fireworks that you could possibly imagine, and Harper and I were staying with the Emlen Roosevelts and their daughter Margaret. But there was a big house party at Sagamore Hill, the President's house, and we told everyone on the Fourth of July that we were engaged. The President was not there then, but when I went back to Sagamore that autumn, I saw him and told him of my intentions to marry Harper Sibley. He said, 'Georgie, *I'm* not surprised. Was anyone else?' And I had to admit, no. 'No, Mr. President, no one except Harper!'"

It was a long engagement, as many were in those days. The following May, 1908, Georgianna went down to visit Alice Roosevelt's half-sister Ethel at the White House. Life in the Executive Mansion was very informal in those days and the children's friends often had meals with the President. Mrs. Sibley remembers having breakfast every morning with him during her visit and seeing him often in between appointments. What she never got over was his fabulous memory and his ability to switch from affairs of state to relatively unimportant events. "The day I arrived in Washington, Ethel met me at the train with her horse and carriage. I hadn't been at the White House very long when her father, the President, walked in and said to me, 'Georgie, I'm so glad to see you. And how is the surprised Harper?' You see, Felicia, this was his great genius. He could instantly switch his attention, and this was one of the many reasons that I grew to love him so. I was only twenty and here was the President of the United States taking the time to make me feel important. He also had the most beautiful manners. I remember when his son Quentin's governess came into the room, he stood up." With a sigh of resignation for a way of life that is gone, Mrs. Sibley said, "That kind of thing is so beautiful. In this day and age you really miss beautiful manners."

In contrast, his daughter Alice seemed to enjoy shocking her father and friends. Mrs. Sibley was a contemporary of hers and remembers a particular incident at Northeast Harbor after Alice had married Nicholas Longworth. They and the Sibleys attended a sermon at the local church on Sunday and it was delivered by Bishop Nash. The subject was "The Tongue Is an Unruly Member." "It was summer and we were about to have a presidential election," Mrs. Sibley said. "The Bishop had just warned us against slander and being malicious. We left church and we all went swimming, and I remember Alice carrying on to our great amusement and saying, 'I love my unruly member. I love my tongue, my unruly member.' She was always a pretty

naughty girl." As if to reconfirm that statement, she nodded her
head and said again, "She really was."

Harper Sibley graduated from law school in 1907, and a month
after her White House visit in 1908, Georgianna and he were
married and began their life together in an apartment at 500 Madison Avenue, New York City. They lived there for four years
and during that time had their first three children. Madison Avenue in the early 1900s was not the business area we think of now.
In fact the store that is now Brooks Brothers was once the home
of Mrs. Sibley's mother and father-in-law.

While Georgianna was growing up, the Sibley family were
busy leading serious lives and amassing a fortune.

The Rochester house that Mrs. Sibley lives in now has housed
six generations and belonged to Harper's grandfather, who built
it over a hundred years ago. There is no mistaking the pride in
the family lineage. Imbedded in the far wall opposite where we
sat in the living room were two coats of arms in stained glass.
"Yes," Mrs. Sibley explained as I guessed their origin, "that's the
Harper coat of arms, my husband's maternal family, and these
are the Sibleys. Now, I don't take heraldry very seriously, but if
you notice those three crescents, they are supposed to represent
three different crusades."

I was curious about the Sibley family and confessed that I had
not known of them. Mrs. Sibley was only too eager to tell me
what is part of the saga of early American history.

"The Sibley family first settled in Salem, Massachusetts, thence
to Sutton and North Adams near Williamstown. My husband's
grandfather, Hiram Sibley, worked his way out to the Midwest
in a canalboat with nothing in his pockets but his two hands
and started some mills in a little town which he called Sibley-
ville. The mills grew, finally numbering about twenty-eight and
he and his wife built a beautiful house there. But he wanted to
get back to North Adams, so he and his bride moved back and
brought the first piano, a spinet, into western New York on a
canalboat in 1827. Hiram Sibley built a very successful business
with his mills and employed about one hundred people, working, grinding grain and mending machinery. He wasn't a real
farmer, although my husband was always interested in agriculture."

Hiram Sibley somehow found his way to Rochester and became a friend of Samuel Morse, the inventor of the telegraph. Mr. Morse recognized in Sibley a man who had business experience and asked him to go to Washington to raise funds to put a telegraph company into operation. This was the beginning of Western Union. Hiram Sibley got President Lincoln to get an appropriation from Congress for the first telegraph link, and it went experimentally from Baltimore to Washington. Mrs. Sibley told me that the first public message was, significantly, "What hath God wrought?" The original telegraph instrument remained in the Sibley family for a long time until they gave it to the Smithsonian. From the first connection to Baltimore, more links were added—Baltimore to Philadelphia, Philadelphia to New York, New York to Albany. My hostess told me an amusing anecdote about Mr. Sibley. He once sent a message home, but he arrived before it did. It cost him twenty-five cents a word and a dollar and a half total.

Hiram Sibley was the founder of Western Union and its first president. His greatest achievement was the installation of telegraph stations across the continent even before the first railroad. On its completion, Sibley dreamed of expanding to Europe and across the Pacific but couldn't figure out a way to insulate the telegraph cable under water. He went to Russia and tried to secure the rights to go across Alaska and Siberia. He had no trouble getting the cable across Europe, but the carry from the Aleutians across Alaska was a problem. According to Mrs. Sibley, at that point the Russian Foreign Minister told him. "Alaska's on your continent. Why don't you buy it?" Hiram Sibley came back to the United States and talked to Seward, Secretary of State under Lincoln, and asked him if the United States bought Alaska, would the government protect Western Union's rights there. Seward replied, "*I* will not, but if it's for sale we will buy it."

Mrs. Sibley's theory of why Seward suddenly bought Alaska was that this was a period of tremendous territorial expansion. The British had just given Canada its independence. Russia was terrified that Great Britain, which had just taken India and South Africa, might also take Alaska, and thus threaten Russia from the east, so Romanoff's suggestion did indeed prompt the United

States into quick action. Whether Hiram Sibley really triggered this chain of events is lost in history, but the family is fond of the story.

The family fortunes picked up as Western Union spread across the country and Hiram Sibley bought various properties that turned out to be lucrative investments. He acquired iron mines in Minnesota and a large tract of farmland in Illinois. It was called Sibley because the whole town was the farm. He also started coal mines in West Virginia and built the Hiram Sibley building in Rochester. Sibley College at Cornell, which specialized in engineering, was a gift of Hiram's father.

Georgianna and Harper Sibley were a wonderful husband and wife team, and Mrs. Sibley made a concerted effort to share her husband's interests, one of which was agriculture. They both took an intensive summer course at Cornell to learn basic agriculture, since the Sibley farms in Illinois were such an important family business.

"You might be interested in knowing how strongly I felt about being Harper's wife," she confided. "I'm always known as Mrs. Harper Sibley, not Georgianna Farr Sibley. It was a definite stand I took early in our marriage. Way back in 1908, there was a movement headed by Mary Stoner to have women keep their own names and thereby assert their special identity. Just in protest and because I felt so strongly that if I cared enough about a man I cared enough to bear his name, my legal name is Mrs. Harper Sibley. I sign all my checks and all legal documents that way. I also took the position," she said very positively, "that whatever my husband cared about, I would become interested in also."

Sibley was offered positions in government while Theodore Roosevelt was President but he turned them down, probably his wife's only disappointment. She was fascinated by politics and, having grown up with the Roosevelt family, was in a position to take an active role. Instead, Harper Sibley maintained a wide variety of interests all his life. He ran the Illinois family farms and received a medal from that state for his contributions to agriculture in Illinois, specifically in developing hybrid seeds. The farms were about 24,000 acres each and all under plow. They were considered the largest single unit of farmland in the

United States under one ownership. Sibley was asked in the 1930s to become President of the United States Chamber of Commerce, President of the United Service Organization, and Treasurer of the Federal Council of Churches.

Mrs. Sibley was twenty-four, a bride of four years, when she and her husband moved from New York in 1912 to Rochester, and in the sixty years she has lived in that city in the same house she has never been inactive. Raising six children and church activity has filled her life. She shared her husband's interest in their church in Rochester. While he was superintendent of the Sunday school, she taught children at St. Paul's Church from kindergarten to high school for twenty-five years. She has also preached from the pulpit of two churches in New York, St. George's and the Grace Church, and in Washington Cathedral. All firsts for a lay Episcopalian woman.

An early interest in the ecumenical movement took the Sibleys to Jerusalem in 1928 for an international conference. As a result of their friendship with John D. Rockefeller and their common interest in the movement and in missions, he sent them on a world mission in 1931. "It was called 'Rethinking Missions,'" Mrs. Sibley said, "and that was September 1931, and the Commission was chaired by the head of the Philosophy Department at Harvard. Ten people had already been sent to India, China and Japan to collect facts for us in regard to economics, agriculture, education (primary, secondary, college), health, women, you name it. We were given forty-two volumes of mimeographed facts to digest, quite an assignment. My husband was one of two men appraising agriculture, and I was one of two women involved in furthering the ecumenical movement."

The Sibleys were gone for nine months, but Mrs. Sibley had a wonderful Scotch nurse who made the whole trip possible by staying on with the children, the youngest being Harper, Jr., who was three at the time of the trip. Between the nurse and Grandmother Sibley, the children were well taken care of.

Many trips followed and carried Mrs. Sibley all over the world. In 1937, her church in Rochester, St. Paul's Episcopal, appointed her a delegate to the Ecumenical Conference at Oxford called "Life and Work." She was one of two women, the other three delegates were men. Earlier in that year she had taken her husband's place, because his mother was ill, as a representative of the American Delegation in Berlin for the International Chamber of Commerce meeting. Thomas Watson, Sr., head of IBM, was Chairman of the group from the United States, and again, Mrs. Sibley was one of two women. The remainder of the delegation was comprised of sixteen hundred men. "At that time we were entertained by Goebbels and Goering and the whole trip was incredible," Mrs. Sibley said. "Incredible because we didn't have the wit to see what was happening in Germany, and this was 1937. We had known that Jewish synagogues were being attacked, and that move alone should have alerted us. We heard that Bishop Debelius of Berlin had been arrested while we were there, and I was in church when his assistant stood up in the pulpit and decried what was happening, and they got him two days later. So we saw it, but we didn't realize what was happening. How stupid we were." In 1945 she represented American Protestant Churches at the United Nations Conference in San Francisco.

In 1948, when Mrs. Sibley was sixty-one, she undertook perhaps her most important assignment. She became a member of the United States Military Government and was sent by the War Department, with a few other lay American churchwomen, on a ninety-day mission to try to rebuild women's organizations in Germany. She was ideally suited for the task, having been a national board member of the YWCA as well as President of the United Council of Churchwomen. Enthusiastic, sensitive, organized, Mrs. Sibley was an ideal choice of our government.

She told me that Hitler had not encouraged any women's organizations under his regime, and with the rank of colonel, she and Katherine Schaeffer, head of Catholic women, traveled all over Germany in transport planes to help German women get back on their feet. She was invited by Czechoslovakian women to meet with them, and through a series of adventures she got to Prague. "I had no knowledge of the language, no Czech money and no transportation. I had to hitch a ride in the back of a truck and sat on my suitcase. Being a Communist country by then, 1948, it was all a bit scary. I went to a hotel I had known about and stayed there until the contact person who had invited me finally came to meet me. And so we went down to Bryn or

Burno, whichever you want to call it, where I was to speak at a meeting. That same night, the woman doctor who was head of the local hospital disappeared, and that really frightened me. There I was billeted alone in a hotel, and the other church-women, who had been there before, told me that she carried fatal poison in her pocketbook in case the Russians should come and try and arrest her. These were very intense moments."

But then, that is what has made Mrs. Sibley. The intense moments, the fascinating ones like her meeting with the Empress of Japan in 1949 after helping raise money with her husband in Honolulu for a new building for the YWCA. She and General MacArthur, whom she'd known as Chief of Staff in Washington when she and her husband lived there, met again in Japan, and he brought her up-to-date on Japanese problems. She left him and went to meet the Empress. "I remember," she said, "her saying, 'We have just gotten freedom for women in Japan and we're having many problems. You've had it for so long in the United States, I suppose American women have no problems.' That was my opening. What started out to be a twenty-minute meeting with only five of us—an interpreter, a lady in waiting, and a chamberlain—turned into an hour-and-forty-minute talk. She was so interested in hearing every detail about American women."

Mrs. Sibley made many trips with and without her husband, all in pursuit of her interests in the church and world fellowship. There is a joke in the Sibley family that if Georgianna and Harper ever had a family crest, it would show a train going in one direction, a plane going in the other, and underneath the legend, "God Bless Our Home."

The Sibleys celebrated their Golden Wedding Anniversary in 1958. In 1959, Harper Sibley died in Santa Barbara of a massive coronary. Active to the end of his life, golfing three times a week, he enjoyed his family and his marriage.

His widow, who has carried on alone for fifteen years, will always feel a vacuum. "We did and enjoyed so much together. I'll never cease to miss him, particularly at five o'clock in the afternoon. That would be our special time together. He'd come home from business or traveling and we'd talk about what had happened since we'd been apart. We led such an active and interesting life. Now I see a lot of the children and grandchildren because I'm very close to them."

Mrs. Sibley believes, like many other grandmothers, that it is more important to keep a relationship of love and confidence, and she resists criticizing them. This, she feels, only brings estrangement. She admires many of the qualities found in the younger generation—their idealism, their lack of prejudice, and their interest in helping minority groups. She tries to encourage all her family's interests.

About death, she said, "I view it with a great question mark and I believe and hope that there will be some contact in another place with the people we love." But she added, honestly, "I have no great assurance. I felt after my husband's death that having been so much the greater part of me, his passing would give me some insight. Some peek into what was beyond is what I hoped for, but death is still that question mark. I admit the old clock is running down." I disagreed and pointed to her boundless energy, which revitalizes her every day. "Well," Mrs. Sibley admitted, "I happen to believe that God is not only power, goodness, love, but also energy. And therefore I believe that one can tap the energy of God, and I do this many times a day with little periods of prayer. I also believe that one must live on the wavelength of that energy, and that anger and pride and all the seven deadly sins, including frustration and overhurrying, separate you from God's wavelength. I also believe in thinking positively. Once Dr. Norman Vincent Peale and I found ourselves sharing a taxi after a luncheon given by the National Council of Churches. Dr. Peale knew that I had attended several other meetings that day and asked me where I got all my energy from. I answered, 'Why, Dr. Peale. It's from you. It's from your book *The Power of Positive Thinking.*' So he said, '*Touché,*' and that's the only time I've ever really thought of the right answer at the right moment."

And still Mrs. Sibley crowds her hours—her ranch in California, trips throughout the country, talks before many diverse groups. Her status in the world's Episcopalian community and the respect she has engendered endear her to her old and new admirers as well as her coworkers. She is genuinely responsive and, at eighty-seven is still willing to help if her presence is called for.

Mrs. William Roth

LURLINE MATSON ROTH, at eighty-four, is respected and revered by Californians as a great lady from a grand tradition, for she has always been her own woman. She still lives in one of the well-known showplaces of northern California, an estate of seven hundred and fifty acres, "Filoli," which is off Canada Road, a two-lane highway in Woodside. Now, because of land development and modern freeways, she is only half an hour from San Francisco and the once open land is a suburban development. However, I remember twenty years ago this same area was open fields dotted with scrub oak instead of houses. It was a favorite spot for horseback riders because of hours of riding on virgin land.

As with acreage everywhere, subdivisions and highways have totally changed the wild, open areas into pockets of shopping centers and rising new communities. But once off the highway, and as you drive through the gates of Filoli, with a sign marked PRIVATE RESIDENCE—SOUTH GATE, it's hard to believe that time has not erased the life style which only the wealthy could and can still afford.

Thanks to her famous father, William Matson, Mrs. Roth and her heirs have inherited a vast fortune which enables Mrs. Roth to still live in the grand manner. William Matson's success was such that his heirs are now millionaires, and the Matson Shipping Line continues to prosper long after his death.

Born in 1849, William Matson was left an orphan at an early age due to his parents' accidental death. Brought up in Lysekil, Sweden, and with practically no education, he began his sailing career. At ten, he began doing odd jobs on various ships, and at fourteen he worked his way across the Atlantic on *The Aurora*, which landed in New York. Already stories of gold in California intrigued this youngster and he shipped out on a sailing vessel called *The Bridgewater*, traveling around the Horn and arriving in San Francisco. Matson became a rugged young man working on barges in San Francisco's harbor and on coal schooners. He became master of a coal barge and also became acquainted with the Spreckles Sugar Refinery and its workers. The company refined sugar which was brought to San Francisco from Hawaii, and Matson became interested in this trade. At twenty-one he was a master mariner. "Captain Matson," as he was called from then on, raised $20,000 from friends to build a ship, *The Emma Claudine*, capable of carrying 300 tons. He filled the hold with goods to sell to the Hawaiians, and in turn they sold him railroad ties, sugar, sandalwood and coconuts. Since railroads were just beginning in the West, Matson seized the opportunity of using native woods to build ties, fill up his cargo space, and sell profitably on his return to California. He became a very successful trader but longed for a large ship with a greater cargo capacity. Again, he raised money and built a brig called *The Lurline*, costing $32,000 and capable of carrying 640 tons. He loved this ship and, as her master, took great pride in all her equipment. In Matson's trading days, the population of the Hawaiian Islands was about 50,000 and the Spreckels Company plant was located on the island of Hawaii. Matson conceived of a fleet of ships, each bigger and faster, to keep up with expanding trade. The sailing ships became obsolete and were replaced by steam-propelled steel boats. In 1901 he incorporated the Matson Navigation Company. His first steamship, *The Enterprise*, was finished in 1902 and sailed around the Horn to establish her place in the Hawaiian trade. She carried 22 passengers and weighed 3,620 tons deadweight. In 1898, Hawaii was annexed as a territory of the United States. The Hawaiian sugar industry became so important that it was to bring about an increase in passenger traffic. Captain Matson foresaw this trend and built a second *Lurline*, which carried 51 passengers and 8,000 tons of cargo. She began service in 1908. Next came the *Wilhelmina*, two years later, with 11 bathrooms, accommodations for 146 passengers, and the first shipboard movie theater on the Pacific run. The Matson fleet was underway. The *Manoa*, the *Matsonia*, the

Mavi, were all added to the Hawaii run. Matson then turned his interest to oil, convinced that it was the fuel of the future. He formed the Honolulu Oil Company to produce and transport oil. He built a pipeline, the first ever constructed in California from an oilfield to a refinery at a seaport. He introduced fuel oil on most oceangoing passenger ships. During World War I, he made three of his ships available as troop carriers on the Atlantic run.

Captain Matson's whole life was the sea. Tough, physically demanding of himself and his crews, the Matson Line prospered. His other interests were in civic affairs. He was President of the San Francisco Chamber of Commerce and had an excellent stable of trotters, enjoying driving a fast horse around the wharves in one of his favorite buggies.

In 1917 Matson died, but the Matson Company still flourishes, headquartered in a sixteen-story building named after the founder in 1924 in San Francisco, and Lurline Matson Roth is the proud bearer of his great name.

There is no number or street address for Filoli, the estate which Mrs. Roth bought in 1937, but my off-duty fireman, who drove me, had no trouble locating the driveway.

"Everyone around here knows where Mrs. Roth lives," he cheerfully assured me. I can count on one hand the number of houses I have visited with half-mile-long driveways.

The entrance to Filoli is like a drive through a private park with heavily wooded areas of eucalyptus tress where sunlight filters through, exposing here and there grazing deer and marvelous old gnarled oaks.

I had arrived on the day before the debut party of one of Mrs. Roth's granddaughters, and preparations for this gala almost postponed our meeting. I could well understand why, when I saw the logistics involved. Four huge rooms of Mrs. Roth's mansion had been emptied for twenty-four hours to make room for long buffet tables and dancing. Two tents were being erected. Caterers' trucks were lined up like cars in a gasoline line. Men were carrying, setting up, or erecting a movie-like set for a one-evening party. Mrs. Roth's own greenhouses had been almost entirely emptied of their flowers and plants, and two or three rented florist trucks looked like flowered floats in the Rose Bowl

Parade. Amidst all these preparations I arrived at the massive stone house, to be greeted by a butler who told me Mrs. Roth would be down in a moment.

I did not see much of the interior except for the room in which we sat and the four drawing rooms, each large enough to hold at least a hundred people. Heavy dark wood paneling was evident, but since the furniture had been put in storage temporarily for the party, it was hard to get a sense of Mrs. Roth's taste in decorating. It wasn't long before this legendary woman greeted me. Even as a child I had heard of her prowess as a horsewoman, her fabled hackney ponies, her dedication to community projects, and so it was that I chose to include her among America's great dowagers, which indeed she is.

We sat in a room filled with potted orchid plants and beautiful oriental porcelain. A simple, charming woman who seemed unruffled by the clamor of party preparations going on in other parts of the house, she was instantly gracious and responsive to my questions.

Born in 1891, Lurline Matson was an only child of a rather reticent mother and a father who established maritime history. But his daughter especially remembers her father's interest in horses, which she inherited and to this day continues to foster.

"You know," Mrs. Roth told me as we talked about her father, "you may find it peculiar, but people who go to sea are often interested in horses. Like many friends he knew, he couldn't swim, but he loved to ride. Father particularly loved to drive standardbred horses. In the early 1900s, all our California fairs in Golden State Park had races for amateur drivers (something they never have now), and Father would also attend auctions. He'd take me with him and inevitably he'd end up buying a couple of horses. Mother wasn't very enthusiastic about the horses, so most of the time he wouldn't tell her how many he really owned. His trick was to parcel them around to different Swedish sea captains he knew because, truthfully, we couldn't afford to have more than two, but somehow he usually had eight or nine."

Mrs. Roth has always had at least two horses of her own, and her father encouraged her to start showing when she was twelve. "I think I was one of the first girls in a five-gaited saddle class at the State Fair. There were only three of us (the other two were men) competing. It was one of the first five-gaited classes in California. I even remember the horse. Father had bought it for me in Tennessee and I was thrilled then. Now that I have more knowledge of standardbreds, I wouldn't think so much of him, but I won the class and they gave me a medal which, I'm sad to say, I've since lost.

Mrs. Roth did not lead the life of a spoiled child. She did what her parents bid her to and accepted and respected their right to do so.

"I should certainly say so," she said with determination when I asked her whether she was brought up with strong moral principles. "Why, everyone was," she added. "I wouldn't have thought of questioning my parents."

Mrs. Roth's mother made her clothes when she was a child, and although they were a middle-class family, they always had staff for their house.

"My father never seemed to worry about money," she mused. "I mean we just lived to the limit, and although we lived well, he would always pinch in some ways, and that's why Mother did most of the sewing. I remember once, when I was fairly young, Mother was hurt because Father had complained that she was spending too much money on the household. Knowing that Father had a soft spot for me, she faced him one night and said, 'All right, if the bills are too high, why not let Lurline run the house,' and I did for three months and he never criticized me once. He really tried to teach me how to handle money. Matter of fact"—and here Mrs. Roth hesitated for a moment—"well, to be honest, I think my father thought of me as a son and treated me like a boy, since that was probably what he had hoped for. And he was really very demanding. If he wanted me home at night, I was there, and if he wanted me to play bridge with him or dominoes, I'd do it immediately. Any schoolwork I had I'd do later. First I would do what he wanted."

Of course, as we commented on this kind of strictness, Mrs. Roth did not mean to infer that she loved him less because of his attitudes. That was how he behaved, and that was that.

Had he had his way, however, he probably would have pre-

ferred that she not marry. Having graduated from the Hamlin
School in San Francisco, her parents sent Lurline to Paris to
study singing for about four months. When she came back she
accompanied her mother and father to Honolulu, as she had
twice a year for years, since the Matson Line was an important
company in the islands. It was here when she was eighteen that
she met William Roth. He was ten years older than she and a
stockbroker, and she says they fell in love at first sight. He asked
her to marry him immediately. When she told her father, his reaction was strongly negative.

"He was really very jealous," she confessed, "because we were
so very close, probably closer than any father and daughter I
could ever think of. He wanted me to wait awhile and used the
excuse that I was too young. I must admit, we kept on seeing
each other anyway, sneaking around until father finally relented
and gave his approval."

Lurline and William Roth were married in 1915 but lived
with her family until 1918, when her father died and they moved
to a house in San Francisco, which is now the Swedish Consulate.
Roth gave up his job in the brokerage business and went to work
for his father-in-law. He and Lurline had a son and twin daughters. The Roth marriage was a happy one and lasted for forty-
nine years, until his death in 1964.

Lurline Roth will always be remembered because of her great
dedication and devotion to fine harness horses. She has not only
been an owner and breeder with a fine show string, but until a
few years ago she showed her own ponies and was nationally
known, having participated in most of the large shows in the
country. "Why Worry" farm, not far from "Filoli" and still in
Woodside, is where the horse operation is still ensconced and
where she still keeps about ten museum-quality carriages and
open rings, maintained in immaculate condition.

"I started the stables on Mother's place in 1922," Mrs. Roth
said proudly. "Mother had wanted my husband and me to name
the property but we couldn't, so she said, 'Well, I'm not going to
worry. I'll call it "Why Worry," since you can't think of anything.' We used to spend our summers there. It wasn't a very big
place. I suppose maybe seventy-five acres, but I sold off most

of the property when we acquired Filoli, and so I just have the stable and ring and carriage house and some paddocks left."

Mrs. Roth has cut down somewhat on the number of horses and the shows attended. But visiting her model stable is an experience that delights every horse enthusiast. The box stalls extend row on row in the large building, which is kept up in the finest tradition of stable management. The tack room is so neat, it is hard to believe that the polished bits and the shiny leather reins and harnesses have ever been used. Show ribbons and photographs of the famous Roth winners and sires are everywhere. The trunks in which the equipment is packed and the van outside give evidence that preparations are always going on to attend another big show.

"Well, generally, I now go to a show with about nine head of small hackneys," said Mrs. Roth. In the old days I used to take at least fourteen." But it is obvious that even though Mrs. Roth is not as active as she once was, the hackney ponies were and will always be her great love, and without her consuming interest, Why Worry farm would not have the national recognition it still enjoys.

Besides her horses, Mrs. Roth is known for her knowledge of flowers and gardens. At Filoli she has a staff of ten gardeners who oversee the formal plantings that lead away from the house, and she is determined to stay and keep up the place, although she admits it's very expensive and probably an impractical way to live these days.

"No, I wouldn't sell Filoli now. It's been my home for too many years, and it's too late to make a change at my age," said Mrs. Roth.

Unfortunately, none of her children and only a couple of her grandchildren share her interest in the horses. And that has been her whole life, more than social events and cultural activities. She would rather donate a trophy to a horse show than gossip at a tea party, and she hopes that she still has enough time to travel and see the countries she missed.

"But the trouble is, at my age, when you're far away from home you may get ill, and that's a hardship for anyone traveling with you. I realize all too well, nobody can live forever."

Lurline Roth made her own life and is fulfilled as a person. She is the only dowager who is known for herself, not because of her husband or children but for her own ability. To successfully run a show string and stable is a talent, and she happily admits she inherited this ongoing interest from her beloved father.

Mrs. Nion Tucker

IF SOCIAL POWER AND PRESTIGE still exist, eighty-three-year-old Mrs. Nion Tucker of Hillsborough, California, is one of the two Old School *grande dames* in the San Francisco area. Her father at one time owned the San Francisco *Chronicle*, and Mrs. Tucker has been active in civic and social affairs for years. She started Guide Dogs for the Blind, she ran the San Francisco A.W.V.S. for four years with a membership of 11,000 women, and she founded and has been the guiding force of the Debutante Cotillion, the most exclusive ball in the city. She has served on the opera and symphony boards and is also a director of the *Chronicle* newspaper and the De Young Museum, founded eighty years ago by her father.

The De Young family was once powerful and part of the elite in the late 1890s in San Francisco, and now Phyllis Tucker is the last surviving daughter of famous Mike de Young and a fine example of the social dowager.

It is hard to believe that Mrs. Tucker is an octogenarian. One would take her for at least ten years younger. She has bright cornflower-blue eyes and short coiffed blond hair. Dressed in her favorite color, blue, she received me at the chic and exclusive Burlingame Country Club, about a half hour's drive from San Francisco. She is the only live-in member of the Club, which is quite a distinction, she has made her residence there for twenty-three years. By way of establishing records, her maid, Dominique, has been with her for forty-six years. For Mrs. Tucker has little left in the way of a family. Her son was killed in World War II; her sole survivors are her divorced daughter and her twenty-one-year-old son. She is the only dowager with little in the way of family and material possessions or personal relationships to depend on.

Women of her age tend to have collected a lifetime of treasures and mementoes, but not so with this lady. Whatever she has accumulated over a lifetime fits simply into a few rooms of a country club residence. She is the living chronicle of a bygone day and life style which is merely an anachronism in the free-living city that San Francisco has become. But present Socialites still pay her homage, for knowing her is proof of being Socially acceptable. "What was Society like eighty-two years ago," I asked. "Well, I was born in San Francisco in 1892 and my three sisters and brother grew up there," Mrs. Tucker recalled.

"My father, Michael Henry de Young, always known as Mike, was born in St. Louis. He and his brothers and my grandparents, who all lived there, decided they wanted to come to California. My grandfather had quite a good deal of money at the time and so they embarked on a riverboat, but halfway through the trip, Grandfather died of a stroke. My grandmother had little interest in money and knew less about dealing with it. She eventually arrived in San Francisco, rented a house, soon acquired her own carriage and horses and many pretty clothes, and ordered a great many more. She didn't give a hoot where the money came from or how she spent it."

The result was that Mrs. Tucker's father, who was three when they arrived in California, found himself seventeen years later without any money. He left high school and started a magazine called *The Dramatic Chronicle*, which gave information on entertainment in the city. He and his older brother, Charles, worked on it together. Originally it was a throwaway tossed in every doorway by newsboys, but the idea caught on, people liked the format, and the De Youngs were on their way. They began the newspaper and lived at home, supporting their mother until they got married. Mike de Young married Rae Deane, a San Franciscan, from the strongly Catholic Deane family.

Mrs. Tucker's mother's ambition was to have been a Shakespearean actress, but the Deanes were extremely conservative—and, after all, in those days, actresses were not considered ladies. She followed her mother's urgings, against her will, to become a schoolteacher, which lasted until she met and married De Young.

It was an odd match; she was a devout and practicing Catholic, and he an agnostic. The De Young children, however, were brought up as Catholics and, as Phyllis Tucker emphasized, it was a strict and old-fashioned upbringing. She and her three sisters and brother never thought to challenge any decisions made by their parents.

Mike de Young favored Phyllis, who was the youngest, and the love between the two is fondly remembered.

"I was very devoted to my father," Mrs. Tucker said.

"In fact, as a little girl I used to walk with him to the office in the mornings, and it was quite a distance, every day. In the afternoon either my mother or I would call for him with the horse and carriage. He was a man of very set rules. He had his breakfast at a definite time and ate what he thought was good for him. I was handed over to my Irish, redheaded nurse at birth, and she stayed until I was twenty-five. When I was seven, my parents put me in a convent in Paris, and then I went to another convent in Dresden, but that was a day school. My aunt and my grandmother rented a pension and I lived with them there. My darling nurse would take me to school at eight and pick me up at five-thirty, and I was perfectly happy despite the fact that none of the children or teachers spoke English, only German. Summers were the only times we children saw our parents, and then we would travel through Europe in a touring car for three months learning about the different countries."

The De Youngs, when they weren't traveling, lived in a large seven-bedroom house in San Francisco. The four children, "Mama Deane," the maternal grandmother, and Kate de Young's sister made up the members of the household. The De Young daughters were encouraged to take up music. Helen was an accomplished harpist, who was asked to join the San Francisco Symphony on a regular basis, but her husband wouldn't allow it. Constance was a violinist, and so was the other sister, Kathleen. Phyllis played the piano and wanted to be a professional dancer. She just didn't have the ambition to make a career out of it, and I doubt that she would have been allowed to. The Social life was the expected one, and San Francisco had its debutante season. As Phyllis Tucker explained, when I asked her if she was conscious of being a member of Society, "Why of course not.

There was no consciousness—you just were." All of her three sisters made their debuts, as did she, in the ballroom of their house, and the endless teas and dances filled days and nights. In between times, Mrs. De Young insisted there should be some time for serious study. "Mother had a wonderful expression," she told me, "that might interest you. She used to say, 'My dear, always remember, never be a tree. Trees die from the top down. Continue taking lessons and learning until you die, languages or music or going to lectures. But whatever you do, never stop learning for the rest of your life.' And so we children did what mother said, taking lessons and going to luncheon parties and wearing pink taffeta dresses—and always a party and more creamed chicken and green peas and ice cream, until two in the morning. One thing Mother did allow us to do was to sleep late until about nine o'clock, and then we could have breakfast in bed. That Mother thought we needed so we could recuperate from the day before and gather strength for the next twenty-four hours."

It was at a party that Phyllis met Nion Tucker, who wanted to marry her right away. She was then twenty and he was thirty. "No, I told him no, several times. I had no intention of marrying anybody. I'm ashamed to tell you that when he pressed me for a reason, I said, "I'll never settle down to one man. I like lots of beaux and lots of flowers and lots of dancing."

"Oh," he said, "you'll get over that someday."

"And I did, three years later riding in a hansom coming back from the theater in New York. He proposed and I said, 'All right, maybe I will marry you. Yes, I guess I will.'" Tucker was an investment banker and an Episcopalian, but he agreed to bring up their children as Catholics and they went to Mass every Sunday. Married twenty-three years, they had two children, a daughter and a son, who was killed at Iwo Jima.

Their daughter Nan, fifty-three, is divorced, something her mother was brought up to believe was unthinkable.

"Yes," Mrs. Tucker said to me, as the word "divorce" was mentioned, "I can remember my mother entertaining in her sitting room at one of her many tea parties. That day a couple of ladies were chatting and Mother mentioned the name of a woman in San Francisco. I remember her saying, 'I'm mulling over in my mind whether to receive Mrs. so and so when she arrives.'

The other ladies were bewildered. What did she mean? 'Well,' she answered, 'after all, she's a divorced woman and she did have fourteen men named by her husband as co-respondents, and I don't know whether I should accept her or not.' Suddenly there was this crisis," Mrs. Tucker continued, "and I never forgot that moment. It made a terrific impression on me."

Nion Tucker died very suddenly in 1950. They had been a close couple and the shock of his death, following her son's, left her bereft. But remembering what her mother would have said if she were alive, " 'Put your head up my dear and go on with your life,' " she said, "And I have, my dear, I have. It does take tremendous courage."

What will Phyllis Tucker be best remembered for? Most probably the San Francisco Cotillion, which she helped start in 1934, and has taken place every year except during World War II. It is one of the last of the super-exclusive balls in America, and it is perhaps the closest event to a private party for today's debutante, a fast-disappearing species. Committees and teas screen out any possible social undesirables, which means almost anything except white, American, Social, Catholic or Episcopalian.

For the first time this year, a "young Jewish woman was invited to be on the Board of Directors. We didn't think of it before," Mrs. Tucker admitted, "although a couple of girls from San Francisco's elite Jewish families have made the list each year. In a city where few Jewish people are accepted in clubs like the Pacific Union, the Garden Club, The Town and Country Club, snobbery is still practiced. Mrs. Tucker thinks it's ridiculous that they are excluded, but concedes she's never thought of resigning from an all-Christian board. "Wouldn't that just be a publicity stunt, like the gentleman who refused his Academy Award because of the Indians—oh, really," she chided me gently. "There are charming Jewish people who are not included in clubs. I know darling old Mrs. Koshland who used to say, 'You know, my dear, I don't understand why people have a prejudice against the Jews. We are such nice people.' " And I'd say, " 'Yes, Mrs. Koshland.' "

Mrs. Tucker still lives with the philosophies and ideological boundaries of the past. From time to time her only grandson wanders through the gates of the Burlingame Club to see his grandmother. Sometimes, Mrs. Tucker admits, he just appears at her door, and then, as if he had just walked in, she says in a generation-gap tone, "Oh, my God, that hair. And I've often asked him why he isn't wearing a tie. One day when his mother was here he came by to please her and me. Turning to his mother he said, 'I'm so famished, can't we go down to lunch?' And I said, 'We can go to lunch but we will not go into the dining room of the Burlingame Club with you looking like that.' My daughter tried to assuage me but I told her I didn't care. 'I'm not going to take my grandson in that room with an open-necked shirt and no tie on and his hair all over the place in a pair of blue jeans torn at the knee and wearing sandals.' 'No, I won't take you downstairs,' I said to him. 'We will go out to lunch.' 'Yes,' he laughed and said, 'Oh, Nanny, you're so silly. It doesn't matter what you wear.' Well, he's twenty-one and it's his life and I try not to keep picking on him."

She's a spunky dowager, but life must be wearing thin, for the Social life was a gossamer one at best, and she is relegated to memories with no real tie to the present. A family name only lives on if the accomplishments continue through each generation. Phyllis Tucker led a pleasant cotillion-type life and now the pace for her is slowing down. Although her presence at a Social event is an assurance that all is still well in San Francisco's dwindling aristocracy. She went to a funeral not long ago and "a man came up to me at the cemetery, a dear old Irishman, and he patted me and said, 'Well, well. You're sure the last survivor of the De Youngs.' I said, 'You're right, I am the last survivor, and I'm still surviving.'"

Matriarchs

THESE MATRIARCHS are a special tribe of women who, as they become widows, wrap their families around them like comforting cloaks. Some are less imbued with the maternal spirit, but all gain deep satisfaction and happiness from close family ties and are duly proud of a successful generation of offspring.

Mrs. Sulzberger is the grandmother of *The New York Times;* Mrs. Buckley, of conservative politics; Mrs. Kennedy, of a political clan; Mrs. Marcus and Mrs. Gimbel, of famous department stores. Mrs. Peabody has had a son as governor and on her own has challenged movements that displeased her.

Mrs. Buckley, Mrs. Kennedy and Mrs. Sulzberger have, because of public prominence, developed clout and power. Their views are sought after, their children are extremely close. All have led extraordinary lives with dynamic husbands and seemingly never faltered. Three have lost children and four are deeply religious. Their apparent strength has been acknowledged by Mrs. Buckley, Mrs. Kennedy and Mrs. Sulzberger as having its roots in extremely affectionate and respectful relationships with their fathers, and the pattern was repeated by Mrs. Buckley and Mrs. Kennedy particularly in their choice of husbands.

The symbiotic relationship of mother to children has had special meaning with this breed of matriarchs, who continue to make the preservation of these remarkable families possible. Very few women of the next generation will want to be matriarchs or take on the responsibilities of scores of grandchildren, and great-grandchildren. The family skeins of my generation have loosened so that these rare *grande dames* have read themselves out of their roles. With the passing, the family unit loses its cohesiveness that they so successfully provided, and there is no one to pass the torch on to. They, the matriarchs, are punctuation points, wonderful to be with and enjoy, unique human beings who cherish character, love and selflessness above all else. Women today could well take note, for these women are successes.

Mrs. William Buckley

MRS. WILLIAM BUCKLEY'S WHOLE LIFE has been family-oriented, first as a child and then as a happy fulfilled wife. Devoted to her parents, she married an extremely successful man, bore him ten children, and now, at seventy-eight, is the matriarch of the well-known Conservative Buckley clan. She is important and impressive to me because she has never felt the need to express herself but remains happily satisfied as mother of eight and grandmother of fifty. Her active, talented children are proof that she gave them a secure foundation, and it is easy to see why she has engendered their love and respect.

Before we met at the Buckley estate, "Great Elm" in Sharon, Connecticut, Aloise Steiner Buckley and I had quite a correspondence. She was spending the winter at her other home, "Kamschatka" in Camden, South Carolina, acquired in 1938. The question was where we would do the interview, whether in New York while visiting one of her children, or in Sharon. The style of her writing indicated a charming, delightful woman, eager to be helpful and only too anxious to receive me. Her letters had established a warm rapport with me, so that when we met on a June day at Great Elm, I felt that we hardly needed an introduction. Instantly gracious and without any pretension we settled into a comfortable conversation. Her dancing blue eyes and eager responses endeared her to me, and it is obvious why she has so many admirers in and out of the family. The typical grandmother, the understanding, sympathetic older woman, she has the facility of giving herself. Being a contented, happy person, her greatest joy is pride in her family. It was, it is, and it will be as long as she can share her life with them.

A descendant of the Lee family through her maternal grand-mother, Aloise Steiner was born in New Orleans in 1895 and is one-quarter German, half Swiss, and one-quarter Scotch-Irish. Her father's family, all of Swiss descent, arrived in Louisiana in the early eighteen-hundreds. Crossing over into France, they had to obtain visas to come to the United States. Mrs. Buckley said, in apology, "I'm not a snob and I don't believe in snobbery, but my father used to say that our antecedents came over, if you'll excuse me, paying their own way. My father was born in 1885 and remembered New Orleans falling to the Federal forces (I used to say 'Yankee' but I don't use that word any more). Both his father and my mother's father fought in the War Between the States. Mother's father, Henry Wassem, after the war, bought some land in Port Gibson, Mississippi, sixteen miles from Vicksburg. He was a tall man, six foot three, but my father was only five foot six. My mother met my father when she was in New Orleans. He was a widower and sixteen years older. They fell in love and he made many trips to Fort Gibson, which was a hundred and thirty miles from New Orleans and the journey was long and difficult on rough roads."

The Steiners were married when she was twenty-two and he was thirty-eight. Aloise's father was a gentle gentleman, and the marriage was an extraordinarily happy one. Mrs. Steiner was the disciplinarian, probably due to her Germanic background. Her husband often deferred to her. According to his daughter, his greatest interest was in books and in writing. He also was one of the few people in the Deep South who went to college after the Civil War.

"My mother went to finishing school in Vicksburg, but my children," Mrs. Buckley affirmed, "are intellectuals, and this trait they probably inherited from my father, who was insistent that my two sisters and brother learn to read properly. As children we were never allowed to read a word which we didn't understand without looking it up in the huge old family dictionary."

The Steiner children were brought up under a strict moral code. "But then" as Mrs. Buckley admitted, "so was everyone else."

"Mother was very strict, and I remember when I was sixteen

a young man began calling on me. He was twenty-one and a lawyer. My grandmother, who had been living with us since her husband's death, was a Lee and very Victorian. She felt that Mr. Outlaw stayed too late at night. 'Too late' meant eleven oclock! Besides, she and my mother (my father never got into these matters) thought that he was much too old for me. Mother told me that I must tell him that he couldn't stay later than ten-thirty, and preferably ten. Oh, I was too shy to tell him that. The next time he was in the house at quarter to eleven an alarm rang. He couldn't imagine what it was. I told him, 'I think it's my signal.'

" 'What do you mean, signal?' he asked.

" 'Well,' I said, 'I'm not allowed to have guests after ten-thirty.'

"He did come back once or twice after that evening, but his ardor was definitely cooled."

Aloise and her sisters and brother were raised as strict Catholics because of their parents' strong religious sentiments.

"My grandfather Wassem wasn't a Catholic, but he died a Catholic," Mrs. Buckley informed me. "Or, as my husband would have said, 'They caught him on his deathbed.' "

Aloise Steiner never went to a Catholic school because her father, an intellectual, did not think that Catholic schools in those days offered the best education, and education was his fetish. The children went to parochial schools, but in those days there were no blacks or minority groups because the schools took the children from the surrounding neighborhood, and the Steiners lived in a well-to-do section. The family wasn't wealthy by present standards, but they had four in help and were considered part of New Orleans Society. But public school offered a more balanced fare than the present city counterpart and Aloise Steiner thrived.

"You see," as Mrs. Buckley explained, "public schools were taught by, forgive me, southern ladies who had been well-educated but who were without means. We were, of course, naturally impregnated with their version of the Civil War. I remember one particular teacher, dear old Mrs. Campbell, saying, 'Now, daughter (we were all called that), the South will forgive, but it will never forget.' Of course," Mrs. Buckley hastened to

assure me, "I've outgrown those prejudices. We had wonderful
teachers, all so beautifully educated, in music and in art. We
really learned an appreciation of these subjects, which one
hardly does nowadays in private schools."

It was during these early years that Aloise Steiner developed
an interest in music. She started taking piano lessons when she
was six, encouraged by her parents, who watched her play at
little concerts. She stopped studying music when she went to
Newcomb College, which was then, in her words, "a private
(I hate the word) 'ladies' college. Now it's the Women's College
of Tulane University." She was only there three years when
she left to marry William Buckley.

Although it wasn't the fashion to go to college, her high-
school teacher called her into the classroom and said, "Miss
Steiner, I would like to speak to you. I would like to talk to your
parents, preferably your father."

"Since Papa was supposed to be the head of the family, he
talked to her," Mrs. Buckley said. "And, although this sounds
very immodest," she admitted, "the teacher said that I was college
material and that I ought to continue my education. I had a few
friends who went to college, but with a father as insistent as
mine that learning was so important, I went."

The religious training of the Steiner children was also left
mostly to their father. During Lent he was very strict and insisted that the family attend church every day.

"We were never allowed to go out on dates with boys during
that time," Mrs. Buckley said wistfully. "Although, I remember
a beau called John Huffman whose mother was a Theosophist.
They're the ones who believe in reincarnation. Obviously, she
didn't have much use for Catholicism. Well, her son John came
to my father and said, 'I'd really like to have a date with your
daughter, Aloise, because I'm very interested in the Catholic
Church' (which he wasn't), 'so would it be all right if I would
accompany you and Mrs. Steiner to the services?'

"Well, my dear Felicia, in the first place I really didn't like
John Huffman and I hoped Papa would say no. But he didn't,
giving me the reason that this might be a chance for a conversion.
He really sincerely believed in the Church and was much more
devout and spiritual than my mother who, being a Mississippian

and having been brought up in a non-Catholic community, only attended Mass once a month."

Although religion and faith are still the foundation of Aloise Buckley's life, in her early years her warm, outgoing personality made her popular in the social circle of her day. She was definitely a member of upper-class New Orleans Society and, as she explained ("And I hope some of my friends won't misunderstand this"), New Orleans Society was very snobbish. The new Americans who came down, the Anglo-Saxon Americans, were never included because they were mostly supposed to be rich and vulgar. My grandmother, who was so gentle, tried to explain how I could go to any party because *our* family was accepted. It was hard for me to understand why even some of my close friends did not get the invitations I did. The great division was in the big carnival organizations. There were the French and then there were the Anglo-Saxon ones. Camus was the most beautiful ball, and it was Mardi Gras Tuesday. And then there was Proteus, Nereus, and the Atlanteans. I remember, you'd receive your invitation and you'd go and sit in an enclosed circle. Everyone was masked and the men wore black tail coats and white tie. It was terribly formal. Your name would be called out as each new dance began and you would be presented to your masked partner. Oh, it was so romantic and usually your partner would give you a very lovely gift. And if he was in love with you, he'd give you a very expensive gift, or maybe even a little bit of jewelry."

You could see by the nostalgic twinkle that this gay little lady had a fun time wherever she went. At twenty-two, she was still enjoying the Social whirl, although her father kept referring to her as a spinster, since her youngest sister had married. It was she who introduced Aloise to William Buckley. He was with the firm of Buckley & Buckley in Tampico, Mexico, where the Lombards lived.

"He was just dabbling in oil because he was so fed up with the big companies," Aloise explained. "So one day in the spring of 1917 the telephone rang and this very nice man's voice said, 'Miss Steiner, I'm a friend of your sister, Mrs. Lombard, and would you have lunch with me at the Yacht Club?' It was right on the lake and so lovely. And then he wanted me to have

dinner with him. But that's where my father stepped in and
said, 'But, Aloise, I haven't met Mr. Buckley and neither has
your mother.' So we arranged for him to come by the house and
meet the family. They were so charmed with him that Papa
relented and allowed me to go out to dinner, but I had to be
home early because I had a rehearsal for a recital."

It was love at first sight, Aloise admitted. She had always liked
older men and Buckley was fourteen years her senior. She
had spent her summers in Mexico City with her sisters and a
family friend from 1915 until she met William Buckley in 1917.
He asked her to marry him six days after he met her. "But I
wouldn't have done that," she confessed and re-emphasized.
"No, I certainly wouldn't have done that, because I was afraid of
my mother, and actually I had a lot of other beaux and was
having a very good time. I remember telling my aunt, 'I'm not
going to be easy to get. I'm going to wait.' And she said that he
was very attractive and had a good reputation and a nice office
in Mexico City."

Aloise and William Buckley were engaged a week later and
married in December 1917. In an issue of the family periodical,
Grelmschatka, edited and written by the Buckley children, there
is a wonderful tribute to their mother and father on their fortieth
anniversary in 1958:

> We had long ascertained that Father, who knows a good
> thing when he sees it, had waited until he was thirty-five
> —that is until he met Mother—to make his first proposal
> of marriage. And we have always known (I guess it was
> Mother who told us) she turned down eleven, or was it
> thirty-six, beaux while awaiting our somewhat laggard
> father. This always seemed perfectly normal to us as chil-
> dren; the possibility that Mother might have chosen anyone
> else to be *our* father was, in fact, inconceivable.

> But now as adults ourselves we realize it was not as simple
> as that. We thank Mother for the resiliency and under-
> standing she has demonstrated in putting up with Father
> for 14,610 days and for a staggering 109,865 days with the
> other ten. We thank Father for his unswerving belief
> through thick and through thin, through braces, pimples,
> through adolescenthoods (ours) and unfinished sentences
> (Mother's) that we were worth it all.

The Buckleys, he thirty-six and she twenty-two, planned to live in Tampico, Mexico, and they did spend a short time there, but with a revolution brewing during Aloise's first pregnancy, they rented a house in Bronxville. (Their first child, Aloise, was born in 1918 in New Orleans en route to the East.) They always hoped to build a house in Mexico. "The old Mexicans just loved Will and we still have so much Mexican furniture," Mrs. Buckley said. But then Buckley was expelled from Mexico because he protested the help Woodrow Wilson was giving President Huerta. In 1922, they bought the house in Sharon, Connecticut, where Mrs. Buckley now lives.

Great Elm has gone through extensive changes and was enlarged to accommodate the brood of ten Buckley children born from 1918 to 1938.

"I'm a great believer in God," Mrs. Buckley said firmly, "and, although I didn't particularly want a large family, I believe in what He wants. It was a little hard on me except for the fact that we had a perfectly magnificent French governess who lived and died in our house and is buried near my husband." There was other help besides—two extra Mexican nurses from whom the children learned Spanish.

When the children were small the Buckleys traveled a lot, but Mrs. Buckley always yearned for a home.

"It was fifty-one years ago that we bought this house, and I remember we put the deed of it on the Christmas tree."

Family life has centered around Great Elm ever since.

William F. Buckley, Jr., known as Bill, nationally known author, TV personality and editor of *The National Review*, talked of his mother warmly and directly and the relationship she had with his father.

"He was more of a perfectionist than Mother was. For example, she would not have rebuilt the roof of the stable eight times. My father did because he didn't like the specifications. In that sense, he was more of a perfectionist than she. Where she's always been perfectly prepared to speak fluent atrocious French and Spanish, Father would never permit himself to utter anything in French because it wasn't good enough for him. He did, however, speak perfect Spanish."

Both mother and son acknowledge that William Buckley Senior was head of the family, and his wife agrees that she did defer to him, "perhaps because I thought he was right most of the time."

Their warm, close relationship, attested to now by their children and friends, gave a secure framework to the childrens' growing-up period. Unhappily, two of them, Aloise at forty-nine and Maureen at thirty-three, died young, and their father outlived them, passing away at seventy-seven.

What makes Aloise Buckley still so vital and interesting is that she is the matriarch of the first Family of American Conservatism, and she has passed on to her eight children her strong Catholic ardor and faith that she and her husband shared. Remarkably enough, the whole family does not covet personal gain or self-recognition. They are crusaders for Conservatism, and William F. Buckley, Sr.'s belief in God and in America and his family strongly motivates his widow and eight children.

"I don't think it's so important to be first and best," Mrs. Buckley said in answer to my question about some similarity between the Kennedy and Buckley families. "It has been said of our family that we were behind the times. Actually, when the children were growing up we thought that what America offered then was better than some of the newer political ideas that were being talked of. For us it's hard to accept change unless it's for the better, and at the moment this world couldn't be worse off than it is."

The eight Buckley children—John, fifty-four; Priscilla, fifty-three; Jim, fifty-one; Jane, fifty; Bill, forty-nine; Patricia, forty-seven; Reid, forty-four and Carol, thirty-six—are living proof of the Buckley legend. Close-knit family ties, total involvement and commitment to Conservatism and their country, they are the best examples of what a woman like Aloise Buckley has contributed as a great wife and mother. John Buckley is now President of Catawba Company in New York City, his family's oil-management company. Priscilla Buckley is Managing Editor of *The National Review*. Jane Smith is divorced and is a housewife in Sharon, Connecticut. Bill, as I have mentioned, is Editor of *The National Review*, a columnist, lecturer, author and a TV personality. Patricia Bozell is Managing Editor of the Conservative Catholic monthly magazine *Triumph*. Reid is an author and lecturer. Carol Learsy is a housewife and does part-time work for *The National Review.* Jim worked for Catawba and has been a senator since 1970.

Her fifty grandchildren each have a special relationship with her, although, as one of her children told me, she doesn't have the fascination for children under thirteen that her husband had.

"She was everything that you would expect of a mother," Bill, her son, told me, "except she never took much of a role in the kitchen. In fact, it was a location with which she was never able to identify. She loves to read and she is very house-oriented. She doesn't really enjoy sports. For instance, she's never been in swimming. She's only been on my boat once, and then with high-heeled shoes!"

Dearly beloved, with religious reverence, Mrs. William Buckley has such strong faith that she is very confident that people whom she cares about, but who aren't as religiously oriented, will somehow find their way back to the good and spiritual life. In a generation that needs beacons, Mrs. Buckley and her public-spirited children are human beings who have found their way.

Someday I would like to go back to Great Elm and see that lovely lady who wrote me so kindly, "I enjoyed our visit and hope we will meet again—less formally. A.S.B."

Mrs. Herbert Marcus

MINNIE MARCUS is one of the oldest women in this book and perhaps one of the youngest-looking. Her unlined gentle face is framed with gray hair and she wears glasses, but at ninety-two she is unimpaired physically and the ravages of time have not caught up to her. Living in one of the oldest, most modern high-rise apartment buildings in the "nice residential" section of Dallas, Mrs. Marcus has no relics around her, no clutter from the past; she lives very much in the present. Her only treasures are her favorite collection of silver miniatures, which is in two cabinets, and in her living room she has a special glassed-in section with the proper humidity and lighting for her favorite hobby, plants.

Minnie Marcus has lived in the building for the last ten years, since her sister's death. She now has a companion and, for staff, a maid and a cook. She recently fired a chauffeur whom her sons had urged her to let go because he was not a good driver. "I finally gave in, since I figured if I ever had an accident they'd be the first to say, 'We told you so.' "

Looking twenty or thirty years younger than her actual age, she does not avert my gaze but listens and unhesitatingly responds to my questions. Dressed in purple wool with a simple gold pin, glasses, gray hair, she folds and refolds neatly with her hands the hanging purple collar tabs. The apartment is a living room, greenhouse, dining room combination with a mixture of Eisendieck's candy-box ladies, a formal portrait of the owner, a small Renoir in the corner, and a back hall filled with photos of children, grandchildren and great-grandchildren.

Minnie Marcus is a gentle Jewish matriarch whose great interest is her family and gardening. The city of Dallas feels she is one of their favorite citizens because she has helped to beautify their avenues with plantings of flowers and trees which she and her family have given as a good-will gesture.

"Mother has an extraordinary green thumb and it is she who really brought Bromeliads to Texas," her son Stanley, sixty-seven and Chairman of the Board of Neiman-Marcus, the unique department store, explained. "On her ninetieth birthday, we, her sons, gave a collection of ninety of these plants to establish the Marcus Gardens as an honor to her and as a memorial to our father. Mother even has her own title, our Horticultural Vice-president, because she still supervises all the greenery in our stores."

"Oh, I've gardened all my life. Even as a child," Mrs. Marcus admitted. "It was an avid hobby of my mother's, and I guess I inherited that primitive instinct. My favorite tree is the crepe myrtle, which is indigenous to the South. I've given these trees to Temple Emanu-El to enhance one thousand feet which fronts on a highway. Temple means a great deal to me. I usually go Friday nights or when I can, but it's so hard to get a chauffeur who is willing to drive at night, and my one disappointment is that my family isn't religious. If they were, I could go with them. That's their only weak spot—an Achilles heel. You see, I was brought up in a totally Jewish atmosphere. As a child I lived in Waxahatchie, Texas. My father's name was Lichtenstein but everyone called him "Lich." He had a grocery store in town and we were only one of four Jewish families in the community. My father was of Russian-German extraction, very aristocratic, very wealthy family but not the smartest people. My mother was born in Russia and she was smart as a knife. She ruled the whole shebang, my father and we children. Papa was the refined, elegant gentleman, and Mama was the one who had guts. She was very strait with us. I can remember at about six, going next door to the Grosses, who were friends. Mrs. Gross had married a lawyer and they lived rather well. They had a cook who would allow my sister and me to play store with the ironing and to touch all the linens after they'd been laundered. That was something Mama would never have permitted, nor did she believe in giving us special privileges. We went to the local public school and I graduated when I was sixteen. My mother always wanted me to go to the State University because she couldn't stand the idea of her daughters going to work. In the 1890s, you see, working women had still not achieved status. Mother said it would be all right to learn to be a schoolteacher. To her, that was the height of elegance.

"One day I met a new young man who had just arrived in town. A girl friend of mine had three old-maid sisters. They were known as the Hernstadt girls. They had invited this man to play bridge in the evenings with them, as he played a beautiful game. His name was Herbert Marcus and I met him one evening when they invited me to join them. I was sixteen and he was twenty and he had just come from Louisville, Kentucky, to Dallas to work for Pacific Mutual Life Insurance. Although we went out several times, he didn't have a nickel to his name, but . . . oh! he was swanky and elegant. One day he asked me what my summer plans were. I told him of the university and my wish to be a schoolteacher. He replied that he had a better plan. A plan that we should get married. I talked to my family but they were against it. My mother believed in saving and had even taught my father. She knew that Herbert was extravagant. He had a trunk full of exquisite clothes and, as my mother put it, 'No plan for the future.' She and my father said, 'He won't amount to anything.' But in time he won them over and we were married in 1902 when I was eighteen. It wasn't that we waited two years. Quite the contrary, I fought him off for two years. He was very anxious but in the meantime he went to work with Sanger Brothers, a general department store, referred to as the Marshall Field of the West (at that time). He was self-educated."

As Stanley Marcus admitted about his father, "He had great ambitions and great pretentions."

"I tried to teach him to put some money away, and we purposely didn't try to have children," Mrs. Marcus said, "for three years. When I did get pregnant, Herbert was making a hundred and twenty-five dollars a month as manager of the boy's department. His brother-in-law, Al Neiman, in New York, was running an advertising agency for country merchants. Herbert told Neiman that he was going to quit Sanger's unless they gave him a raise. Philip Sanger offered my husband a dollar and a quarter a week more and Herbert turned it down, although Sanger thought he ought to stay and was certain 'That dang fool kid'll be back soon.' But Herbert had another plan. Neiman asked him to come to Atlanta and run his office. We moved there when Stanley, our eldest, was two months old. Al and Herbert were very successful, I thought. They would go to little country towns and make a big to-do about a big sale. I don't even know if their company had a name. They had nothing to sell but their reputation and a desk. After two years, Herbert, who had dreams of a kind of elegant life, became dissatisfied and he talked Neiman into selling out. They advertised that their advertising business was for sale and someone offered them two choices. One was to take over a concession for a new drink that was coming out called 'Coca-Cola.' The other was taking twenty-five thousand dollars in cash for their business. They made the latter choice." And as Stanley Marcus was to say years later, "Neiman-Marcus (although now a thriving, world-famous store) was originally founded on poor business judgment, if you look at what's happened to Coco-Cola since my father turned down the franchise."

But Neiman and Marcus took their cash and returned to Dallas. In 1907 they started the store in Dallas and by 1926 they had doubled its size. It's still growing, with six other branches across the country. They were both known to have good taste, and Herbert Marcus insisted on stocking merchandise of very high quality. Today his thirty-five-year-old grandson, Richard, is President of the store, and it still carries on the tradition of "The Best of Everything."

Minnie Marcus' trust in a man her parents did not have high hopes for proved her right. Herbert Marcus became an extremely successful man, and his "little country girl" wife, as she refers to herself, learned about good taste and acquired culture.

"She couldn't help learning from my father," Stanley said, "because all he ever talked about at dinner was the store—what was happening in fashion, what Mrs. so-and-so didn't buy, et cetera."

Herbert Marcus was, from all reports, a strong person and a demanding one. As his son reflects, "He was, as Oscar Wilde once said, 'easily satisfied with the best.' He expected the best as a matter of course, and if he brought two people home for dinner at

6 P.M. or 8, the meal, he assumed, would be perfect. My father's interest was in the end result, not in the actual working. He wanted big trees and was unwilling to plant small ones and wait for them to grow. Mother had patience; she was willing to do the spade work and help them grow." Much as she did with her sons, she devoted her life to bringing them up, and today she is the matriarch of the Marcus family.

While her husband was alive, her family agreed that she was willing to bask in his reflection, learning self-confidence as her husband's achievements and finances grew, but she was quietly clever. Her belief was, and is, that women should have a subtle influence on their husbands and children and that influence should manifest itself in love and affection for the family. Backing it up should be a sense of values and determination that children live up to standards set by their parents.

Herbert Marcus died after a long illness in 1950; they had been married almost forty-nine years. Minnie feels that her husband was the most important influence in her life, but it was her mother who, with her high principles, set the example for her daughter. The idea of conscience, a word we don't often hear these days, was the fiber from which Minnie took her credo. In the early 1900s, conscience was a very important moral factor. Frugality, which her mother had practiced all her life, was an inherited trait. A grandson notes that his grandmother, true to her European background of making the most of what they had, never threw away a piece of string. "She always wound it up and put it in the 'string drawer' because, as she said, 'You never know when you'll be needing a piece.'"

Minnie Marcus never tried to be anything but a good mother and wife. She has always been conservative, even now in later years when she can afford anything she wants to. She is a careful manager of her own money but very generous with it when she feels people are in need. She continues to stress "character" as an important facet of a human being. Her four children, eight grandchildren and fourteen great-grandchildren think of Minnie Marcus in a loving, affectionate way and respect her homely virtues of insistence on character building, her adherence to principles. "That comes before everything else," Minnie told me. "I once told a young man who came into our family rather unwel-

comely (we all have that happen): 'You know, it isn't money that
I care about, it's that my children have to have a goal and they
must be honest.' I agree with ol' man Shakespeare, 'Thou shalt not
be false with any man.' I also believe in being fair with all one's
family."

Stanley's greatest compliment to his mother is that she has always recognized the strengths and weaknesses of her family. "She
tried to compensate for the weaknesses in each and helped develop
our strengths—always trying to keep things equal. Mother lived in
a period when fidelity was considered a virtue much more than
it's considered today—in a period when even divorce was rare. In
her day you married a man because you loved him. You brought
up children according to a family code; whether right or wrong,
you never deviated."

Minnie Marcus at ninety-two had the deep love and affection
of her husband, despite his demanding character. After his death,
she emerged with greater strength and self-assurance. She has become stoic about old age.

"Of course I have aches and pains. You can't get to be ninety-
two without having them, but you learn to overlook them and
keep your problems to yourself. I'm like all old people. I'm fussy
and expect a great deal of my grandchildren. Sure, I'm healthy,
as health goes, but deterioration is not a pleasant thing to contemplate. I don't contemplate death with any pleasure, but I don't
fear it. I've learned a lot in my life. Most women outlive men because wives plague their husbands to death. I learned from Herbert (I mean 'Herb.' Oh, when I got real strict and hoity-toity I
called him Herbert, but mostly it was 'darling' or 'sweetheart')
not to ask men too many questions. A man likes to have secrets."

It isn't just the Marcus family who look to Minnie Marcus as a
binding force and a warm, wonderful lady. She has endeared herself to the whole Dallas community. On her eightieth birthday
the city showered her with affection. Mayor Thornton declared
a Minnie Marcus Dallas Day and gave a big luncheon for her, the
first woman in Dallas history to be so honored. As Minnie
fondly recalls, "The Mayor was such a doll to have done it. After all, there were women much more important than me. I was
deeply touched."

Back to the present, fingering her purple wool neck scarf, she

found humor in herself. "I just had the flu, you know, before it
was chic to have it. My companion is sick with back trouble and
went to the hospital. I've let my chauffeur go. I have nothing
right now. Poor little rich girl." And you knew from her twin-
kling eyes that the grocer's daughter who had risen to be one of
Dallas' beloved citizens still hadn't lost her sense of values or her
sense of perspective.

Minnie Marcus is really Dallas' favorite grandmother. She can
call much of the city her own private garden, between what she
has given and her family has donated to the city in her name. She
engenders in strangers and family alike a genuine motherly feeling and a strong respect for principles from the Marcus of each
generation and from a city that takes pride in her very presence.
Beauty is what she learned from her husband, and she wants to
share now that love with friends and family.

Mrs. Joseph Kennedy

PROBABLY AMERICA'S most celebrated living matriarch, Rose Kennedy at eighty-four is an example of a remarkable octogenarian. Few women have played as many roles: daughter of a mayor, wife of an ambassador, mother of a President and nine other children, and grandmother of twenty-eight grandchildren. Her life since early childhood has been filled with every facet of human drama and emotion, the joyous heights, the despairing depths, yet she is an extraordinary example of how a person can tolerate suffering and still rebound publicly whole and strong, ever the symbol of motherhood, ever a morally and spiritually dedicated soul.

A tightly structured woman, she has found that religion and self-discipline are her best defenses against mortal suffering. She has developed incredible concentration, and although a public figure, her life is her communication with God and her family. Her daily winter routine is in itself a study: breakfast after early morning Mass, lunch at 1:30, dinner at 7:15. Punctuality is maintained daily. Working with her secretary in the morning, she reserves the late afternoon, around five-thirty, for an hour of energetic walking along Lake Worth in Palm Beach. The routine varies little.

In the day and evening that I stayed with Mrs. Kennedy, she and I were always alone together. Her staff—a housekeeper, secretary, chauffeur and discreet bodyguard—were only in evidence when their duties called for them to be. We had four meetings; two were taped interviews, one was my tagging along on her daily walk, and on a purely social basis we talked before and during dinner and later until about nine, when we each went to bed.

Always co-operative and polite, Mrs. Kennedy never let down the façade or expressed an impulsive thought. It seems Kennedys rarely do, even when life's script is altered by unexpected incidents.

It was three o'clock in the afternoon when I arrived at Mrs. Kennedy's. I went up a few steps, through an unlocked door, up onto a terrace with a screen door that opened into the house. I rang the bell a couple of times before going in, but there was no answer. I called Mrs. Kennedy's name and then decided to go inside. A small hallway lay ahead, a living room to the right and a dining room to the left. The windows all faced onto a large lawn and the ocean. I enjoyed a few moments looking at all the photographs in the living room and then walked through the kitchen to the pantry, expecting to find a maid or someone.

"Hello," I said to the emptiness, feeling I might be arrested any moment for trespassing in the Kennedy house unless someone soon came to identify me. A voice answered, "I'll be right there." It was the secretary, Sue Sulad, and since she had typed Mrs. Kennedy's letter to me and obviously had read my responses, she didn't seem like a total stranger. She showed me to my room, referring to it as the President's bedroom, and told me that Mrs. Kennedy was resting but would be calling me on the telephone at 4 P.M. Before leaving me she showed me the book Mrs. Kennedy had left for me to glance through called *The Founding Father*. I had read it, fortunately, but her notes in her own handwriting in the margin proved fun, more interesting and much more useful to me than the text. There are so few Kennedy articles or books that Mrs. Kennedy deems worthy of attention, but this one book seemed to meet with her approval more than most others, and the facts that displeased her were noted as erroneous and a correction made in her handwriting.

Being an inveterate snooper, I observed the room. Utilitarian English commodes with white linen runners on the top—twin beds (I wonder which one the President slept in) with simple white organdy spreads; gray-green walls—like the rest of the house, which I was to be more familiar with later, simple and comfortable. A Mizner-built house with Spanish tiles, by no means the kind of pretentious decorating found in home-furnishing magazines—in fact, totally the opposite. A family had lived and enjoyed the spaciousness of the rooms with no special interest in promoting the interiors. The bathroom had Mrs. Kennedy's white towels with her monogram in blue. The books on one of the bedroom tables were a varied lot: *The Rosary in Daily Life;* a *Reader's Digest* Condensed Book of *Winds of War, The Runaways* and *Amazing Mrs. Pollifax;* and *The World's Great Letters.*

It wasn't quite four o'clock, so I wandered back into the living room to have a closer look at all the tables filled with photographs —Jackie in her wedding dress, a family group of Rose and Joe with their eight children, Teddy in wartime uniform, Bobby with Ethel and baby in a hospital, the President with John and Caroline as young children at the White House with their famous pony "Macaroni," Rose Kennedy at a masquerade ball, another at Kennedy Center with Teddy, Pat Lawford with three children, Bobby in scuba gear, Kathleen and her English husband, Ambassador Kennedy and Morton Downey. On one wall hung a wonderful photograph of the President and son John, and at the opposite end of the room an oil painting of Kennedy, Sr., in a bathrobe relaxing on a chaise longue by the pool. In the corner of the room there is a large piano and one is struck immediately by the two frames side by side on the polished top— photographs of the two portraits by Stickler that hang in the White House, one of the President and the other of his wife Jacqueline. Fortuny-print chairs and sofas and oak furniture complete the room. There are no fresh flowers, but a few fake arrangements here and there, because Mrs. Kennedy told me later that so many of the family had allergies.

The buzzing of the intercom in my bedroom interrupted my ogling and I walked quickly back to pick up the phone. I glanced at the bedside clock; it was ten minutes to four. "Felicia," Mrs. Kennedy's familiar voice greeted me, "welcome. Have you everything you need?" I assured her I did. "I'll be coming downstairs to see you at four o'clock." And then she hung up.

Armed with my recorder and prepared with my preset questions, I went back into the living room, sat down on the couch by the fireplace to await Mrs. Kennedy. It was only a matter of minutes before she came into the room behind me and I rose to greet her. She was immaculately dressed, every hair in place, and I was struck by her simple makeup and youthful, healthy looks. Her manner suggested that she was ready to get down to business. After some preliminary social tacking, we sat down, almost by stage direction, in front of my recorder. We taped for about an hour and I sensed that she was getting restless. I suggested that perhaps we should stop. "I usually take a walk about now," she said, relieved to have a break, and asked me to join her. I said I certainly would, with an enthusiasm my family would have noted as being totally phony. They know I loathe walking, but I didn't want to miss the opportunity of perhaps catching her off guard. She excused herself to put on something warmer. Although it was seventy degrees and April, I'm always cold and had come forearmed. I put on my white coat and a scarf, but my feet had no equipment for the exercise ahead. I had sandals, with a thong between the toes, that clearly were not made for a brisk trot, and I got a beautiful pair of blisters to nurse for a week. Mrs. Kennedy met me in the hall. So far we were twins, scarf and coat, but she had sensible walkers on and, due to recent arthritis in one ankle, had foregone temporarily her favorite sport, golf, which formerly was part of her afternoon activity.

We stepped right out on North Ocean Boulevard. Her house is on a curve and it wouldn't be difficult to be hit by a car. I can see why her family worries about these outings, which she usually takes alone. Through Eden Road and development houses, we walked to a dirt path onto the paved bicycle road along Lake Worth. Mrs. Kennedy walks so quickly that there wasn't time for chatter, and I was very grateful when we walked up onto a hole on a nearby golf course and sat down on a bench on one of the tees. It was only a few minutes' rest and off again with my sandals flapping. When we returned to the house Mrs. Kennedy was revitalized. I was exhausted. We each went to our rooms to change and she asked me to meet her in the library at seven. She had thoughtfully inquired as to whether I'd like a cocktail (she doesn't smoke or drink), and I told her I preferred just wine at dinner.

I arrived in the library before seven, having realized that punctuality was a trait she and I both shared. She came into the room in a long lovely dress, carrying her pocketbook. Her makeup was flawless. "How do you like my hair, Felicia?" she asked, "I had a permanent two days ago but I don't know . . . What do you think? Should I wear it up? I always did, but I want to change my image. I'm tired of looking this way." I told her honestly that I thought she looked lovely. We small-talked our way through a simple dinner. Mrs. Kennedy cannot eat roughage, so she had her own menu of soft foods because "I have a sensitive tummy."

The conversation was generally about children, which must have set her thinking about her grandchildren, for the next morning she wanted me to know how she felt about her relationship with them when we met at ten o'clock. Before parting at 9 P.M., she did ask me to tell the cook what I wanted for breakfast and left a message for the gardener to put the cushions out by the pool in case I wished to get some sun the next day. She also produced two black notebooks filled with clippings of all kinds of articles that have been of interest to her over the years. I asked if I might borrow them and look them over to return to her the next morning. She agreed and I spent about four hours that evening making notes, and when we did the interview the next morning at ten I checked with her to see if I might use them. From these black books and the conversations we had, I hope there emerges some new insights into this tenacious woman who has guarded her personal feelings and her life from the curious and the press.

Mrs. Kennedy's whole life has been and still is steeped in her family. The values that are so precious to her now she traces back to her mother and father, and it was her father who was the greatest influence in her life. This is a matter of record, but it is also the basis of the Kennedy philosophy.

"Mother and Father were in different departments, of course. My mother was very calm and deeply religious. Devoted to her family, she had good common sense and all those characteristics that I admired as I grew up and value more as I grow older. She also taught me, and I inherited this idea from her, that the man of the family worked hard and when he came home he was deserving of all our love and approbation and everything that we could give him." Years later, Mrs. Kennedy applied this principle in her own marriage and unselfishly and happily gave of herself to her husband, for this is how she saw and still sees a woman's role.

John F. (nicknamed "Honey Fitz") Fitzgerald, Rose's father,

was quite a different type from his wife, Josie. They lived in the
North End of Boston and were part of a large Irish-Catholic
community in that city. That he was a somewhat boisterous political type and openly exuberant were not qualities his daughter
stressed to me.

"My father, of course, was a great extrovert and he was terrifically interested in Boston and the history of Ireland, but he had
so much more to give. He'd talk incessantly about the United
States and about places of historic interest. He loved literature
and music. As a child, he stimulated my interests. When the opera
came to Boston, he'd always go and take my sister and me every
Saturday afternoon." As if clicking into a memory track, Mrs.
Kennedy, in that singsong accent that has come to be immediately familiar to all members of the family, continued: "I went to
hear every singer that came to Boston Symphony Hall. And when
I went to Europe, Father encouraged me to try different steamship lines so as to know what the German, the French, the British
and the American lines were like. He also encouraged me to take
an active interest in many things. He had a great, probing mind."
Then dropping her voice and with self-assurance she said, "and I
think I inherited that."

Her own positive qualities of energy, determination and flair
for anything tackled, coupled with tremendous self-discipline
and the drive to instill ambition and achievement in one's family,
were obviously directly traceable to Honey Fitz and to her strict
Catholic upbringing.

"I had always been interested in language. I studied it, of
course, in school. I always wanted to go to Europe to study, so
one day my father said, 'Rose, you've been talking about going
abroad, so I think that this summer we'll all go, and you stay over
there and go to school.' The Sacred Heart Convent I went to was
known all over the world. It sounds snooty, but the children who
went there were usually from very good families. They were
well brought up and attractive to know as well as to study with.
All the French convents were closed, so I went to Aix-la-Cha-
pelle. I had already had six years of French and four years of German in this country, but I wanted and did get my ear trained at
the convent so I could speak and understand the language. I read
Goethe's *Faust* in the expurgated edition, and I still keep up my

French. You see, I go to Paris every year, and we used to have a house in France. I love to speak it when I'm there; I go like a streak and say '*Où est l'église?* (Where is the church?),' and every time, to my great disappointment, they answer me in English. I remember the time I took my daughter over and I said in some store, 'This child has traveled three thousand miles and would you please speak French to her.' But, as usual, the Parisians wanted to perfect their English so they could get the best clients, and so my daughter didn't get much practice.

"But to get back to my schooling—I liked to study, I really did, I liked to get good marks. I was fortified by my father's interest and I wanted to know as much as I could. Like Sarah Bernhardt. She came to Boston when I was living there, and I would go and see her perform or whoever else there was who was new and exciting. I wanted to participate in everything that was stimulating, and that was a natural-born gift. I suppose. I tried to pass that on to my children. And I think I did."

In Mrs. Kennedy's youth, Boston was, as she has told me, divided into two different sections, and the Fitzgerald family did not have the lineage or credentials to be part of the city's Society. There were the Irish, the descendants of the Irish immigrants who had left their home country; and there were the Protestants, the Back Bay Bostonians, a conservative, staid, prejudiced group. The two communities were completely separate. At her friends' debut parties, Mrs. Kennedy recalls, there were no Protestant girls. "Nor could I get into the Vincent Club, an old Boston social institution, so I founded my own called The Ace of Clubs. It was the best, and Ace was an English term that meant finest. I was its president for seven or eight years."

The Kennedy family has often been accused of having been rejected by Boston Society. But Rose notes in the book *The Founding Father* by Richard J. Whalen: "As a child I had no inferiority complex. In appearance and education I think I've held my own. Why did I want to be part of Boston Society? I knew all the Catholic girls who had gone to school with me and their brothers and their beaux. I ran dances with our own group, including nieces and nephews of cardinals. I was completely happy. I wanted to marry a Catholic. Mixed marriages were very much frowned upon."

It has been said that the Fitzgeralds were not pleased with their daughter's choice of Joseph Kennedy. Mrs. Kennedy admits that they favored another beau who was financially much more successful, and they thought with him she would have a great many more advantages.

"I was just seventeen when I met Joe, and I guess my family was right to a certain extent. I mean, after all, you just don't marry the first man you meet. But we kept on seeing each other, and from the day that we got married in 1914, we hardly ever disagreed about anything. Of course, when the children were young, he was away a lot working, but we knew how we wanted to bring up our children. We came from the same religious ideas about going to Mass and going to Communion every Friday."

Mrs. Kennedy and I talked about the changing role of women today and how marriage doesn't have the same meaning it used to. "I have always said my role was just to make everything very happy and comfortable at home for my husband and the children. That was my fulfillment, but at the same time I developed my own potential as president of my club, and we enjoyed going to the concerts at Symphony Hall. I loved reading French books, and I had a very pleasant family life. My husband had the responsibility, and he had to go to work. I, when he got home, was perfectly happy to do what he wanted, and if he preferred to take a walk at night or go out to dinner or whatever, I was perfectly content. I never wanted a life of my own. I don't quite understand why people can't get along better these days. Of course, now it's much easier to get a divorce, and I suppose it makes marriage more difficult because many young people don't feel any obligation to settle down and be wives and mothers."

Mrs. Kennedy told me a story about when she was growing up. She knew a girl who had been divorced, and there was such a social stigma to it that she couldn't live in Boston any more. Like divorce, she has no patience with the motives of Women's Lib. Almost angrily she said, "What is the point of trying to get out of the house? For what? All this business about becoming a person in your own right. Women go out and what do they do? What's so glamorous about getting a job outside of the home, being a secretary for somebody or selling dresses in a clothes shop? Don't you think being a wife or a mother is being a person?"

These are the ground rules by which she has lived, and her question is totally appropriate to her own credo.

The family now, as it did years ago, totally absorbs Mrs. Kennedy.

"When the children were small I tried to encourage them in everything they did. Their father gave them opportunities to further their interests and to support them in whatever they were trying to do. For instance, when we went to see the Pope crowned in the Vatican in 1939, our older son was in Madrid at the time of the Civil War. But why was he in Madrid? Because he had been interested in Spanish history at that time, and the revolution was going on and he wanted to be there. He had expressed a desire to go and it was made possible. These unusual opportunities to go places and see history in the making were given to all the children. But if they hadn't been given this urge and knowledge when they were small and growing up with me, they wouldn't have been ready to accept new challenges or face up to them. If they hadn't been brought up this way, the moment my husband had given them this opportunity, they might have been reticent about trying new things and meeting people. Once Joe said to Bobby, 'You're going on a boat to Europe and I see that Lord Beaverbrook will be on the same ship. So go and speak to him.' And Bobby, of course, was then only seventeen or eighteen and rather in awe of Lord Beaverbrook, but his father requested he introduce himself, but Bobby knew his father well enough to know that if he didn't follow the suggestion, Joe would be very disappointed. So Bobby went about it. So there was this encouragement all the time and this purpose in life and this interest. We'd all get together and we'd exchange ideas. My children are perfectly happy. We talk about everything. We walk. Even now, when Teddy comes down here on weekends, we've taken long walks at night. We've discussed the Senate. We've discussed his children, who frankly don't know their catechism too well. As for my hopes for my daughters, I just always wanted them to be married and live happily ever after."

But what was Mrs. Kennedy really like as a mother, I asked her only remaining son, Edward, in his Senate office in Washington. His answer was sober and perhaps more for posterity than the spontaneous response I had hoped for. In fact, it turned out to be a well-contained minispeech and I was the audience.

"My mother gave me plenty of attention when I was growing up, and despite the many demands upon her by all the children, she even found time for children's stories at night. She was very much involved in my life, primarily looking after me and making sure that my religious instruction was kept up, particularly when I was going off to a Protestant boarding school. Her presence was very much felt. It was a presence that included all the love and understanding and warmth which a child looks for in a mother. It was a presence that also represented the stern hand of parental guidance at times. I recall walking home from kindergarten one day when I was told to wait to be picked up. When I arrived home my mother was very upset that I had not followed her instructions. I received a good spanking for it with a coat hanger. But I remember her explanation for the spanking, that my walking home created undue consternation to other people, who did not know what had happened to me, and who worried whether I was safe and secure from the dangers of walking along a big highway crowded with cars and trucks. She made the chastisement seem quite understandable. She did not use just a hanger to spank me. On occasions she would use a hairbrush. I think that, with Mother, discipline was always immediate to the particular infractions. It never was really resented. And her discipline never really bothered me or my brothers and sisters. Mother and Father had a very complementary relationship in the bringing up of the children. My father was the one who provided the paternal love and, for the most part, the discipline and inspiration and the expectation. The sense of duty and compassion and understanding to other people came from both. My mother assumed the role of spiritual leader in the family, making sure we kept abreast of our religious education and obligations. This role she even extends to her grandchildren. She asked them in Palm Beach why Lent is forty days, and how long did the Lord stay after Easter Sunday, and what He did during that period of time. They did not know the answers, and when we left and returned home they were stimulated enough to seek the answers from their Bible teacher. In a positive and constructive atmosphere she tries to stretch the knowledge of the grandchildren as she did with her own children.

"If a political situation arose, such as a decision to enter the Wisconsin primary, the consultation would be with my father. But, if you relate decisions that went into early childhood and the teen-age period, I found that both my mother and my father were equally involved. I was born in 1932 and Father retired in 1941, so he was an active parent at home until the time he became ill. He probably was around more than the fathers of many of my friends. My mother had, and has, a very special way with people. She thoroughly enjoys them. She values their friendship. She is always looking for the positive and hopeful signs in people. She is an exciting and stimulating person to be with, and always brings out the best in people. I think it followed from her that we children became interested in people and their problems. It comes from an interest in history and events, and this is what, I believe, stimulated our interest in public affairs.

"Mother never shows disapproval as disapproval. I felt more that, if I disappointed her, it was my failure to live up to an expectation. She never actively disapproved if we erred, but always gave us the idea that life was a challenge to be dealt with positively. My mother is a perfectionist and works at studying and making speeches on behalf of mental retardation, and in being well-dressed, and in doing whatever she decides to the best of her ability. I know she does not approve of long hair and the modern dress which the children sport at Cape Cod, but she has never chided them about it. She is always prepared to explain to them her own views. I think her greatest strength is her faith, the kind of inspiration she was able to provide to all of us, and optimism toward life. To a great extent the essential aspects of those qualities had a profound effect on both President Kennedy and Bob in their approach toward problems, and I think it was a very inspirational force in the lives of all of us. My mother had such a kind of concern and caring about Father when he became ill, as anyone would have, seeing someone you love experience great unhappiness and discomfort. When Father died she took comfort in knowing she did all she could for him in his lifetime. Her life now is not really that different. Her interests have not diminished. She has a full life. She'd rather read than entertain or make small

talk. She has lasting friendships which she maintains. She probably doesn't see as much of the grandchildren as she would like,
but she conducts open and friendly exchanges of conversation
with the older ones. My mother doesn't keep tabs on all of us, but
I think everyone feels that she is someone who has been and is
very special. All of us tremendously enjoy her company. She's
stimulating and exciting to be with and it's very, very natural
that she would be the focus of our family life. We all see her at
different times. In past years all of us would get together on my
father's birthday and on Thanksgiving and the other holidays.
Her birthday is a big event for the family to gather and celebrate. I visit with her in Palm Beach three or four times in the
winter and weekends on the Cape. My sisters see her quite often.
She enjoys spending time with all of us individually rather than
having twenty children surrounding her at one time. She has had
a difficult number of challenges, but her strong faith and belief
have sustained her and she has kept her sense of purpose." My
time was up. The Senator's next appointment was at hand.

While Ambassador Kennedy was alive and before his health
failed him, no one will disagree that he was a very powerful man,
both in business and within his family. No major decisions were
ever made without him, and many conferences were held in
Hyannis and Palm Beach in order to seek his insight and gain his
support or help politically. It would have been unthinkable not to
consult him or ask his advice, and Joe Kennedy had the drive and
power to see that they did. One of his favorite quotes was:
"Things don't happen. They're made to happen." He also said,
in some notes his wife made: "The boys might as well work for
the government, because politics will control the business of the
country in the future." "Yes," Mrs. Kennedy said, "I think he
said that in 1926, and he also said, 'Take the top spot. Don't interest yourself in anything else. Win the race. Don't come in second,
for that's no good.'" A Kennedy has always surmounted every
obstacle except fate.

Competition, ambition and strength are Kennedy traits. With
wealth stirred into the brew, power is inevitable. I asked Mrs.
Kennedy if it wasn't true that after the death of her husband the
power he had generated had now been transferred to her. Her
answer was interesting. I expected a denial. Instead she said, "But

I don't use it any differently. I have my work to do. What power would I want than the power I have? Yes, I guess I do command power, but I've always been spoiled, first as the daughter of a mayor and then being married to a successful husband." But she indicated that women could put power to useful means. "I've gone along in my own way, using common sense and bearing responsibility. I've tried to cooperate with people who were trying to develop useful projects. I've also tried to help others or do something for the community or the parish. For instance, today I visited a school for mentally retarded children. They were having an outdoor athletic event and I felt that by my presence I could focus interest in their cause and encourage the mothers of these children and they themselves. I was only too glad to accept the invitation and co-operate. And I've always done that."

The Kennedy family fortune, due to Mrs. Kennedy's husband's astuteness, is well-known. I wondered whether wealth had any great effect on any of them. Would the course of their lives have been altered had they not been so fortunate. "Well, not basically," Mrs. Kennedy answered. "We still would have had our interest in the community, much as my father had, but the children and I would never have had the opportunities that their father made possible. I think that one cannot just accept wealth, that there are great responsibilities that come with it. I quote from St. Luke: 'Of those to whom much is given, much is to be expected.' That about sums it up. I think all the children understood this and have passed this philosophy to their children. For instance, Kathleen, Bobby and Ethel's daughter, went to Arizona two or three summers ago and worked with the Indians, and of course they've all worked in campaigns, and some have had jobs in Africa. Caroline spent a couple of months in Appalachia. Most of my grandchildren have had different projects during their summer holidays, and they've spent time at a camp that Eunice started for the mentally retarded. All of my children were encouraged to give money to help support those in need. I don't know what they each do personally, but we've got the Kennedy Foundation, which gives to different schools. And then, for example, Ethel is working now on Bobby's memorial, and each year they have a big tennis tournament, and Eunice and Sargent have been very active in the field of mental retardation. They've done

a lot, but, my name being Kennedy, I get the credit and the publicity. But Eunice is the one who has really done the work.
Teddy is a champion of health-care reform, Jean is interested in
the Kennedy Center in Washington, Pat Lawford is concerned
with the sports program for the mentally retarded called the Special Olympics. All of the children are involved, and they've tried
to spread their interests a little bit so that they'll embrace different things, but of course with half the family gone, we all have
more responsibilities than we would have had, had they lived. Or-
dinarily Joe, or Jack, or Bobby would have been there to do their
share."

It often seemed to friends and associates that when Ambassador
Kennedy was alive he was more demanding and more critical of
his children than was their mother. Congressman Torbert Mac-
Donald, a classmate of President Kennedy's at Harvard, knew
the family well and we talked about Rose and Joe Kennedy. "I always thought of the Ambassador as being the commander, the
captain of the ship, and Mrs. Kennedy obviously was a very relied
on and very important executive officer. He was the brains of the
outfit, I felt, and she was the heart and soul. She loves people
and she gives wise counsel. She was never just a decorative adjunct to the Ambassador. He quite properly could be described
as an autocrat, especially at the dinner table when he would
choose the subject of the night to discuss. He was smart and he
knew everything, and for somebody like me who just read in the
newspapers about people, the Ambassador would be first-naming,
without name-dropping, most of the important people who were
currently doing things in the United States and abroad. They
were all friends of his.

"I remember one time when I was about seventeen or eighteen
and Mrs. Kennedy had just returned from a visit to Russia.
Communism and the Russians were not Mr. Kennedy's favorite
cup of tea. I was at lunch with the family—I guess this was
before 1940. Mr. Kennedy was whacking the Russians and trying
to alert us to the danger that we might find ourselves in. Mrs.
Kennedy indicated that she had met some Russians and sort of
liked them. I think she was trying in a small way to talk about
her contact with them, and she wanted him to know that she was
going to discuss her trip at some group meeting. Mr. Kennedy

was not particularly keen on having her do this. But she didn't
bat an eye. She was not an argumentative woman at all. I think
her husband, like any married man, saw signs that she wasn't
about to give in, so he changed the subject and I recall him
asking me directly about what I thought of the Communist
system as it then existed in Russia. I can remember my answer
because I wasn't trying to ride the fence, but I merely said,
'Well, it's done an awful lot for the Russians in the short period
of time since they took over,' and he gave me one of his famous
scowls. But Mrs. Kennedy agreed with me. Perhaps that's why
the whole incident stuck in my mind. She's a strong-willed
woman in her own right."

Mrs. Kennedy tries not to interfere or criticize her children.
"I wouldn't because I don't know what the trend is now. Just
like Teddy's hair. I thought it was rather long, but I would
think he'd know whether to cut it or not at his age better than
I. He knows how people are wearing their hair. But one day
he had a haircut in the dining room here and the light wasn't
very good and he couldn't see that it was getting shorter and
shorter. So when he got out to the hall," and she pointed
behind her, "he looked in the mirror and was rather stunned.
I think Joan knows about clothes, and if she wants to dress in
a certain way, that's up to her. It isn't as if they were twenty-
two years old." Her voice indicated that she had nothing further
to say concerning public criticism, except, "You just can't let
it upset you. I've had so much publicity all my life, I just
don't magnify it."

Mrs. Kennedy's religious faith has kept her together during
all phases of her life. She was brought up as a strict Catholic
and still goes to Mass every morning. "We learned to make
sacrifices in the Catholic faith. Now a great many of those are
not demanded any more. We didn't used to be able to eat meat
on Friday. Now you can, for instance. So much has changed.
During Lent you were supposed to fast. Now many Catholics
don't. You rarely hear about making sacrifices these days. I,
on the other hand, grew up with that idea, that it was a worthy
thing to do and that it was expected of you. It wasn't anything
to be just attributed to one's self or because you were a Catholic
family. It wasn't to me, because I might have been more devout

than others. It was just a rule of the Church. Just like you didn't
eat before Communion. Now you can eat up to an hour before.
I wouldn't have thought of going out and playing golf. My
boys, my sons wouldn't either until they've been to church.
They go, like I do, about seven or eight o'clock in the morning.
But so many others go to church the night before. So many
restrictions have been relaxed. Life has been made easier. The
Church doesn't demand as much as it used to from you. Now,
is that a good thing?"

One hears that if Mrs. Kennedy were to ever reveal any
disappointments about her children and grandchildren, it would
be in the area of religion. No one could be more devout than
she and, if possible, she would have liked to instill that strong
feeling in them. Whenever she has a chance to explain or inform
them, she does.

"I usually try and see as much of my grandchildren as I can
now. A few years ago I didn't have a very close relationship
with them, and I was thinking about that last night. In the first
place, there were twenty-eight members of the family and
they'd all come to Hyannis or Palm Beach at odd times and
they'd usually come in groups. It would have been different if
one or two had come to spend their holidays and stayed with
me, but each year the groups change. This year my four
youngest grandchildren were here. At Easter, Eunice is bringing
two or three. I don't know, maybe her daughter Maria. A
couple of weeks ago Caroline was here with Pat's daughter
Sidney. So it varies. And then, when Mr. Kennedy was ill, of
course they never stayed in the house at all. They came and
saw him and were told to be very quiet and they were. But
when we are together, we never have any big family rows,
where they talk back to each other. They've never been told,
'You do this and if you don't you can't go to the movies.' They're
all very respectful. If they use the sauna here for instance—my
grandson Bobby Kennedy does, but he always comes to me
and says 'May I use the sauna?' He never assumes that it's all
right. So they've been really very satisfactory. More than satisfactory. I like having discussions with them. Right now we're
talking about Easter and why it's a different date every year,
or why there are forty days of Lent, or what they're doing in

schools. I like to know what books they're reading. Of course they read different books, from the types I'm used to which are far in advance of what we used to read, or at least that's what they say. But I'm trying to find what they are in advance of."

I asked Mrs. Kennedy if she had ever talked to her older grandchildren about sex and drugs. "No," she said, "I've never discussed sex or pot. We have the chance in Hyannis when we see more of each other, but I spend all winter here in Palm Beach and they're in school. In Hyannis they come over for lunch and dinner, but I don't think it's my business to tell them what to do. That responsibility belongs to their parents and they are the ones who are with them all the time and know the current trends. They're much better equipped than I am. I don't think I know enough . . . I know I don't know enough about all their problems. But I try to be *au courant*. I used to say '*au courant*.' Now," she said, pleased with herself, "now I say 'with it.' The one who knows all these expressions much better than I—and I was so humiliated after I'd talked to her the other day—was Evangeline Bruce. She had all these expressions . . . plus. I asked her where she learned them and she told me, 'From my children. I telephone them. I pay for the calls or I wouldn't hear from them.'"

Mrs. Kennedy's black notebooks, which she has kept for many years, indicate the breadth of her search for knowledge. The color tabs designate her different categories: Definitions, Men, Music and Art, People, Places, Politics, Quotes, Religion, Women, and Phrases. From my nocturnal perusals of these books, I picked out some of the items and have listed below a sampling of what Mrs. Kennedy chose to include in these categories. They seemed to me indicative of her own philosophy and wide range of interests. Under "Definitions," she had listed the special words and some of their definitions: *pluralism, aquarius, hedonism, nihilism, harassism, rococo, paranoia, parsimonious, Ms.* (pronounced *miz*), *courage*—'an often renewed evidence of our capacity to transcend what we just are.' Modern lingo—rip off, dig, dude, throwing the egg, funky, brother, to do a number.

The second category was "Men," and here she had included a clipping of a review of Robert F. Kennedy's book *The Enemy*

Within, and had underlined, "He was available and truthful—his frustrations, political."

The third category was "Music and Art." Note: Plays 1968–1969: "Aspect of past season has been prolific use of nudity as a theatrical function. Nudity became an obsessive substitute for plot—nothing of enduring value—the year will also be remembered as a moment in cultural history when black theater came of age."

The fourth category was "People." "Half of all the Jewish people in America live in New York" clipping. Also, Jews had won more Nobel Prizes than any other people.

The fifth category was "Places."

The sixth was "Politics." A special sample statement she clipped: Protocol—Mrs. Kennedy ranks after the Vice-president and the Chief Justice and their wives. Clipping re Walter Annenberg: "Dear Mr. Ambassador Plenipotentiary. You may be the diplomats' choice of the century, With talent to spare on matters vice-regal, But please, if you will, sir, don't harm our poor eagle."

The seventh category was "Quotes." DeGaulle: "I am never bored when I am alone with myself. When I want to know what France thinks, I ask myself." "It matters not so much where you sit as what your mind and heart enable you to see." *A Pilgrim's Way* by Lord Tweedsmuir: "Public life is the crown of a career and to a young man it is the worthiest ambition. Politics is still the greatest and the most honorable adventure." Sigmund Freud: "Immortality means being loved by many anonymous people." Malraux: "Man is not made for defeat. He may be vanquished and destroyed."

The eighth category was "Religion." Psalm 8 recited by astronauts landing on the moon. "We are troubled on every side, yet not distressed; we are perplexed, but not in despair; persecuted, but not forsaken; cast down, but not destroyed" (II Cor. 4:8–9).

The ninth category was "Women." "Woman at home often finds that affluence makes her a manager and decision-maker rather than a laborer, but she is no less harried" (*The Harried Leisure Class*).

The tenth category was "Phrases." "Grief: Begging the Good

Lord to give you the grace and strength to carry, with patience and resignation, your latest cross of bereavement."

I culled some of the notes Mrs. Kennedy had noted in the margin of *The Founding Father*.

Rose was thrilled that the older Kennedys served as godparents to the younger ones—"very important" she noted.

Rose always believed that her children should have the same allowances as their friends at school and on the Cape, the same clothes as their schoolmates.

Montagu Norman was the smartest banker her husband, Joe, ever met.

The reason Joe never went back to reunions after his graduation is that he hated to see his classmates grow old. It made him realize that he, too, was old, so he preferred to stay away.

"My husband had the great facility for getting along with princes or paupers, chorus girls or Society matrons, Catholics or Protestants—East Boston or Back Bay, businessmen or dilettantes."

She noted her husband's temperamental conservatism and her son Jack's dispassionate liberalism.

Rose writes that during his Senate days she didn't believe that Jack even thought of becoming President. He would enjoy power but not handshaking. Mr. Kennedy always said, "Take the top spot—don't interest yourself in anything else."

But what of the woman herself, who admits to being a perfectionist, who has kept house for sixty years and has a remarkable ability to accept the tragedies of life, pace herself and never let down the front. I wonder how many people, even in the family, have ever seen her show her emotions. I did, briefly, when we spoke about her daughter Rosemary, whom she never really talks about publicly. "I usually just mention that we had a retarded child and there was no help then." As we began to talk about Rosemary and mental retardation, she became very emotional and her voice trailed away and she broke down for a few seconds, but then she recovered quickly and went on to talk about the work her daughter Eunice was doing.

I understand more about Rose Kennedy because I learned how she deals with different matters. Exercise, swimming, golfing when able, religion and walking are her ways of dealing with

problems. She uses these times to collect herself and face the
frightening moments with calm and serenity. I remember when
the President was killed, reading the stories about her walking
and golfing alone at Hyannis, her own private way of dealing
with grief and her unshakable faith, which transcends everything in her life.

She is always pulled together, mentally and physically. Even
when we were just the two of us, after dinner, she checked her
makeup and added more lipstick. If her hair doesn't look just
right, she will wear a hat. She is such a perfectionist that if she
is to give an interview, she wants the questions in advance so
she can be well-prepared, and if they aren't suitable, she is quite
frank in not wanting to waste her time or yours. She will check
inaccuracies and will not respond until she is thoroughly convinced that her answer is as it should be. She wants to correct
the criticisms leveled against the family and tries to set the
record straight. It would be impossible to catch her unawares;
at all times she is in control of the situation. The only exceptions
are due to her physical ailments—her arthritic ankle and, most
recently, a short hospitalization, all of which annoy her because they cannot be dealt with in her usual fashion.

She is unsure what to do about some things—the Palm Beach
house, for example, because now that she's alone it's too big.
The pool needs repairs, the curtains need redoing, but she
really doesn't want to spend the money to fix them up because
she knows her children will never want the house. It has been
said that Teddy told her to keep the property, which is very
valuable, and raze the house, but I don't think she is quite ready
to give it up. She patches it up here and there and gets estimates
for renovations, but she hasn't gone ahead with any overall
plans.

As she has gotten older, she fusses more about her public ap-
pearances. She never leaves her upstairs bedroom until she
is content with her image. She cares tremendously about clothes
and goes to Paris every year for fittings. Every dress must be
just right, everything in its place.

She told me that when she makes speeches she is very conscious of her delivery. Is she talking too fast or talking about
herself too much? In the past she planted spies in the audience

to find out what the people's reactions were afterwards. She has a routine before a speech. She remembers to gargle first, then she places herself in front of the microphone, careful not to get too close to it, and she reminds herself not to make a lot of unnecessary gestures with her hands. Her goal is always to improve herself, to gain new knowledge, for that is the key to success. I don't really know, but I would surmise that Mrs. Kennedy would have little patience with incompetence and a low tolerance level for laziness and inaccuracy. She expects a lot from people because she has always demanded, and continues to, the same from herself.

She is ever mindful of her family, and they in turn are ever thoughtful of her. She is very fond of Ari Onassis, and he is the only person to call her "Rosey." Her other in-laws call her "Grandma." He and Jackie have spent a lot of time with her. She has often been on the *Christina* in Scorpio and when she's in Palm Beach. Often the Onassises lunch with Mrs. Kennedy at her house, but they are mindful not to put her to any trouble; they bring their own staff, food and bartender from the ship so as not to inconvenience her. On Sundays, when Jackie is there, she and her former mother-in-law go to church together. Once Jackie had the children with her, and because of them, there were a lot of security men around. Mrs. Kennedy is often overwhelmed by crowds. This time they were waiting for her arrival and made it impossible for her and Jackie to get out of the car, so Mrs. Kennedy decided to go on to another church in West Palm Beach, leaving the security guards to sit through two Masses in the first church, where she had been expected. One of the men confided that he didn't mind the fact that he had to sit through such a long service. "It was really because I had to contribute twice each time they passed the collection plate!"

Mrs. Kennedy is as fond of Jackie as she ever was. "She was such an asset to Jack," she told me. "She always loved poetry and used to read aloud to him. When she accompanied him to France, I thought later, no one could have been better prepared as a President's wife than she. She had done her historical homework. She spoke French, loved the ballet, and was dazzling at the dinner given in their honor at Versailles." Jackie, in turn, obviously has great love and respect for Mrs. Kennedy and enjoys being with her whenever their schedules permit it.

I was alone, packing and getting ready to catch a noon plane home. Mrs. Kennedy was resting upstairs after our last interview. I went back once more and stood in the living room. So many family conferences had taken place here, so much Kennedy lore hung in the air, yet the rooms are all empty now. The screen doors blow open with the ocean wind. No one enters. A security guard walks by on the lawn. The ocean is as near this house as it is in Hyannis—the ocean which saw so many of the family sailing and swimming. "We like the water," Mrs. Kennedy said, "and when the children were young we wanted to keep them occupied. We've always had houses by the sea because we liked that kind of life."

I was ready to leave and I called to Mrs. Kennedy to say goodbye. "I'll be right down, dear," she said as the chauffeur took my briefcase and suitcase to the car. I had my Instamatic camera, hoping I could take an informal picture that could be used for the book. My hostess appeared in a linen slack suit and with a hat in her hand. I thanked her for her hospitality and help and asked if I might take some pictures. She reluctantly agreed but wasn't satisfied with her hair and put her wide-brimmed hat on. We went outside and she stood with her back to the house. She struck a pose with her head turned to the side. I took two pictures and then she said firmly, "That's enough. I'm quite tired, Felicia." She walked me back down the covered steps to her car waiting on the street. "That's a very pretty dress, dear." And we kissed goodbye. I got into the car, closed the door and she waved and turned to walk back up to the house —surely to renew herself in solitude and reflection and prepare to face with determination whatever lies ahead to challenge an indomitable spirit.

Mrs. Malcolm Peabody

THE PEABODY NAME and Boston are synonymous. Quiet, ultra-conservative, they are revered by their peers and those who put great stock in family and the "Proper Bostonian" tradition.

Mrs. Peabody's mother, Frances Parker, was born in 1855 in New Jersey and brought up at the time of the Civil War. She was a great beauty. As her granddaughter, Marietta Tree, recalls, "She was a real bluestocking, a tremendous flirt, and she was famous for being temperamental." In contrast, her husband, who pursued her for ten years before their marriage, was a nice solid man, a sensible, conservative Boston banker with great charm, but clearly no match for his rather headstrong free-thinking wife. Mary Peabody admits that her mother was the stronger of the two and, having been brought up in New Jersey, she was more worldly, more liberal. "She was the kind of woman who attracted gentlemen wherever she went, but she didn't marry Father until she was twenty-five."

Mary Parkman went to school until she was sixteen, when her parents took her out because they didn't think she was developing properly physically. She had one more year at Miss Porter's School in Farmington, and she regrets that her education ended there. Like other "Proper Boston" girls, she was brought up strictly. "We were taught to tell the truth, never lie or cheat, and do what you could for other people. Sex didn't enter into any discussions. It wasn't even *thought* about."

Mary's parents were older than those of most of her friends in her adolescent years and she had very little rapport with them. The key to her personality is that she accepted the fact that they were not very demonstrative or openly affectionate with their children. It might have been their age or the Boston emotional climate, but she herself inherited that trait, which her cousins quickly recognized and in many ways have had problems adjusting to. Left probably to develop on her own, Mary Parkman became a strong woman but certainly not the feminine center of attraction as had been her mother. She did all the things that nice Boston girls did, belonging to a sewing circle (in which she still is active), and she grew up with a strong sense that her life lay in the service of other people.

"We were all good church people, you see, and through the church one became involved in other things. I was very interested in missions and I think my first work was with a class at Emmanuel Church in Boston. I was also President of the Junior League. And then I decided I wanted to marry a minister. I think I wanted to be married because it was expected that girls did marry and want children, but I would have liked a career of my own besides. I figured out the only way that would work was to marry someone who had a career in which I could have a part."

She did indeed meet such a man while on a world cruise. She went with Mrs. Harvey Bundy (Mac's mother), who is still her closest friend, and Mrs. Harry Shelley. She was twenty-one and of course the families of the girls had seen to it that the young ladies were well-chaperoned. Mary said indeed they did have a chaperone. "But we ran her because she was an old lady. She followed us around and gave us security, supposedly. That we didn't need, but she did lend an air of respectability," she said with a twinkle. She saw Malcolm Peabody on this trip, although he remembered her from long before with pigtails walking on Commonwealth Avenue as a child, and she did remember going to a Hasty Pudding dance with him once, although he hadn't made much of an impression on her then. She saw him again in the Philippines, during the cruise, where he was teaching as a missionary. On his return to Boston, he decided to be a minister and told Mary of his plans and romance blossomed. She married him at twenty-four and their first home was in Lawrence, Massachusetts, where he took the post of curate in the local parish. She never came back to Boston until she was seventy, and has lived there ever since in an unpretentious house with antimaccassars on the chairs and a dark tufted old-fashioned velvet sofa.

Mary enjoyed the role as her husband's helper, after Mr. Peabody became minister, in between having five children. She was terrifically conscientious in all civic works and in activities related to the parish. Marietta, her daughter, remembers being taken to the church when she was two or three and being parked in the corner somewhere while her mother attended a committee meeting.

"She was really a partner of my father's and I can hear everybody always saying, 'Oh, Mary, aren't you wonderful!' There she was helping in church, doing all the housework as well, hauling the food home and taking care of me and my brothers. Mother was always conscientious, believing that you couldn't have a good life unless you worked for other people and progress. She never went for the glamorous jobs, more usually the dreary ones: envelope licking, concentrating on meetings and always the wish to help."

Her children don't feel that she had much fun out of life, that their father got a good deal of satisfaction from his career and his life but that Mary never felt secure as a woman, perhaps because her own mother never gave her much assurance.

It wasn't until Mary's husband retired, at seventy, that she had more free time for herself, to pursue her own interests. Her son Sam felt that the problems of child-raising were difficult for her because of her being so self-disciplined and undemonstrative. "She's got a good sense of humor and she can laugh at herself, but her favorite trick is finding your weakest point and then teasing you about it. This takes time and understanding to accept." She was, and is, apt to make biting comments about her family's clothes, which aren't always well-received. She also has strong opinions on what is appropriate and what is not.

There is a wonderful story about a wedding present that was given to the Peabodys by Isabella Gardner, a close friend of her mother. It was a beautiful Degas painting of a theatrical scene: a lady sitting in a box overlooking the stage with a curtain coming down over a lot of ballerina legs. She had a very amply exposed bosom. Mary, it seems, was not overly fond of Isabella

Gardner and she thought that a painting of such an inappropriate subject did not fit into the life of a churchman and his
wife, so she gave this valuable work of art to a rummage sale.
The family never knew where it ended up, and, as far as anyone
knows, she never regretted this action.

Both Mary and Malcolm Peabody were very principled, but
their chief tenet and strongest adherence was in their belief
that lying was not to be tolerated and honesty was of the utmost
importance. Sam grew up, as did the others, having been repeatedly told that one must not lie. "When I was a small boy," he
said, "I remember stealing some money out of Mother's pocketbook. In my haste to get it the bills stuck together, and instead
of taking five dollars I took ten. I was going to a fair, and when
I got there I suddenly realized I had two bills instead of one. I
couldn't resist spending them. Mother, meanwhile, had to go to
the hairdresser, and when it was time to pay she realized there
was money missing from her bag. She knew that I had been in
her room earlier, and when she got home she asked me if I'd
taken it. I guess I was about eight and I said, 'Absolutely not.
No sir. Not me.' She said, 'Well, how did you buy those
things?' noting my new purchases from the fair, which I was
clutching. I told her that I'd found them and made up a whole
story which I was sure I'd get away with. She was bound to get
me to confess, but the more she pressed me the more I denied
stealing. As a result, it was a draw and she never punished me,
but, looking back, it seems to me her main object was not
punishment but for me to admit my guilt."

Mary Peabody's strength, which often rankled her children,
was often a source of comfort. When they had problems, when
they were depressed, she was able to relate their disappointment
to her own life and she listened. Her unflagging spirit to make
the children reach for certain intangible standards and her emphasis on their positive qualities were markers, but what they
missed was the ability to really help and affectionate emotional
support. These qualities in their mother, in later years, burst
beyond the children's control and made them seek psychiatric help. Although Mary denies bringing the children up to be
competitive, they nevertheless felt that she believed in achievement and that they must each do their best to gratify this need.

Mrs. Marjorie Merriweather Post.

Mrs. Post in costume. Photo by Bert and Richard Morgan Studio.

Mrs. Lytle Hull. Photo by Felicia Warburg Roosevelt.

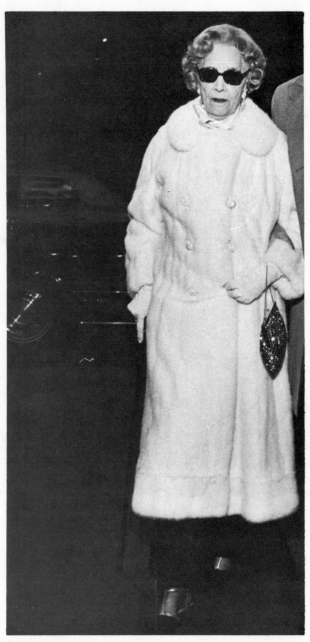

Mrs. William Woodward. Photo by Bill Cunningham.

Mrs. Harper Sibley. Photo by Jim Laragy.

Mrs. William Roth. Photo by Felicia Warburg Roosevelt.

Mrs. Nion Tucker. Photo by Felicia Warburg Roosevelt.

Mrs. William Buckley. Photo by Felicia Warburg Roosevelt.

Mr. & Mrs. William Buckley, 1949. Photo by Jay Te Winburn.

Mrs. Herbert Marcus.

Mrs. Joseph Kennedy. Photo by Felicia Warburg Roosevelt.

Mrs. Kennedy.

Mrs. Malcolm Peabody. Photo by Pamela Peabody.

HELP US
CELEBRATE
MOTHER'S
80th YEAR

JORDAN POND HOUSE
SATURDAY, SEPTEMBER 4th, 1971
5:30-7:30

MARIETTA & RONNIE TREE
ENDICOTT & TONI PEABODY
GEORGE PEABODY
SAM & JUDY PEABODY
MIKE & PAM PEABODY

R.S.V.P.
Sam Peabody
North East Harbor, Maine

CIVIL RIGHTS BATTLER
CIRCA 1964
MRS. MALCOLM PEABODY

Invitation to Mrs. Peabody's eightieth birthday.

Mrs. Malcolm Peabody. Photo by Pamela Peabody.

Mrs. Bernard Gimbel.

Mrs. Arthur Hays Sulzberger. Photo by Arthur Ochs Sulzberger.

Marian Anderson. Photo by Bill Cunningham.

Mrs. Hazel Hotchkiss Wightman, 1973. Photo by Dr. Harry Richelson.

Clare Boothe Luce on her seventieth birthday, April 1973. NEWS-
WEEK photo by Robert R. McElroy.

Louise Nevelson. Pace Gallery, photo by Al Mozell.

Lila Acheson Wallace. Photo by Kenneth Wilson.

Diana Vreeland. Photo by Bill Cunningham.

Peggy Guggenheim. Photo by Fotoattualita, Venezia.

Alice Roosevelt Longworth. Photo by Sir Cecil Beaton.

The Peabody marriage was a long and harmonious one (until his death the summer of 1974). No one disputes his wife's aid and support nor the fact that he was very proud of her work in her fields of interest. When they were first married and her husband was running the parish in Lawrence, World War I broke out and Malcolm enlisted as a chaplain. She ran the parish while he was gone. When he returned, St. Paul's Church in Philadelphia, a very rich parish, wrote him asking him to leave Lawrence and join them. He really didn't want to leave, because he enjoyed it where he was. They came to see him and asked him again if he wouldn't reconsider and come in six months. Instead of a response from Peabody, Mary answered, "Of course, he'll be ready to come then." From the post at St. Paul's he was elected Bishop of Central New York; they lived in Utica for two years and then in Syracuse for twenty.

Mary Peabody not only had, but still continues to have, great physical strength. She never believed in pampering herself. When she and her husband took a train trip, he would get a berth, but she would sit up all night in the coach. Today she is well into her eighties, but she continued to do all the housework while caring for her ailing husband, until he passed away. He was almost childlike for a long time and she tried to keep him going, but his focus got confused and her life became more confining. "I never went out in the evening. Up until a couple of years ago, I had people to the house. The children are worried I don't have enough life of my own, but I've had a good life and, after all, a pretty long one, so I don't mind giving up this part of it."

Mary regrets many things, and her role as matriarch of the Peabody family, although recognized, is not totally what she would like it to be. Her "Proper Bostonian" background has forever gotten in her way. Although the strands of her earlier life still remain, her Sewing-Circle-of-1910 friends have dwindled. She feels now that she's breaking up and every part of her has something wrong. She tries not to give in to the aches and pains. The stalwart spirit won't give in, so she busies herself constantly with the day-to-day job of living.

In March of 1963, after her husband had retired as Bishop,

Mary's decision to go to Florida made national headlines. She tried to explain to me the reason for this trip. "I've always been interested in reform. The civil rights issue always bothered me and a whole group of us decided to go down to St. Augustine. We were all bishops' wives and we were going to make it a Bishop's Wives Crusade. I guess it was because my son Endicott was the reigning Governor of Massachusetts that I got all the publicity. And that was good. We really did something." And the something eventually landed them in jail for the night. "MOTHER OF GOVERNOR PEABODY AT 73 JAILED WITH BLACKS." The papers had a field day Her original intention had been to mingle with blacks, walk into hotels and bars with them, and when the authorities asked them to leave she would let them know her strong stand on civil rights. She knew she ran the risk of being jailed. She told Marietta about her trip, and Marietta encouraged her to go and stand up for her principles. At that time, Marietta and her husband, Ronald Tree, were in Barbados entertaining Britain's Queen Mother Mary. It appears that Marietta spent a good deal of time listening to the radio for news from St. Augustine. Ronnie turned to the Queen Mother and apologized for his wife's absence. "You must forgive Marietta. Her mother is taking part in a demonstration and I think Marietta would like to see her arrested, since it would prove an important point." When it was time for the Queen Mother to leave, she said goodnight to Marietta and added, "Mrs. Tree, it's been a delightful evening and I do hope your mother gets arrested soon."

Three generations of Peabodys now annually get together on Thanksgiving and Labor Day, making a gathering of about twenty-five, and Mary Peabody is still anxious for the various grandchildren to come to their Maine summer home in Northeast Harbor. She quietly resents not seeing more of the grandchildren, although several confrontations and her critical nature put them off. One granddaughter who appeared in a bikini once has never forgotten her grandmother's vocal shock and horror. Mary realizes these shortcomings and truly longs for a rapprochement. "I think we communicate all right, but I think they just make fun of my old ways and power."

Sadly she concluded, "I always expected the children and

grandchildren to spend part of the summer with me, but now they always want to do something else. Always want to go cruising together, or be on their own. My children and their young, they just don't want to visit their grandmother as much."

Her "old ways" included decided opinions about society, religion, psychiatry, marriage, children—you name it. She is very straight and outspoken on any number of questions.

On Boston Society—"You see, the Roman Catholics are of Irish peasant background; that goes back a couple of generations. It takes three generations really to amalgamate a race, I think. Now, I don't think people are so conscious of this, but in Boston Catholic girls still have a hard time getting into the clubs."

On her granddaughter Frankie Fitzgerald and her prizewinning book *Fire in the Lake*—"Imagine having a man of Averell Harriman's stature saying that he thinks it's the best book he's read on Viet Nam."

On religion—I wish my family were more religious. I believe it's a tremendous stabilizer and anchorage for people. I wish every child had it growing up."

On psychiatry—"I don't believe that it's necessary to go to psychiatrists to get yourself ironed out. I still think that the New Testament can do that for you if you have the sense to let it."

On her children—"You see, I wasn't aware that my children were having problems when they were growing up. I've come to realize, with them as well as the young, that it's important to keep the line of communication open. I used to admire my mother-in-law tremendously for this. She had a wonderful way with young people. She really got them to talk and confide in her. I don't talk easily. I don't have that skill. My family likes me all right, but I don't think I have the relationship with the young that a lot of grandmothers have."

On power—"I've never thought of it in terms of myself. I suppose I've had power and I suppose I've used it, but not consciously. When I lived in Syracuse for so many years and worked with the Russian Relief Organization and then the American Field Service, I suppose I might have influenced people more. But that's a dangerous thing to do, too. I don't know whether I'd have used personal power if I had realized then that I had it. Certainly as the wife of a bishop one must be awfully careful *not* to use it."

On interests—"When my husband became Bishop I felt that there was little left for me to do. In fact, what I really missed when he became Bishop was that I was not involved in his work except in going to meetings. As the wife of a minister I had a base and a point of reference. So I decided to work in other areas—in resettling Christian refugees from all nations. That took up a lot of time."

On being a mother—"I don't think I *was* a very wonderful mother, really. I was always interested in other things and I didn't put all my energies into the children. Some women do nothing but talk about their family all the time, and I know I didn't. I'm afraid what I did was put them down a lot and I didn't do enough to build them up. You see, lots of people know about how to bring up children now. They've had the advantage of Dr. Spock. In my generation we were just doing what we thought as right and with more emphasis on trying to make them do what was right. I think I was too strict and didn't give them enough encouragement."

Nevertheless, despite a strong mother and a rather unrelenting conservative Bostonian outlook on life, the five Peabody children have all made outstanding contributions to society. Marietta, the oldest child and only daughter, has been interested in world affairs since 1942. She was with the United Nations from 1961 to 1965, finally assuming the position that Mrs. Roosevelt had as United States representative on the Trusteeship Council with rank of Ambassador. An active Democrat, a longtime friend and supporter of Adlai Stevenson, the mother of two well-known daughters, she is now the only woman member of the Board of Directors of CBS.

George, the bachelor son, was a former clergyman and lives in New York, where he works as a consultant to corporations on dynamic psychology and group motivation.

Mike works in Washington for the United States Department of Housing and Urban Development (HUD).

Endicott is the former Governor of Massachusetts and now practices law in Washington.

Sam has been an active schoolteacher in Westchester and New York. Recently focusing his energies on the field of drug abuse, he and his wife, Judy, have been leaders in a rehabilitation center called Reality House. Interestingly enough, notwithstanding a firm upbringing and open ideological clashes with their parents, the Peabodys are all interesting individuals. Being individuals, they may have more difficulty than some families whose members have more of a herd instinct, but there is no question of the deep respect they all have for one another and their parents. Mary Parkman Peabody has been a grand, inspiring matriarch in whose blood the seeds were planted to lift up her children's sights. Her greatest strength is her individuality and her interest in the world around her. Wealth and luxury are meaningless to a woman for whom character and simplicity are everything and who has been buoyed by her innate faith in the Church and the goodness of man.

Mrs. Bernard Gimbel

ALVA GIMBEL had just taken her poodle, Pepe, for a walk on Fifth Avenue as I waited for her in her city home at the Pierre Hotel. It was early winter and she, like many wealthy widows, would soon be leaving for her house in Palm Beach. "Chieftains," the last of the large estates in Greenwich, Connecticut, is where she spends spring and fall weekends and summers.

Maintaining these homes for her late husband has always been her life, and the hurly-burly affable man who had more fun in a steam room with the men than in his many drawing rooms, enjoyed Alva's care. As the head of Gimbel's Department Stores, which was founded by Adam G. Gimbel, his grandfather, in 1817, Bernard became a rich man, and although he and Alva enjoyed very different people and interests, they had a happy blend of companionship and integrity that gave their long marriage meaning.

I had known them and their children for thirty years, and although Mrs. Gimbel had seemed rather feisty and abrupt as I was growing up, the years have mellowed her and softened her responses. A typical example of her earlier retorts was a story concerning her great interest and ability as a rider. A girl friend of one of her children was spending the weekend at Chieftains, which, among other assets, was known for its beautiful stable and show hunters. Mrs. Gimbel was an accomplished horsewoman and rode and hunted sidesaddle. Both her daughters, Carol (now Lebworth) and Hope (now Solinger), were well-known competitors on the horseshow circuit. On this particular weekend, the children's friend expressed an interest in riding and Mrs. Gimbel suggested that the guest ride her own special horse. Not being a particularly experienced rider, the girl was rather apprehensive and said to her hostess, "I'm really so flattered that you trust me with your beautiful hunter."

Mrs. Gimbel, never at a loss for a quick put-down, answered, "My dear, I don't trust you, but I trust my horse."

Now at eighty-two and considerably more tolerant, Mrs. Gimbel makes the best of a wealthy widow's life. "I hate living alone, Felicia," she confided. "Loneliness is the most horrible thing. It took me a long time to get over it after Bernard died in 1966."

Born in New York in 1893, Alva Bernheimer was the youngest of three children. Her mother was eighteen when she was married, and her father thirty-three.

"She was a woman of very warm feelings, who always called me 'baby,'" Mrs. Gimbel said, "but when my father at fifty-two died, she collapsed completely. He had always spoiled her and she didn't know how to do anything. Looking back, it seems pretty strange, but she immediately took me as her companion and not only asked my advice but listened to me, and yet I was only a child. I went to private schools, on trips to Europe with an institutrice, which is more than just a governess. Actually, she was kind of a teacher who tutored me in all subjects and especially the arts and literature of the different countries we visited. I was fifteen on my first trip and I guess a rather spoiled child."

Alva was influenced rather early by Christian Science, since this was the first school she went to. She was Jewish, but the only time she and her mother went to Temple was Friday evenings, for the Memorial Service and when the time came for the mourners to rise, she remembers that her mother and she would stand up. This impressed her about the service, but little else. Christian Science seemed to have greater meaning for her, although she could never go along with its denial of medical aid. In fact, in later years, Alva's most important project was her interest in medical rehabilitation.

"My favorite childhood memories are of riding sidesaddle at the age of seven, and in fact we always had horses and carriages until Mother bought the first automobile," she happily recalled. "I loved riding at our place in Elberon, New Jersey, and also at Durland Academy in Central Park. It was a sport that I loved and continued, and only stopped a few years ago. I showed and hunted with my daughters, Carol and Hope, who became accomplished horsewomen. But up until the day I was seventeen, I was always chaperoned. I met Bernard when I was sixteen. He rang me up the next day to ask if he could come and see me. Of course, I said that I'd have to ask my mother first. I'd gone to a dinner given by Mrs. Rothschild, whom my mother knew because she was a sister of one of the Guggenheims, and my sister Grace had married Robert Guggenheim. Mother refused because she said I was too young."

So to please her mother she started doing work at the Henry Street Settlement. She learned how to knit, but before starting teaching, she would go to Gimbels, where she knew Bernard worked. He was the fourth generation in the store. She told me that she would call him up and he would help her get the wool that he thought pretty, and then she would go downtown on the elevated railroad, "to teach those poor unsuspecting pupils how to knit." She saw Bernard on and off. He came to her debut, when she was eighteen, at the Plaza Hotel. "I had lots of boy friends. I was, really, I must say, quite popular. But Mother, being the strict person she was, felt that I should only be with boys my own age. She also refused to let the orchestra play a fox trot. It had just come into fashion and it was considered a very naughty dance. But some of the girls defied my mother and went straight up to the orchestra and told them to play it, and of course they did. But I remember Bernard being so much more mature than the boys at the party. He was seven and a half years older than I, and of course my poor mother thought that was dreadful. I wanted to start going out with him right after that night, but I got scarlet fever soon after and my mother shipped me off to Europe. Very cruel, really, but when I came back the next year we met again at a little dinner, and within the month I fell in love with him right away, and he said he did too."

Her mother softened and really came to love him, but she never liked the fact that the Gimbel family had just come from Philadelphia only a few years before, for the Bernheimers from Fourteenth Street considered themselves quite a swell Jewish family. Alva told me that her father was in the wholesale cotton business, and a merchant from out of town was not what Mama had in mind as a husband for her daughter Alva. He wasn't cultured or as traditional as her family, and he didn't like music much. As Alva recalls, "My mother had opera seats every week, and she would see that he had one right next to us. He stood it for about two months and then told my mother that one night someone in a box above had dropped their opera glasses. Why, they might have hit him on the head, he said to Mother and begged to be excused from further attendance. He got his way, which he usually did, and so we got married. Really, you know, he was such a dynamic person."

Sports were his great interest and at one time he had wanted to be a professional boxer, but his parents talked him out of this. Bernard's other energies were spent on building up Gimbel's, but even after a hard day's work he would always go to the Athletic Club—every night all through his life. When the Biltmore Baths were built in the Biltmore Hotel Bernard Gimbel and a group of ten or fifteen men such as Jim Farley and Mike Lerner would all get together there. They'd work out and then Bernard would go home to Alva.

"He'd come in around seven-thirty and I used to say, 'Well, tell me the news, because I know you've been gossiping the whole time you've all been in the steam bath.' That was one of the ways I'd hear what was going on in New York. I also became involved with woman suffrage. I made a tremendous cardboard sign saying, 'Votes For Women'; and I'd drive my Model-T Ford around the country and my friends and I would try and convince people of our cause. But not many listened."

As if to fill in the years, Alva completed the picture.

"Oh, my life was full. I had three children very quickly. Our first son, Bruce, now head of the Gimbel stores, then Hope and Carol, who were twins, and another set of twins, Peter and David. David died tragically of cancer in his thirties."

Bernard adored the children. It was he who piqued their interest in sports. The girls were riders and tennis players. Bruce learned to fly and still does, and Peter developed the skills he now uses on his deep-sea-diving escapades: the *Andrea Doria* and the search for the rare white whale. He is a recognized expert in this field.

"While Bernard was pursuing his sports and encouraging the children, I did what I enjoyed—going to museums and reading,"

Alva continued. "We had great happiness because we were both devoted to our children. We traveled a great deal together and we enjoyed people—not always the same ones, but we respected each other's interests. That's the key."

Alva became very interested in the Institute for Rehabilitation in New York, which Dr. Howard Rusk founded, and the Rusks and the Tunneys became their closest friends. Traveling and speaking for the Institute for years, Mrs. Gimbel and her house tours have raised hundreds of thousands of dollars.

"We had a great closeness with our grandchildren," she wanted to remind me. "I love young people. I like doing things with them the way I actively did with my own children."

The family house, Chieftains, was and still is the gathering place for two generations of children. Eighty-two acres—stables, swimming pool, bridle paths, tennis court, and a wonderful old stone house where friends would meet, celebrities from the sports and art fields all thrown into a happy potpourri in a large but conversationally arranged seating plan. You might find Gene Tunney and Arlene Francis in one corner, always a dog, always a son or daughter, usually grandchildren, Howard Rusk and his wife, all ages, all interests. Bernard and Alva ran an informal salon where at any chair you would find a lively conversation going on.

A woman of very definite opinions, Alva is not very impressed with Women's Lib. "Ridiculous," she told me when I asked her what she thought of the movement. "Why, I never felt any restrictions, nor did other women after they got the vote. I believe women have been independent for a long time."

Certainly Alva's children and grandchildren, from a vantage point of one and two generations, have always felt her strong will and determination.

Hope Solinger, one of her first set of twins, had her mother well pegged. "Mother is a stormy type with quite a temper. It flares up and then subsides, and she's not to be crossed easily. 'Pops' used to call her 'Baby,' which had been her mother's nickname for her, but at other times he would call her "General." He used to say she had black boots on and, cracking her whip, would try to regulate other people's lives. But when she would try it with him, he'd quietly say, 'Now, Baby,' don't play General with me,' and that would be the end. Nevertheless, she was terribly loyal to him and to all of us children. Let anybody say one word against any of the family and she'd be the first to take up the cudgel like a lioness."

Alva, more than her husband, encouraged the children in their sports activities, even if there was danger involved. When their son Peter was in his thirties he organized a diving expedition to explore the *Andrea Doria*, which was lying on the bottom of the Atlantic Ocean. Bernard tried to talk him out of it and told him he was stupid to try, but his mother never questioned his desire. She was far less critical. And when Bruce, their eldest son, took up flying, Alva went up with him just to prove to her husband that their son wasn't completely mad.

She remembered the flight, and I, even now, had to admire her courage. "Yes, of course I flew with Bruce. It was one of those small two-engine planes and he was piloting it from New York to Denver," she paused. "Oh yes, there was a terrible storm. A terrible storm. I'll never forget. We had to land at the first airport we could find. Bruce was at the controls, of course, and I was sitting in back of him. When we finally landed, after bouncing around a lot, Bruce patted me on the knee and said, 'Mother, you're wonderful. You never made a sound!' I really had great confidence in him, but I didn't want to admit the reason why I never spoke. I was actually too frightened."

Since Bernard's death, Alva has become the matriarch of the Gimbel family. She keeps up relationships with her grandchildren and makes a point of bringing them all together so they can see each other. Christmas and New Year's are family occasions. She even threw her own eightieth birthday party so the clan could gather around.

As with many widows, Alva has come into her own as a forceful person. Without anyone to curb her, as Bernard would at times, she has assumed the head-of-the-family role. Her reasoning for this is that she feels strongly that families should stay together and be together and do things together. She likes to organize the occasions, and if there are any family tiffs Alva is there trying to patch up the differences. She is known to be a strong intercessor with her five children, fourteen grandchildren, and seven great-grandchildren. In fact, she shares with all matriarchs the overwhelming *raison d'être* for living fully these later years—a deep emotional involvement with family.

Her grandchildren find her totally unshockable. One of them, Faith Summerfield, expressed her opinion of her grandmother in admiring terms. "Mimi is so interested in what is going on today. She's really with it and much more understanding about our generation than many of my own contemporaries. She's very tolerant of drug addiction, abortions and young people living together. And she enjoys traveling with me and my cousins. I can't help but admire her verve, and she can carry things off that most of us wouldn't dare to. I remember when she took me to Greece and we were going someplace, to a very chic club for lunch, and we were following our hostess' chauffeur in a taxi and the taxi got stopped by the police, the Greek police. We were late and Mimi wanted none of this and so she stepped out of the taxi and, in her best Greek, which is utterly nonexistent, started talking to the taxi driver and the police, and I kept saying, 'Just leave them alone. You're going to make everything worse.' And she realized that they didn't understand her, so she tried Spanish, German, French, Italian . . . any language she could come up with. They took the taxi driver's license away. They actually unscrewed the license plates off the car. I was sitting, shaking inside the car, and fifteen minutes later we saw the police screwing the license plates back onto the car and off we went, everybody smiling. I don't know how she did it, but as you know, she's really incredible."

To other grandchildren, however, Alva can appear enormously strong and dictatorial. And there were instances when we talked that I shared their feeling, such as my statement that she and Bernard had been married for fifty years. She fairly bristled. "Of course, I was married fifty years. In fact, it was fifty-four." It was my mistake because I had indeed been present at their Golden Anniversary celebration at the Pierre, in the ballroom. Several hundred of the Gimbels' friends of all generations gathered for a buffet supper. That was the last time I saw Bernard, as he died several years later at eighty-two.

But *au fond*, Alva's great strengths outweigh any of her momentary flashes of temperament. Civicly minded all of her life, she has spent years helping people who are physically underprivileged, and the list of her interests has no bounds. She feels that she can never do enough, and there's always somebody or some object that needs her help physically or financially.

Her great interest of the moment is encouraging young artists by buying their works, if she likes them, and by lending them money if they are sorely in need.

"I've always used my own judgment in choosing art," she conceded after I commented on pieces set about the living room. "I gave a Picasso to the Museum of Modern Art and a Degas to the Guggenheim. And now I am starting to dismantle many of my earlier discoveries and finding new artists. I like pre-Columbian pottery, and you can see I have an Italian *avant-garde* painting, a South American modern bronze, and a sculpture from Rhodesia."

Her artistic interests carry her on trips with the International Council of the Modern Museum and on the Archives of American Art trips with her friend Eloise Spaeth. She's been all over the world and still shows no signs of slowing down.

"My family doesn't think anyone can keep up with me," she confesses. "They say I'm going all the time. But you know, Felicia, I have a secret." Eager to hear what it was, she shared a story which exemplified it. "The secret is to relax completely, and I seemed to have learned how to do it. I once went on a trip with Dr. Rusk and his wife Gladys. They had been invited by President Eisenhower to head a medical team to Korea. The Rusks invited me to join them to represent the blind, as I had worked for many years for the Lighthouse in New York. Gladys always said she couldn't sleep on a plane, particularly crossing the Pacific with no place to land in an emergency. But it didn't bother me a bit. The man sitting next to me was Jack Taylor and I turned to him and said, 'You look comfortable. Do you mind if I put my head on your shoulder?' And he said, 'Of course not,' and off to sleep I went."

Alva Gimbel at eighty-two is an indomitable spirit whose energies thrust her tirelessly through the ensuing years. Updating herself constantly, even her attire is quite mod, and her jewelry is bold and massive compared to the conservative, traditional models of her younger and middle years. She's a game, fearless matriarch for whom the Social life has never meant much but to whom dedication to those less fortunate has been a crusade. Bibelots and Society, although available to her, have never lured her, and although wealthy, her money has never been spent ostentatiously. She exists for a handful of close friends, family, and special projects which give meaning to her life each day.

Mrs. Arthur H. Sulzberger

THE NEW YORK *Times* is probably the best known newspaper in the world, and three generations of Iphigene's family have been its publisher. It was founded by her father, Adolph S. Ochs, in 1896, who was succeeded by Iphigene's husband in 1935 and by her son-in-law, Orville Dryfoos, in 1961, on whose death in 1963, Arthur Ochs Sulzberger, Iphigene's son and present publisher, took over.

There is no question that Iphigene's life has been deeply involved in the newspaper business, and had circumstances been different, Iphigene might well have been an active and visible power. However, her great talent is that publicly she has supported the policies her menfolk have espoused, but no one doubts the strength and intelligence that is brought to bear on issues that she feels important. Were it not for the fact that Iphigene has never been personally ambitious, the masthead of the *Times* might look quite different. She has always been an esteemed member of its Board and is respected by prominent leaders throughout the world as an astute and charming lady, and as an added compliment, her family feels the same way.

Iphigene Ochs's family was rooted in Chattanooga, Tennessee; well-respected German Jews, they were not to make their real fortune until the mid-1900s. Adolph Ochs, Iphigene's father, was not only the man who gave the world the slogan, "All the news that's fit to print" and esteemed *The New York Times*, but he and his wife produced, after ten years and two miscarriages, a remarkable, sensible, and always beloved daughter.

"I was very fortunate in my parents," Iphigene said. "Some parents are never around, so they're a negative influence. But mine were unique. Mother was the daughter of Rabbi Isaac Wise, who was the founder of the Hebrew Union College and the Union American Hebrew Congregation. He was sort of the leading reform rabbi of his day, and reform was then regarded as the wave of the future among Jews. Mother was the eighth child and her father remarried and had four more, so she grew up *en masse*. She had great sweetness and loving qualities that made people want to do things for her. She should've been a queen with a large retinue, because everyone was always dashing around trying to wait on her."

Adolph Ochs was quite the opposite and came from sterner stuff. His mother was a very positive, domineering woman. After they were married, Adolph and his bride lived for fifteen years with his mother and the rest of the family.

"I once asked my father why he didn't have his own house. He answered that he couldn't afford two, and obviously his mother wanted her son with her." Like all mothers-in-law of that era, she never gave an inch, nor did it occur to her to let her son's wife share the responsibilities of housekeeping. Fortunately for the matriarchs of the 1900s, they were never challenged by their daughters-in-law. Iphigene remembers her mother saying to her, "Change what you can, and the rest you put up with," an attitude that would send present-day feminists out to battle.

Iphigene, a small, prim woman with decided ideas, sits perched in a large chintz armchair in her Fifth Avenue apartment. Evidence of a full life is all around: photographs of children and grandchildren, and two large oil paintings, each inscribed with a gold plaque to Arthur H. Sulzberger—from Dwight D. Eisenhower a street scene, and from Winston Churchill a European sea scene. Photos of Kennedy, Johnson and Roosevelt, also inscribed to Iphigene's husband as well as mementos of her trip to China, are on other tables. A secretary works in the library, and Iphigene's papillon dog, having just returned from the park with his mistress, scratches away on a sofa, unnoticed, trying to make a comfortable place to lie down.

As we talk, it is hard to imagine, so far removed from the presses of *The New York Times*, that Iphigene has been involved behind the scenes in the newspaper business since she was a child. She has probably met every head of state during her eighty-two years, since it has always been a custom for all important foreign visitors, as well as Americans in positions of power, to attend the weekly roundtable lunches with the Publisher. First, as his daughter, then as his wife, next, as mother-in-law, and presently as his mother, Iphigene has sat in and participated at the four different Publishers' request. She has been on the Board of *The New York Times* and attended all their meetings until recently, and has had a strong voice, albeit not the final one, in all decisions affecting the paper. Vocal and making her views known, she does not hesitate to let management know her sentiments. She has written Letters to the Editors on a variety of subjects, from decrying the unnecessary killing of rabbits to stating her liberal Democratic views. Many times she uses deceased relatives' names, unknown to the public but self-evident to the editorial staff. Had Iphigene been brought up under a less strict and old-fashioned father, she might well have taken over the paper. Certainly she was and is qualified. Yet, in a time when women like Dorothy Schiff of the New York *Post*, Katharine Graham of the Washington *Post*, and Buffie Chandler of the Los Angeles *Times* have long held power, Iphigene has deferred to the men in the family. Her father would have shaken less confident daughters than Iphigene. But coupled with his great love for his only child and her total respect and admiration for him, his philosophy strengthened and imbued her with restraint. The power she has always had, yet because of how she was brought up, she has never exercised it. Somehow she has dealt it out to support the family but with remarkable restraint. She has not exercised her clout. Therein lies the great secret. For Iphigene's smile belies the role she plays. As the largest single stockholder of the *Times*, she is a millionaire more than a hundred times over. Yet, she is totally unassuming in her private life and not given to the public displays of her vast wealth. She, more than anyone in this book, is the living example of how a strong father can, by suggestion, influence his daughter's life. His principles she still proudly follows, although time has tempered many of the more rigid attitudes.

The Ochses left Chattanooga when Iphigene was four and moved to New York in 1896. Adolph Ochs is part of New York history now.

"My father was one of the strongest men I ever knew. He had an extraordinarily strong character, but he also possessed great imagination and personality. He never let me make dogmatic statements. In fact, I raised my children and grandchildren on a passage from Ben Franklin's *Autobiography*, which he used to make me memorize if I couldn't back up a point. 'What is your source?' he would ask me, 'Are you sure of that?' If I persisted in saying, 'I just know,' I would have to recite a long passage of Ben Franklin's theories of cultivating various virtues. He made a list, not of those he had but those he wanted to have. Then a Quaker friend told him he was very vain. So he decided to add humility to his list and he practiced not making dogmatic statements by saying, 'It seems to me . . .' or 'I apprehend . . .' or 'From my knowledge of the case . . .' In other words, qualifying his remarks. I never forgot that adage."

Adolph Ochs believed in old-fashioned principles—"sticking to the virtues you learn at your mother's knee, the Ten Commandments, and being honest." He was keen on Iphigene getting an education and going to college, which was not as common for girls then as it is now. And Iphigene did indeed graduate from Barnard. But he was of the old school of males who didn't believe daughters should work, and by no means at *The New York Times*, which by this time he had worked up to owning after small beginnings as a printer in Chattanooga. He would not have minded if his daughter became a teacher, "but he didn't want me near the *Times*. Once I said I'd like to and I got a friend to give me a job, which lasted exactly two hours until my father heard about it and I had to give it up. The only time I really worked at the paper was during World War II when we were shorthanded and my husband, then the Publisher, asked me to help out. But I learned how to put a newspaper out from my father. I was like a little puppydog at his heels. My mother really had her own interests. She loved opera and concerts, which my father didn't. She like to read and stay at home while I just tagged along with my father. He'd take me through the press rooms and particularly the composing rooms. Some of the men in the printers shop were the same ones who had started with him as boys in the South."

Much of Iphigene's strength comes from her faith. Not religiously active, she still carries with her the background of teaching she was given. Her first brush with religion came from her Swiss governess, who was a strict Lutheran, a Calvinist. Mr. Ochs, believing that his daughter needed a little English discipline, hired a cultured and charming Irish lady and strict Catholic, Mrs. Macdonald. Iphigene was sent to Sunday school but didn't like it, so no one bothered to push her.

"I did, however, go with Mother to the synagogue on Friday nights. She particularly liked the evening service, I think, because there was no sermon. We all went to Atlantic City because the family had taken a summer house there. I used to have to go to temple regularly with my aunts there, and if I'm not strongly religious it was due to them. It was very hot and I was squeezed in between them. Those were the days when ladies wore corsets, and if I wiggled I would hit armor plates on one side or the other, so, between them, religion was not made very attractive. But Mrs. MacDonald, whom Father had hoped would elevate me intellectually, was shocked that I really didn't have any religious beliefs, so she started to teach me. Her idea of Judaism was Catholicism without Jesus. Well, the result was a little disastrous, because I got hold of Thomas Paine's *Age of Reason* and decided I was a Deist and didn't believe a darned thing. I told my father this. I guess I was about fifteen and he said, 'Well, if you don't want to believe, I'm perfectly satisfied that you give up your religion. But what I object to is that you're giving up something you don't understand and don't know. I suggest you go to the new rabbi at Temple Emanu-El, whom I used to know in Louisville. He's a very learned young man and it might be a good idea if you asked him to give you lessons.'"

Being, as usual, an obedient daughter, Iphigene thought she'd try it. As she now recalls, the lessons were fascinating, and she went once a week for about two years and read the Bible from beginning to end. The Rabbi had great rapport with his pupil. He began by asking her what she didn't believe. "Well, I said, I don't believe the world was created in six days, I don't believe Noah and the Ark, or Abraham, or Jonah and the whale. I hadn't gotten very far on my list when he interrupted and shocked me by saying, 'Who do you think does believe these stories?' Of course, I had gotten them from my Calvinist nurse and from Mrs. Mac-

Donald and her strict Irish-Catholic point of view. 'You mean to tell me, Iphigene,' he said, 'that you don't know the difference between mythology, folklore, history and religion? This is shocking!'" And, as Iphigene told me, he began to go through all the books of the Bible. "I'll never forget those lessons. I remember particularly that he told me the books of Ruth and Esther were novels and that Job was an epoch poem of Babylonian origin. I really found out what religion was and its essence. That's what was important to me. Frankly, I don't go to temple much any more because Judaism seems to have retrogressed. I think Hitler, making the Jews suddenly very self-conscious, has forced even reform Jews to become overly ethnic. They're beginning to go back to wearing those old skull caps and prayer cloths, chanting in Hebrew. I'm not at home there any more. Then, I object to the prayer about the Lord always taking care of the Jews and freeing the captives. I told the Rabbi we ought to have that prayer out of the book. 'Where was he at Auschwitz and Dachau?' I asked. 'Oh,' he said, 'you're too literal-minded.' 'Well, I feel ashamed to say this, even to mumble it. I keep apologizing to the Lord. I don't know what he is, but I apologize every time I read that prayer.'"

Iphigene waited to get married until she was twenty-five. She had met Arthur Sulzberger when he was at Columbia and she at Barnard. They went out together on and off for about seven years. It has often been said that the Ochses disapproved of Sulzberger. His family had been in the cotton business. Iphigene knew that her father would probably discourage the idea of her ever getting married, but she was very attracted to Sulzberger, who was handsome and charming.

"Father never really understood why I would want to get married. After all, I had a good home and he liked having me with him. He also thought that nobody was worthy of his one and only darling. My mother was all on my side, but Father tried his best to delay our plans. It was during the war and he thought I should maybe wait until after it was over. Well, we didn't. We were married in 1917. Arthur was in the Army. Eventually, Father got used to the idea. He even said that having picked a husband with an interest in newspapers and the *Times*'s interest at heart, I couldn't have done better."

Mr. Ochs never gave his son-in-law a specific job on the paper. Sulzberger began as an assistant to George McAneny, the Editor.

"Arthur was an energetic young man, and he told me he got his early training picking up what everyone left undone. He went through the different departments but not in an organized way. He became Publisher after my father died in 1935."

The Sulzbergers had four children: Marion, Ruth, Judy and Arthur, who was nicknamed "Punch" because of his next sister. Marion's first husband, Orvil Dryfoos, was Publisher after Sulzberger's death. Dryfoos died at an early age and Punch succeeded him. Judy went into medicine and became a doctor, and Ruth runs the paper in Chattanooga. All have been married twice. (Marion was a widow for a brief period before she married Andrew Heiskell, Chairman of Time-Life.) All have been community-minded, and they are an extremely close, noncompetitive family. Iphigene did not believe in any hard and fast rules in raising her children. "It seems obvious and sensible that if you want to raise children to adjust in a changeable world, they must keep an open mind. 'What does the Lord require of thee? To deal justly, to love mercy and to walk humbly with thy God.' I believe in teaching children that. And to take every opportunity you can to be of use and service to your fellow man. Jesus said it is more blessed to give than to receive, and he was right. It's no fun to be on the receiving end. It's often an obligation and sometimes an embarrassment. It takes a lot of character to receive graciously."

The *Times* has a charitable foundation, and the family's contributions come out of it. Iphigene has given time and money to her alma mater, Barnard. She's been on many boards—the University of Chattanooga, Hebrew Union College in New York, the Girl Scouts of America, the New York Botanical Gardens—and she was for years President of the New York Parks Association.

It has not been the good works or her own interests that have given her the greatest enjoyment. She believes that a woman's greatest role is in being a good wife and devoted mother. Christmas and birthdays and other holidays are still reasons for a family get-together. On her eightieth birthday the family gave Iphigene a party. Her granddaughter, Susan Dryfoos, Marion's daughter, read a tribute she had written, which really spoke for all the family:

"God in his infinite wisdom, has seen fit to bless us with success and good health. What more could we wish for?" Your father spoke of those words on September 19, 1892, the day "his precious lump of humanity," when you, Granny were born. "I realize I have prospered beyond my desserts and merits," he said on that occasion, "and can account for it only by my good luck."

It is of that moment, when you came to life with black, curly hair, the cutest of hands and undoubtably sneezing in a soundless, funny way, that we, your grandchildren, celebrate today. And for us the soft, handsome lady you are in this moment of becoming eighty years old brings the same feeling of preciousness your father expressed so beautifully. For us that preciousness lies not so much in what you've been in the past, but in what you are today, in the way you touch us now and will touch us tomorrow.

You're a living human, not just a human being. You take us traveling abroad and we buckle up with indigestion, cramps or old-fashioned fatigue, and you're full of energy, bringing us meals in bed, fluffing our pillows. We tour museums, historical sites, you question the guides with the curiosity of a child, relate unheard-of historical tidbits and invite strangers to speak of their lives. We dine with dignitaries in chandeliered suites or lunch in self-service, fly-swatting cafés, and you're a classy lady and our best friend.

You're involved in beautifying parks and streets, preserving wilderness and wildlife, restoring historical landmarks, supporting the creative skills of craftsmen, advising reporters and relatives on the welfare of *The New York Times*, providing relief to the Indians, and the poor in Harlem and slums around the world, and yet, you're never too busy to spend time with us. You come to graduation exercises, phone to invite us over, write a postcard from abroad just to say "hello." And when we're together we're never generations apart. You're right there, listening with your heart, speaking of your confidence in our ability to grow, supporting our goodness and asking only that we move, toward the "humanness" in being. With you we're not ashamed to flop, to launch unedited thoughts and feel safe, as if we were alone. With you we're never ashamed to ask for a book, a car, money or a hug. You invited us to be ourselves, to laugh at our silliness and confront our mistakes. You never touch us and we touch ourselves. We take your gifts, but never get around to saying how much they mean. They are very precious. We love you for all the meaning you give to our lives, for being our friend, for just being.

> SUSAN DRYFOOS
> September 19, 1972
> On the occasion of Mrs.
> Sulzberger's eightieth birthday.

A matriarch of the Old School, loving, yet wise, Iphigene doesn't really subscribe to Women's Lib. "Men and women have separate roles and it's perfectly absurd to me to go against nature. After all, nature didn't develop two sexes to make them exactly alike. And we know we aren't alike. Of course, women should have equal job opportunity and equal pay, but to pretend that being a mother and having a home is demeaning or not worthy, I think, is ridiculous. Why should you want to go dashing out and enrich the lives of somebody else's children in a day nursery and abandon your own? It doesn't make sense. I think young people of today are taking chances with their future. Immorality, drugs, abandoning standards. I think they'll regret it later. On the whole, human beings are really like herd animals. We have to live together and you've got to have certain rules and regulations. Society goes to pieces if you don't have certain moral and spiritual standards."

Iphigene never felt that she had to prove herself. She was, and is, happy with her feminine role in a large and powerful family. She has never aspired to a more dominating position, but she has inspired her children and grandchildren to turn to her and to make the most of their own lives. There is an easy exchange of ideas between the generations which sometimes surprises people. "My friends often say, 'But, of course, you can't advise so-and-so or tell Punch . . .' Well, of course I tell all of my family. I tell them everything that comes into my head. And they, in turn, are completely free to ignore it . . . no hard feelings. If I want to tell Punch something about the paper, it's my privilege. It's his privilege to choose what he wants to do about it. All of my family enjoy each other, thank God, and we're friends!"

Iphigene Sulzberger votes in New York because, as long as she is a part of the *Times,* she feels an obligation to keep her legal residence in the city. But she has a special feeling about her house in Stamford, Connecticut, which she's had for about twenty-three years. Here is where the Sulzberger clan gathers and one sees a truly great matriarch with her children and grandchildren. Not addicted, as most ladies are, to gardening, "I don't like digging and getting my hands dirty. I just don't like the feel of earth." She enjoys walks in the woods and having friends and family around. "I never was the sporty type and I've never been lonely. If nobody's around I just love to read and never have enough time to catch up with the papers and books, but I do love people."

Her associates and friends love Iphigene too. They appreciate that she has never thrown her weight around and that she has always acted like a great lady. If she has faults, no one will admit them, for she has always been composed and led by example. She can make light of her own failings. "I'm now off all of the boards that I was on because I think you should have a retirement age. Younger people must be given a chance to take responsibility. Besides, you never know yourself when you're beginning to be an old fogey. I think it's better to retire before the other fellow thinks you are." With a sweet smile, this benign matriarch had some very wise words: "One thing I will say, when you're eighty, I've discovered that there's a heck of a lot I don't know anything about, don't understand, can't understand. So I might as well accept it. I've got my limitations."

Achievers

AMERICAN WOMEN in the last century have, in increasing numbers, achieved tremendous personal success and, due to the rapid growth in communications, have been acclaimed during their lifetimes. Encouraged by the examples of thousands of celebrated women, others less noted, but certainly of comparable ability, have made important contributions in all fields heretofore dominated by men.

I have chosen five achievers from different backgrounds and of diverse philosophies, but all of them able and wanting to fulfill themselves. There were many other women, among them Margaret Mead and Cornelia Otis Skinner, who are missing from these pages. I spoke with them but, since they have both written several autobiographies, I felt that there was little new I could add to the public's knowledge of their careers.

Mrs. DeWitt Wallace has gained power and recognition, although she has certainly not courted publicity, and indeed prefers to bestow her largesse in meaningful but not self-aggrandizing ways.

Clare Luce is a product of her own creation whose beauty and brains were, and still are, a definite asset among less ambitious and effacing women.

Louise Nevelson felt, even as a child, the stirrings of an artist, and despite obstacles, being a woman and the expectations of trying to be a wife, created her own image. One of a kind, an individual whose sculptures are molded from a penetrating sense of self-purpose, she has become a special figure even in a world where artists are expected to be a different breed.

Marian Anderson, besides developing her own talents to the

fullest, believes in people and life, and in her own way has responded, ever so graciously, to all the demands that have been made on her. Her great religious faith has made her equally recognized as a musician as well as for achieving the highest ideals of human character. Saintly in disposition, with quiet serenity, she reflects none of the stridence or dominating traits that so often characterize successful people.

The perseverance and determination of Hazel Wightman, a tiger of the tennis courts, has given her the sense of purpose that still keeps her going. A remarkable example of what you can do for and with yourself if you really try, is this spunky woman. Not endowed with wealth or beauty, she was determined to find her own special niche and fashioned her own tools to achieve it. And the tennis balls are still bouncing in the Wightman suggested tennis rhythm.

Of the above five women, all have been married, two happily, two unhappily and one successfully. More often than not, women who have talented lives to fulfill find it difficult to be the expected model of a wife and mother. The key to the luckier ones, it seems, is in having husbands who are not interested in competing and who are self-assured enough to lead their own lives in peaceful support of their partners.

Women who have power usually cannot expect to win on all fronts, and many have admitted that, for them, marriage and careers were the combinations they did seek. The careers were achieved, the harmonious marital relationships often were not.

The important fact is that they have created their own special legacies and, even though the road is short, have enjoyed making their own roles and still continue as sages in their special fields. All have enjoyed avocations of their own choices and have managed, some better than others, to be successful in their professional fields as well as in their domestic lives. This duality of roles was not as accepted in the 1900s as it is today, and yet these women rose to the challenge to fulfill themselves with a sense of confidence that deserves great admiration from succeeding generations.

Marian Anderson

MARIAN ANDERSON is one of two women in this book who are still married—to their original husband. She and her husband live in Danbury, Connecticut, and have been married for thirty-four years. At seventy-two Miss Anderson is still a remarkably handsome woman. Tall and erect, she radiates composure, inner beauty, and a boundless soul. One of the most renowned singers of this century, she has made more concert tours throughout the world than any other musician and still has found time to write her autobiography, work at the United Nations and make lecture tours.

I found her warm and gracious and with a unique language style. Her sentence structure is stylized and lengthy and she never apostrophizes her words. Her diction is perfect and every word is pronounced individually, as if she were waiting for the listener to absorb every thought before continuing to the next.

When she spoke to me about her childhood, she referred to herself as "I," but then as she progressed to the beginning of her musical career, she began to use "we." For a while I assumed she was including another person, which she actually was. Only the other person is "God." Miss Anderson avoids the use of the first-person singular because it is almost too personal and egotistical. As with everything she refers to in her life, she is incredibly modest and gives herself no intended credit for her talent and success. She seems to have inherited her strong sense of morality and her gentle disposition from her warm and loving mother, whom she remained close to until her death eight years ago. Her father died when she was still a child, yet her early years are filled with affectionate recollections of family

life. Her parents gave her a sense of values that she is still proud
of today. The family budget was meager but their spirits were
high, and she and her sisters were endowed with the joys of
living and learned the meaning of happiness in giving of themselves to their church, to their family and to their neighbors.

Miss Anderson's father worked at the Reading Railroad ter-
minal in Philadelphia in the refrigerator room, and as a second
job, sold coal and ice. He was not averse to hard work in order
to support his wife and three daughters. Miss Anderson's mother
was born in Virginia and met her future husband at her sister's
house in Philadelphia. Prior to that, she had become a schoolteacher in Lynchburg, Virginia, but gave up her job when
she married. Marian was the first child and was born in 1903.

When she described her father, it was a beautiful word picture.
"I felt that he was a very strong character and I admired him a
great deal. I was, of course, very impressed that he was so tall
and good-looking. He was really quite handsome and well over
six feet. There were few youngsters in the neighborhood who
had a father who looked quite as well, as elegant, as fine as my
father did. He dressed in a conservative manner, and he was very
careful with the way the trouser hit the ankle. In the back it
would almost touch the ground and you could barely see the
bottom of his heel Oh, he was just grand."

He certainly impressed his daughter, and although she recalls
that he wanted all the good things for his family that he
could provide, we wondered how he made ends meet. Marian
isn't sure even what his salary was. "I would hate to say even if
I knew, because in this age one couldn't conceive of working so
hard for the small amount of money Father then received. Only
with two jobs was he able to do the things he wanted, but I'm
sure that his total income never exceeded twenty-five dollars a
week."

He never complained, Miss Anderson said, and he enjoyed the
few beautiful moments with his daughters that were his exclusively—special trips to the circus, and in the summer a day's
outing with a group to the park. "Whether it was with a church
group or others," Marian said, "it was a family event in which
Father was an important part. Particularly Easter. Father would
tell my mother that she could get our clothes, but he wanted to

buy our hats. He would always buy us broad-brimmed ones that turned up somewhat. They usually had flowers galore and streamers on the back." Clearly, Mr. Anderson loved dressing up his girls, and they in turn enjoyed the attention. "Another thing that fascinated me about Father and was perhaps my first introduction to music was his singing of one song, 'Asleep in the Deep.' There were only a few bars that he sang, but they were enough," Marian said firmly.

Mr. Anderson was very interested in the Union Baptist Church, where he served as head usher. He and his mother and sister would often take the children to church. Marian became a member of the Junior Choir at the age of six.

"But at home when we were quite young we had little sings," Marian recalled. "I think Mother played a few chords on the piano now and then, and we did too. We used to make up our own harmonies and in the beginning we sang mostly Negro spirituals. They were the easiest and everybody seemed to know the tunes and the words. We would even have our own four-part harmony."

When she was eight, Marian's father either bought or inherited a piano, which his daughter used to play. She had never had any lessons but learned from a card that was marked with notes. "I don't know whether those cards exist any more," she confessed, "but it was made of white cardboard and the notes were in black and white. You put it behind the keyboard, and if you cared you could write little numbers to show you where the keys were. Father was so happy when the piano came. He wanted us, he said, to teach him how to play. He was, of course, just humoring us because he was that kind of a person. We even thought we could teach him, and I remember one time trying to show him something. I would take his finger to put on a key and he would always let it slip to the side so he'd be striking two notes at a time. I suppose he was pretending that I could do much better than he."

Mrs. Anderson was a devoted mother and homemaker. Realizing the family finances were in need of help, she did laundry for the neighbors from Monday to Friday, perhaps adding four or five dollars to the weekly income. Of her mother, Marian told me that she did this, as other things in life, because it was necessary and it was her way of helping. The children too went out and did odd jobs to earn a little spending money. From their way of life, Marian learned the value and the sacrifices families make. "I've found this out in life," she said, clasping her hands, "people can manage. You cut your garment according to the cloth. I do not remember a time that we needed a piece of bread or wanted anything that wasn't somehow forthcoming from someplace or another. Somehow my mother instinctively knew how to cut corners here and there and make things last."

Marian's mother seems to have had the strongest influence on the children. Innately good herself, she tried to pass on the virtues she felt were so important, and judging from her eldest, she more than succeeded.

"My mother never had to talk to my sister and me and tell us what she expected. I think what she wanted was to build a beautiful and firm foundation and the importance of being true to yourself and to others. She never insisted that we do anything special, nor did she steer us in any particular direction. I think this was very good, for so many people rebel when they do not want to be pushed. We lived in the kind of atmosphere where the family and the home happened to be our whole world."

The first home Marian knew was in South Philadelphia. The neighborhood had once been black but it was in the process of changing. Except for two other families besides the Andersons, it was a block of mixed nationalities. To Marian, they were all neighbors; a sickness in one family concerned everyone. One of her closest friends was Louise McIlvaine, whose uncle was a white politician. He would often come home late, so Louise would spend the evening with Marian until Marian was put to bed, and then curl herself in the Morris chair to await her uncle.

Many of the children in the neighborhood joined with Marian and her sisters in trying to make a little extra money. After scrubbing the steps of their own houses, they all went and scrubbed the others in the neighborhood.

"Mother always said, 'Now, if you're going to do something, do it well, and if it takes you a little longer than someone else, take the time, but do it well.' That philosophy never left me and has remained with me all my life. We didn't always do things as well as we might have, but we always made the effort."

Marian didn't mind scrubbing steps. "There wasn't any status symbol to us about not doing it. We did our own, since we couldn't afford to pay someone to, and if a friend next door asked, 'Would ya clean my steps? I'll give ya a nickel or a dime,' well, we never gave it another thought. We went about the task joyfully, and I recall we'd even play jacks as we were working. We'd earn our money and Mother would be our banker. If you gave her five cents, no matter when you called for it, it would be there. Day after day, week after week, month after month, and I suppose even for years after. She was our bank and she kept our money in a little box."

Marian never had any musical training, to speak of. In secondary school she sang with the class. She also at this time developed an interest in medicine and had a strong urge to become a doctor, because if anyone was hurt she was always there ready to bandage or help.

Few children have a rare gift which, without training, is recognized at an early age. Marian Anderson was six when she joined the Junior Choir at the Union Baptist Church. Alexander Robinson was the choral director. Devoted to the church and without any pay, he encouraged the youngsters individually with their singing. It was Robinson who gave Marian and a friend, Viola Johnson, a copy of the song "Heart of a Shepherd" to memorize and perform as a duet. This led to her being billed, as a baby contralto at the age of ten, for frequent concerts at various church functions. While still in high school, friends collected money to put into a Marian Anderson future fund. Mary Saunders Patterson was Marian's first voice teacher. But Marian, through the church choir at the Union Baptist Church, would often sing in other church events. With no professional training, she would receive anywhere from fifty cents to one dollar fifty, depending on what the audience could spare for a particular cause. She was only fourteen and her repertoire consisted of two or three songs. Sensing that she needed professional help, she once tried to become a pupil in a music school, but the results were disastrous. They turned her down because of her color.

"Yes," she said, when I asked her what response was evoked when she was refused admission, "it did have a profound impression on me, because in my teens I was still very naïve. I did not understand why in a beautiful setting like that music school, with a beautiful girl receptionist, a whole moment could be shattered by this person saying, 'we don't take colored.' She seemed so happy to tell me that, you know, and it was so bitterly disappointing to me. Many people would not have moved until they had had their say. It was such a shock that I was speechless, terribly hurt, and a bit numb about the whole thing."

Marian's immediate response was to go home to her mother. She had learned long ago that to have made a scene would not have changed the decision. She felt, as her mother had, that one had to believe in the fact that if you cannot help a situation, you shouldn't aggravate it.

That incident and another, when she was put in a Jim Crow car en route to an engagement in Washington, served, as she said, "to mark my growing up. It was part of my training to become a professional."

Marian would have liked to go on to college after high school. This is when she began using "we." "We went to Chicago for a conference of the National Association of Negro Musicians," she said. I asked, "Who went with you?" to get at the meaning of "we," and she said she honestly didn't remember who. From that point on, she referred to herself collectively. "After the performance there were several people who felt we should have some help in musical education," she ventured. "It was decided that I should go to college and, as I remember, my tuition was even oversubscribed. I was thrilled to death about the whole thing."

But for unexplained reasons it never happened, and Marian was amazingly restrained in her reaction—a typical grandiose gesture to people who had let her down. Instead of criticizing, her remarks seemed to exempt them from blame. "As often happens, the enthusiasm of the moment doesn't always carry the person to achieve their intention. The obligations they might have made under emotional circumstances are not always followed through. "So," she said with a sigh and a pause, "the money was not there when the time came for us to go to Yale, and we did not have it to get there, so I never went."

The first teacher that Marian studied with, as her school career was ending, was Mrs. Mary Saunders Patterson. While a pupil of hers, she gave her first major solo performance, under the auspices of the Philadelphia Choral Society. Later, friends helped her to study with a then great voice teacher, Giuseppe Boghetti. He prepared Marian to enter the competition which launched her singing career.

Marian has never forgotten that moment. "It was 1926 and three hundred contestants appeared at Lewisohn Stadium in New York. There were several warmups before the actual tryouts. One place I remember particularly was Aeolian Hall on West Fifty-seventh Street. Boghetti, my teacher, was not as experienced as others in competitive events, and Reba Patton, another of his pupils, and I waited a long time with him for our audition. Finally, it was brought to his attention that we had to have a card with a number on it. He went up to the stage and got the first number he could, which was 44. That was how long we had been waiting. He got a second ticket, 44A, for me, and by the time my turn came along, the aria which I was to sing had already been performed six times. We had also learned, from the long wait, that the judges would make a little clicking sound if they had heard enough of a voice. But Mr. Boghetti had told us not to stop, no matter what they did until we came to the end, because we had a special trill which," as Marian modestly put it, "wasn't the worst one that he'd ever heard! He insisted that we get that in. We were lucky in that we were allowed to finish. Reba had been disqualified and we went back to my teacher's studio. Within a half hour the phone rang and they told Mr. Boghetti we had been one of the sixteen chosen from the original three hundred contestants. Then we had to go back and they chose four from our sixteen, and then one from the four. He was very thrilled when we won. The prize was a concert for me at Lewisohn Stadium with the New York Philharmonic."

In the late 1920s and on through the '60s, Marian Anderson became world-famous. She gave everything to her musical career, traveling thousands of miles through Europe and Asia on concert tours.

Marian Anderson's concert tours and engagements were the fulfillment of a dream born of dedication and hard work. Her voice became her greatest asset, but to achieve a career as a singer, being black and without financial resources, was a challenge she rose to with her particular cheerful ardor and quiet determination.

An inspiration, Marian Anderson's life is a tribute to the heights to which a human being can aspire, despite handicaps and obstacles which might have discouraged less courageous individuals.

To her belong all the superlative adjectives that are attributed to people with magnificent character traits. These have obviously brought her great acclaim and success in the musical field and she well deserves the title of being a great humanitarian. From her beginning training with her teacher, Mr. Boghetti, to contests, simple recitals, then later achieving the ultimate, gaining an accompanist, Billy King, each step gained her more prominence. Marian Anderson never took any engagement for granted and never was content to accept the gratification of the moment. Her great artistry comes from her great humility and total dedication to giving the best of herself and reaching for excellence in performance standards.

There is no question that Miss Anderson's inspiration and happiness of spirit were rooted in her deep attachments to her family and to her church. She was cherished and lovingly followed a long and righteous path because of the strong feelings and comfort that these relationships have brought to her. She does not believe that she would have had the career she enjoyed or have accomplished what she has without God's help.

From her first trip to Europe and her concert in England on September 16, 1930, her schedules of engagements began to steamroll. From the fall of 1930 and for the next five months, nineteen concerts were scheduled. For the next thirty-five years, Marian Anderson toured the world, and her collection of press notices would fill a trunk.

All the years of touring were interrupted only once, in 1958, when Miss Anderson was appointed United States alternate delegate to the United Nations. With her usual reticence, she told me that she accepted the job, although she did not really feel qualified. "I did not see myself as admirably prepared, and when you go to the United Nations you do not put forth your own ideas; rather you are there to express those of your country," she admitted. "You see, it was a little confining, since I was used to my active concert schedule. Anway, music was my first love, and so after the UN I resumed my career until I gave it up after the 1963–64 season."

It was in Wilmington, Delaware, at a concert she gave at the age of eighteen, that she met her future husband. He was known as Razzle Fisher. He wanted to marry her when she was still in high school, but the marriage did not happen for nineteen years because her musical career took precedence over everything else. All of her traveling made any kind of romance impossible, for she was dedicated to becoming, first, a successful artist.

It did not disturb her that their lives were totally separate. She told me, quite dispassionately, that that was a fact she accepted. "I knew he was always there because I knew that he was an interested person and I was interested in him to a degree, but at that time music was the most important thing in my life. He had his own career as an architect, and we would see each other from time to time or he would write, but it was not often."

Razzle Fisher was not one to be put off and was constant in his devotion, although rather impatient about waiting.

They were married when Marian returned from a concert tour in 1940 and moved to Connecticut, where they have lived ever since. Each has pursued separate careers successfully, although they have missed not having had children.

"My great desire," Marian said thoughtfully, "if I could have had a family, was to devote as much time to our children as my mother did. If we had been half as successful as she was with us, we would have done a very good job. Having children is a great responsibility, and we sincerely believed that they would have been a great joy to both of us. We have been sorry that when we decided we wanted a family, it was a bit late."

As with all other facets of her remarkable life, Marian Anderson has led a totally contented married life, and now that the frenetic pace of her career has quieted down, she enjoys being, as she calls it, "a homemaker." "We're very interested in the young people and in encouraging singers to appear in the auditions for the Marian Anderson Scholarship Fund that is still held annually and was set up many years ago with a grant of ten thousand dollars, but of course more has been added in order for it to exist. My husband belongs to the Urban League and we belong to the NAACP."

I asked Miss Anderson whether she thought that great progress had been made in opportunities for Negroes in the professional fields.

"Yes," she said thoughtfully, "I think Negroes have even become more aware of knowing and being proud of people of their own race, starting with children in school who identify more with Negroes who have achieved. Serious performers are better rounded than those of my day and are knowledgeable in fields other than their own particular profession. Because of more education and greater interests, I know that many of our young people now can start at a higher level than they might have years ago. Many people really and truly deliver in a most gratifying way."

After our interview was over and Miss Anderson left, I thought about the time we had spent together. This was the second interview we taped (for about two hours), but unfortunately when it came time to transcribe the tapes, they turned out to be blank due to a faulty recorder. How to tell Miss Anderson that her trip into New York at my request had been a total loss took a month for me to resolve. I called her and explained my terrible dilemma and fearfully asked her if she could possibly give me another chance to meet with her. Her gracious affirmative response was heartwarming, and fortunately, it gave me another chance to meet with this truly superb woman. Hers is the real American success story; but more than this, being privileged to have spent the time I did with her, I felt that I was in the presence of a human being who had developed herself and her skills to the best of her ability. Her achievements reflect the extraordinary heights to which one can aspire. Miss Anderson is an example, against seemingly unsurmountable odds, not of a successful Negro but of an extraordinary human being.

Hazel Wightman

TODAY WOMEN TAKE PART in almost all of the competitive sports,
training long hours and working their way up through the amateur ranks. Tennis is no exception, but back in the 1800s tennis
was a social game played almost exclusively by boys and men.
Hazel Hotchkiss, born in 1886 in the small town of Healdsburg,
California, didn't intend to become a ranking tennis player. She
watched her brothers and, with the zest of a gym teacher, plus
ability, she became a champion. Using only the space between
two dormer windows as a backboard, and with nothing but her
own competitive spirit, she, a totally self-taught young woman,
won the U. S. Singles Championships in 1909, 1910, 1911 and
1919.

Hazel credits most of her abilities and purposefulness to her
early family life, and growing up with brothers who encouraged
her.

"We lived in the country, as everybody did in those days, and
we had a nice big house and a great big lovely place in front to
play baseball and other children's games, because of course there
was no TV. There was no cement around the house, just gravel
and rosebushes. The public school was within walking distance
and so was the local high school, which I attended for two years
before we moved to Berkeley in 1902."

Her childhood years were happy ones and Hazel delighted in
the attention her brothers gave her, even though everyone told
her mother, "Oh, Emma, your boys are so handsome. It's too
bad Hazel is so plain."

"I heard that from the time I could breathe, you know," she
said by way of information, and unself-consciously. She was al-

ways small, five feet tall, and obviously a tomboy. Her adult weight, 110 pounds, is the same as it was when she was in her teens. But, as a child, to make up for her lack of looks and to be useful, she took to helping out in the family.

"I waited on my brothers hand and foot. Everyone, including my father would say, 'Sis get this' or 'Sis, get that,' and I was really happy to oblige. I've always enjoyed doing something for somebody else."

She was well-rewarded, for her brothers, as she told me proudly, would bring home boys and they "always had me show off what I could do. Me climbing the ladder. Me polevaulting. They'd praise me and make me first on their teams, which was a great compliment. It meant that I was even better than a boy."

Hazel really craved approval and wanted to be needed. That remark was gratifying and satisfying, so she helped with the housework whenever she had a chance. Her parents were both very strong-minded, and from them Hazel developed determination and dedication. But it was at the age of fifteen that Hazel, quite by accident, discovered the game of tennis, which was to bring her the success for which her ego hungered.

As we sat at the card table in her present home in Chestnut Hill, Massachusetts, she recalled how tennis came into her life. "I'd seen one game of men's doubles in Berkeley and had seen the Sutton girls, who were well-known, play a few times. The game looked like fun but we had no tennis court at home, only an old dilapidated barn, hardly a place to practice. Someone, I can't remember now, lent me a racket, which in those days had no resemblance to the present ones. It was almost square with a very short handle. I found, however, to my surprise, that I could hit a ball against one of the barn walls and keep it going, and that was a great accomplishment and I liked it. I used to run into our house and tell my mother, 'Imagine, I kept it going ten times without missing.' She didn't know what I was talking about and was not very encouraging because she was so busy with the housework and taking care of a large family. But Hazel persevered with a persistence for which she has always been known, bouncing the ball and hitting it against the wall, day after day. One day in 1902, one of her brothers heard about a local doubles tournament. He had a college friend who had a sister who played tennis. None of her brothers had ever seen their sister play, but they were eager to have Hazel enter the fray despite her inexperience, even though she had never been on a court before.

"I met my partner going over to San Francisco the morning of the tournament," Hazel vividly remembered. In fact, there isn't a lapse in any part of her agile memory. "I wore a long skirt, down to here," she indicated, pointing to her ankles, "and long white stockings and a top with long sleeves. I especially recall the long sleeves, as it was hard playing in them. We won anyhow," she said proudly.

"But in 1909 Mother made me some dimity dresses with short sleeves. This was to free my arms so I could volley better and run around. Nobody had ever volleyed before. Women used to stand in the back court and hit the ball back and forth for hours. I played in Philadelphia and won there."

It is remarkable that Hazel ever won any match, being completely self-taught and never having had a lesson.

"I think the reason I did so well was because nobody told me what to do or how to grip the racket a certain way. I just did it instinctively." This even today, is the advice she gives to youngsters.

Hazel started playing in tournaments all over the country after 1903. She won practically every state tournament, including 1906 in California, where one by one she took on each of the five Sutton girls and beat them all. Since they had been champions, Hazel Hotchkiss had her proudest moment. She played all during her college years, and after graduation, in 1910, her father, who was President of the Central California Canneries, took her East. She met her husband-to-be on this trip. David Nyles, a Bostonian, whom she had met at a tournament in Seattle, introduced her to a friend, George Wightman. Hazel and George met at a prearranged tennis game and then went on to a Harvard football match. He chased her for about three weeks, but they didn't get married until 1912 when he was in law school. The marriage produced five children, all of whom Hazel breast-fed and raised.

But the marriage didn't last.

"I think that he kind of became jealous of my tennis and I really couldn't figure out what was wrong when he asked me for a divorce. It took me a little time to figure out. I thought we'd been happy going to the theater Saturday nights, and we did have the interest of the children in common. I was home a lot, wrapped up doing things with and for the children. I'd even had three miscarriages. George and I drifted apart, and I think the thing that made me finally agree to divorce in 1939 was that he lost interest in the children, and they were my whole life. Tennis never played an important part in my life then except for local tournaments. I never believed in traveling while the children were growing up."

Hazel was game all through this period of difficulty. The breast-feeding was hard and she often had to give up because she felt sick. Once she was asked by the great Bill Tilden to play in a doubles tournament.

"I was just getting over a miscarriage and I didn't feel right. I just had to turn him down," she said regretfully. "I also took full charge of the children, and you figure it out. I never even had a nursemaid. We lived in Brookline until 1939, when I moved here."

For five years when her children were growing up she taught at Pine Manor Junior College nearby, and she is proud of a pamphlet she wrote, which is still being read, entitled *Better Tennis*, which was published by Houghton Mifflin.

"They wanted me to publish a big fat book, which would have cost about four dollars. That was a lot of money in those days and I probably should have been sensible, but I said 'No' because I thought something simple would be more effective, and instead I just wrote down some information while waiting for my children at school." Some of the tips, like "a tennis racket is just an extension of your arm," and timing and ability, she feels, are more important than a lot of stylized movements. She doesn't believe in the new, fancy steel rackets, preferring her old wooden one.

This is a woman without any pretenses. With the simplest racket in her hand, coupled with seriousness of purpose, she has won forty-three national titles. As she was just five feet tall, the secret of her court tactics was clearly not a booming serve but her ability to, as she says, "be ready," and her strength was in returning volleys between the base line and the net, then running up and putting the ball away. Her early training at her California house in Volleyina was on a makeshift court whose base was the gravel on the driveway and whose net was a rope stretched from the rosebush to the house. Later she practiced on a court at the University of California, but she had to play before 8 A.M., as women were not allowed to play later than that.

Hazel was persistent, and although she didn't win every match, the sheer enjoyment of the sport has carried her through. Long after she gave up competitive tennis, she took up teaching —rivals like Helen Moody and Helen Jacobs, and protégées, whom she encourages even to this day. For forty years she taught group classes at Longwood, and she still teaches children in her garage behind her house. And her house is something you shouldn't miss. Filling the glass top of the door is a white crocheted cloth with H.H.W. embroidered in it. Inside she shares her quarters with another family, now that she lives alone. Her living room is a happy jumble of trophies, photographs, plants, and an old card table. The simplest necessities seem adequate, and her greatest thrill is to have a good old gabfest about her favorite sport. Her children range in age from sixty to fifty but aren't vitally interested in tennis. They leave that to their garrulous and independent mother.

A perfectionist, still not content to be just a sportswoman, Hazel has made time to work for the Red Cross, which awarded her with their sixty-year pin, which she proudly showed me.

"I've worked all these years and never did anything badly. I did it because I wanted to help, and I especially enjoyed the canteen work. I never had the kind of money to contribute but I played in tennis tournaments to benefit the Red Cross since 1914. I was never paid, but the people who came contributed to the cause."

Hazel never tires of tennis talk.

"I'm the smallest tennis player our country has ever had, without a doubt! And I've labored under many disadvantages. When we were young, tennis balls were a great treat. I took care of a single ball like it was gold. Nowadays, kids can't play a tournament, they think, unless they have twelve balls. I guess my secret is that I grew up appreciating everything. I took pride in my sport. To encourage tennis between America and England, I donated the Wightman Cup in 1924, and it has been a source of great pleasure to watch our American team defend the cup against the British for the last fifty-one years. Last year the tournament was in Boston. People really came to watch, even though it was steaming hot. In the old days, people who wanted to play tennis, did it without an audience. Nobody then wanted to sit in a bleacher on a hot day if you could go swimming instead. Now it's a big spectator event."

Hazel got up from the card table. Her silk stockings were rolled at the knees. Her gray hair cropped short, arms akimbo, legs apart, knees flexed, she wanted to show me how age has not changed her athletic pace. "So much has changed," she sighed. "Would you like me to show you how I look holding a racket? See?" she said, holding a small one, "you've always got to be ready. You have to judge your distance. But there aren't any fancy rules. Remember, you can't make a champion. A person has to have 'it'!" Hazel is full of her own maxims and even her own alphabet:

Always	Alert
Be	Better
Concentrate	Constantly
Don't	Dally
Ever	Earnest
Fair	Feeling
Get	Going
Hit	Hard
Imitate	Instructor
Just	Jump
Keep	Keen
Less	Loafing
Move	Meaningfully
Never	Net
Only	Over
Praise	Partners
Quash	Qualms
Relax	Rightly

Stand	Straight
Take	Time
Umpire	Usually
Vary	Volleys
Work	Wiles
Xceed	Xpectations
Yell	Yours
Zip	Zip

Hazel Wightman, an unconventional tennis player, is still full of bubbly enthusiasm, and correspondence from new and old fans kindles her energy. What she has learned she wants to pass on to others, and her competitive spirit through the years has given tennis the impetus that eight decades later acknowledges that women players like Chrisy Evert and Billie Jean King can give any man a good court battle.

She, admittedly, may not now be the best-known tennis player in the United States. "But I've been around longer at eighty-nine and I've played with all the greats—Helen Wills, Sarah Palfrey, Helen Jacobs, to name a few." But what impresses one about this energetic 110-pound woman is that her life is as it was when she was a child, defined by the traits and character that make an athlete and by the relationship between her and her competitors. She enjoys the rivalry, but she is also interested in helping an opponent learn new tactics after a match, even though she may be beaten next time by her very own teachings.

Clare Boothe Luce

CLARE LUCE typifies the American woman with that rare combination of power, beauty and brains, and still, in her seventies, she is as electric and fascinating as ever. Her reign in the 1940s and 1950s in circles where women heretofore had feared to tread, had made me more than anxious to meet her. I wanted to talk to her and probe her motives and see for myself a woman who was perhaps more hated and feared than loved. Respected, yes, but being a verbal sniper herself, the barbs came back many times over and less strongly motivated. Not that it isn't still all there, even with a fever and the flu—Clare Luce in her dressing gown is still a madonnalike figure.

We were sitting in Bill Benton's suite at the Waldorf Towers, where she was staying to enjoy the revival on Broadway of her play *The Women*. She apologized about her health and said she almost canceled the interview. It had taken many months to arrange, since she lives in Honolulu and has been suffering from poor eyesight, so her travels to the mainland are fewer and fewer. Despite occasional coughs, constant cigarette smoking, and an explained exit from the room to take some medication, what I expected to be a brief encounter turned out, three hours later, to be a riveting disclosure of a brilliant mind. No part of those 180 minutes were at all disappointing.

What still intrigues me is that this exciting lady, who is still sought after for her political acumen and advice, had a fitful childhood with little in the way of emotional or financial benefit.

Her father, Will Boothe, was the son of a highly respected minister in Mount Holyoke, Massachusetts. Her mother, Anna

Clare Snyder, was the daughter of Catholic-Bavarian immigrants living in Hoboken, New Jersey. Not only was her mother's marriage to Will Boothe frowned upon by her family because of the then intense prejudice among Catholics against marrying Protestants, but also because they were married by a Justice of the Peace. Clare remembers her grandfather and grandmother on her father's side not tolerating the union because Anna Clare was part of a frowned-upon profession, the theater, and worse yet, she was in the chorus line.

"Both of my grandparents on each side refused to accept the marriage," Clare said, "the consequence of which was that I never saw my father's parents once, although I did see my mother's. When my father did something worse, as far as his family was concerned, like deciding to become a musician, and of all things a violinist (which nothing but Italians or foreigners ever became), that was the end. But Father didn't seem to care. He and his brothers were all musical and they started the Boothe Piano Company, which still exists in Philadelphia. Only my father elected to take the money that he was getting from the piano company, because he wanted to play both piano and violin and get a job. But with an American name like Boothe, the only work he could get was as 'fiddle' in a theatrical orchestra."

It was while working in some musical that Will Boothe met his future wife, who had been a child actress. After they were married, their first child, David, was born in 1902 in an apartment on Riverside Drive, which was the scene of Anna Clare's birth the next year.

Simple surroundings and rather Bohemian parents with never enough money marked Clare's earliest years, but Will Boothe did, with practice, make it up to becoming first fiddle with the Chicago Opera Company. It was during this period, his daughter recalls, that he fell in love with Mary Garden, the celebrated actress. "That just about tore it as far as my poor little mother was concerned. She was about twenty-five when Father left the family, having found another woman, and Mother got a divorce. The only time I heard from him was when he wrote me from Los Angeles saying that he was ill and dying. Prior to getting sick someone told me he had run a music school in Los Angeles and was considered, curiously enough (though this means nothing to me, because I don't know anything about music), the first master of fingered tenths. I think the phrase has something to do with how far you can spread your fingers on a violin.

"My mother never discussed her own divorce, or my father or his parents, and would never have asked them for help, although it was very difficult for her raising two children without a job. I vaguely remember her receiving two or three thousand dollars a year which Father sent her, although my brother and I were not supposed to know where the money came from because, after Father left, Mother simply told us he was dead, but somehow she was able to send my brother to military school in Wisconsin and later to a military academy in New York. During this time she and I went to Paris and lived in the Pension Balzac. I must have been nine or ten, because when World War I broke out in Europe we had to come home on a ship. Great excitement! I've always remembered—one does recall such things as the boat. She was of the old White Star Line called the *Carmania* and the captain's name was Barr and he took a tremendous shine to me. Yes, now it comes back," she said, reaching mentally into the past. "I had my tenth birthday party on the ship and I was the little birthday girl. Up until now I'd had no schooling. A little Huguenot had taught me French and my mother had hauled me through museums and galleries. But I'd never been in a classroom and always felt very lonely without any playmates.

"My mother always had a clear idea that reading books was very good for lonely children, and although we never had much money, the one thing I always had were books. I remember whole sets of them: the blue, red, white, and green fairy stories. And the Oz books and the Rover Boys and Rover Girls. I also remember that by the time I was thirteen I also had full-length sets of Dickens and Thackeray and Dumas, and I read all of them. I had nothing else to do, and for me, reading was everything. Where other children had cozy playmates, all I had were my books."

Finally, Clare's mother put her twelve-year-old daughter in a boarding school, St. Mary's on Long Island. Having had no formal education, Clare, by taking a test, was placed by Miriam Bytell, the headmistress, into the eighth grade, two grades higher than most children her age, but her voluminous reading had stood her in good stead. "As an interested teacher, Miss Bytell started me really thinking. She was an old-fashioned, ladylike, but tub-thumping suffragette, and she really believed that once women had the vote (which at that point they didn't) they would become emancipated and the equal of men in all professions."

Clare was admitted on a scholarship, and to this day her two greatest friends are Elizabeth "Buffy" Cobb and Helen Atwater, two of her classmates at St. Mary's. After two years Clare moved to the Castle School in Tarrytown and, whether through the good offices of her mother's then rich beau, Percy Frowert of Philadelphia, or what, somehow the private-school tuition got paid. Clare remembers Frowert, who had three children and was President of Black Starr and Frost. "Unfortunately for Mother, he was married and his wife wouldn't give him a divorce—one of those simple stories—and so the romance just petered out."

Clare did very well in school and always wanted to be a writer or an artist. "I never really had any other ambition. The ideas that many young girls have, that they want to be movie stars or ballet dancers, never interested me. I produced my first play at thirteen in 1917 in Old Greenwich, Connecticut. I remember it was summertime and Mother had bought a house on the outskirts of Greenwich. This was our first real home, outside of two-room apartments, that David and I ever had. I had such fun doing the play. I dramatized a fairy story, directed it, put together the cast, and found a theater. I still have a clipping that shows the play made fourteen dollars and ninety-two cents, and I gave it to the Red Cross, for whose benefit it was being played."

Nineteen seventeen seemed to be the happiest year of Clare's childhood. The new school, the six-room (albeit rundown) house in Old Greenwich, and an interested headmistress helped Clare to bloom. "It was great to be in the country after all those hotel rooms where Mother and I cooked over gas jets. But the school added something very positive to my character. Moreover, Miss Cassidy Mason contributed a great deal to Clare's interest in her new school, The Castle. "I had one remarkable teacher called Miss Pulver. She taught me history and, between her and my French teacher (those were World War I years), really set my mind in the direction of politics and history. I remember that my graduation essay, written in French, was *Qui sème le vent*, *recolte la tempête,* 'Who sows the wind, reaps the whirlwind.' I still have it and all my old papers. I have always been a real squirrel because as a child, having no home and moving constantly, I got in the habit of taking my little treasures and stuffing them away in little boxes with ribbons around them. Eventually, all these boxes have found their way into one vast trunk that I still haven't opened, but I will one day."

But what was Clare aiming at during her formative years? She says she was aware of the economic insecurity because her mother was a victim of it, and the only way you could get around it, Mrs. Boothe suggested, was by getting a good education and marrying someone of substance. A woman with a profession of some sort, or able to take on a job, was definitely an asset. Clare was brought up to believe that education and marriage to a man who could support you made the best combination.

Until the right man came along for her daughter, Mrs. Boothe had entertained hopes that Clare would become a great actress, fulfilling vicariously her own disappointed ambitions. "I tried out the movies after graduating from school at sixteen, but it was the silent days and I was just no darned good," Clare said. "Actually, I felt an inner resistance to it. I tried the theater because Mother thought I was rather pretty and might have a chance on the stage. I understudied Mary Pickford in *The Good Little Devil,* but I never got a chance to go on, as she never got sick. After that, I understudied a child called Joyce Fair in *The Dummy,* and I actually played it once but the management wouldn't put my name in the program that night, so no one knew it was me. Finally, Mother sent me to Clare Tree Major's School of the Theater, and there I was utterly convinced that I was never going to be an acress, but I got the idea that maybe I could write plays. During this time something wonderful happened. Mother met and married a nice dear country doctor, I suppose you'd call him—a general practitioner—Dr. Albert Elmer Austin, who later became the Congressman from Fairfield, Connecticut. He was a bit on the stiff-stuffy New England side, but we moved after they were married, and this was a two-story, four-bedroom house and the first real true family home. Of course I was intoxicated."

Dr. Austin was Chief of Staff of the Greenwich Hospital and

President of the Greenwich Bank and Trust Company, and Clare's family finances were definitely on the upswing.

In 1920, Clare's mother and stepfather sailed for Bremerhaven and a sojourn in Europe. Clare had become a beautiful teen-ager. She was five feet six, with long blond hair and strong blue eyes. She acquired many beaux on this trip, but on their return on the *Olympic* Clare met Max Reinhardt, the threatrical producer, and Mrs. O. H. P. Belmont, the avid suffragette. Mrs. Belmont saw in Clare a new member to enlist in her cause, and by the time the ship had docked Clare had agreed to play the part of a nun in Reinhardt's production of *The Miracle* and also go to Washington with Mrs. Belmont to meet Alice Paul, the head of the Women's National Party. "She really is the mother of the Women's Liberation movement and she was the one who got me to distribute handbills out of a rickety old airplane over Schenec-tady, New York. She is a truly remarkable old lady at eighty-seven."

Mr. and Mrs. James Cushman were also on the *Olympic* voy-age. They were a Social couple and childless, and he was a very religious man. They, too, took an interest in Clare and kept in touch with her after the trip was over.

Clare was eighteen. Her picture had been in the New York papers, reporting that on that famous European trip she had won a beauty contest on the Riviera. It was 1921, and suddenly she was being taken up by notable people. She never got to play in *The Miracle*, because, as a result of an invitation from the Cush-mans, she met George Brokaw, a forty-three-year-old playboy, very much a part of Society and very wealthy. He immediately fell in love with this budding young beauty, although Clare's feelings do not seem to have been as strong toward him. Perhaps armed with the philosophy that marriage and wealth would bring her happiness and with urgings from her mother that this would be a suitable alliance, they were married in 1923, when Clare was twenty.

She and George led a heady Social life and Clare's only child, Ann, was born of this marriage. Six years later Clare took her daughter with her to Reno to get a divorce. "I probably would never have left George except, boy, could he drink! He was such a nice fellow but a periodic drunk. He was one of the ones who had to be dried out for a couple of months at a time," Clare said. "And then when he'd start drinking again, he'd wind up in a straitjacket, and when you're young, like I was, it's a horrible experience. But if I hadn't married George I don't know what my fate would have been, because at least he gave me entrée into a world in which later I found my place. The minute I got a divorce I had no doubts. I said to myself, 'By God, I'm going to be my own woman.' I was shattered and unhappy and ill over all those years with George, so as soon as I was divorced I went and got psychoanalyzed. That was the thing to do in those days, to find yourself. But right in the middle of my analysis I just got off the couch and walked out of the doctor's office. I didn't feel I needed analysis. I felt the real problem was that I needed a job!

"Being a woman with no college education and no talent for the theater, I went to Condé Nast, my friend, who was head of *Vogue* and *Vanity Fair*, to ask him for a job. I had met him at one of the many dinner parties he used to give. But he refused my request and sent me to Edna Chase, the Editor of *Vogue*. She turned me down too—and I hope this doesn't sound vain, but they both used the same excuse, saying, 'It's absurd that a girl like you, looking the way you look, is going to stick to anything.' Condé said, 'I know your type, Clare—the first time you get a glamorous invitation to Palm Beach you'll be off.' "

Clare Brokaw didn't need the money, although she had settled with her millionaire husband on an income of around twenty-five thousand a year, less than she might have gotten if she had pressed for a larger settlement. But she genuinely wanted to work and wouldn't be put off by Mr. Nast and Mrs. Chase's brushoffs. 'I pled so hard with Edna Chase, who said she was going to Europe, as was Condé, and I did elicit from Mrs. Chase the promise that she would discuss a job with me when she returned, if I was still interested."

Clare's next move was a chance coincidence that only someone like her could have angled, and the incident launched her on her writing career. "I left Edna's office, and on my way back through the halls I saw, sitting at a desk, Nancy Hale, who later became quite a well-known novelist. Nancy was sitting at this desk and I nonchalantly asked her what she was doing. She replied that she was writing captions for *Vogue*. I think it was around lunchtime and I asked, looking around at the empty room, 'Well, who sits at all those other desks?' And she said that there were only four other girls working. Well, I said, sitting down at an unused one, 'Then, this is mine.' And she said, 'Oh, yours?' And I said, 'Yes, this is mine.' In a few minutes the woman in charge of all the copywriters came by and she just looked at me. I told her that I was the new caption writer and she said, 'Oh, fine,' and from that moment on she began to give me work to do. I remember the first caption I ever wrote, very clearly, and it was called, 'What the Well-Dressed Baby Will Wear.' Somehow I stayed at my desk for two weeks, and without being challenged, but then at the end of the week it almost looked like my game was up. It first seemed that it was office procedure that every Friday afternoon a girl would go through the offices with a wire basket in which there were little yellow envelopes with your paycheck. The first Friday she stopped at my desk and asked my name. I told her it was Clare Brokaw. 'Well!' she said, 'we don't have a check for you, Mrs. Brokaw.' 'That's all right,' I said to her, 'my salary is being arranged by Mr. Nast. When I saw him we didn't decide on what I should be paid, so I'm sure he'll let you know when he gets back from Europe.'" Clearly a moment of triumph for Clare.

In any decade this cheekiness and nerve would be strongly resented. But even in the retelling Clare stated quite coolly the whole story without apology or meekness. In fact, she actually kept the job, because when Nast returned he assumed that Edna had hired her, and vice-versa, so she just went unsalaried for about six weeks because she was afraid to bring it up and be discovered. "One day I met the Managing Editor of *Vanity Fair* magazine, and I suppose he thought I was attractive and he took me to lunch and I finally made my ambitions known to him. He was a brilliant young man called Donald Freeman, and eventually he gave me job on his magazine, first in 1930 as an assistant editor." Six months later Frank Crowninshield promoted her to associate editor. After Freeman's accidental death, "Crownie" made her his Managing Editor with a salary of $12,000 a year.

There is so much Clare accomplished during her *Vanity Fair* days. She wrote satirical pieces on Society, gained an insight into politics, and soon became involved with the new National

Party, a third party which would not be partisan. Clare went to the Democratic Convention in 1932 to convince Democrats to join the new party, and her seat was in the box of Woodrow Wilson's widow. It was here that she met Bernard Baruch, who became a lifelong friend and supporter of this beguiling woman who was using her intelligence along with her native beauty and sex to get ahead.

She wrote a play, *O Pyramids!* It never went into production, but she did do a layout for a new picture magazine to be titled *Life*, but the editors did not think it financially feasible. Clare resigned from *Vanity Fair* in 1934, a not unfriendly parting.

She had met Winston Churchill with Baruch, and after she left the magazine she visited the Churchills and also wrote a column for the old Paul Bloch newspaper syndicate. She was expected to write the comings and goings of the Social Set, but being bored with that idea, she interjected instead her feelings about the European political situation and she was shortly fired.

Playwriting followed a book she wrote called *Stuffed Shirts*. As she began to write the play an incident occurred that was to change her life. She met Henry Luce at a dinner party given by Thayer Robinson and sat next to him. He was then the boss of *Time* magazine. "I didn't like him and he plainly didn't like me," she admitted. "We didn't see each other until a year later when Elsa Maxwell invited me to a party honoring Cole Porter at the Waldorf."

Luce was still married and it is unclear whether Clare's maneuver to go up and talk to him that evening was planned or not. She decided that she was really going to get even with him because of his inattention to her at the dinner party the year before. She was at her provocative best, and it only served to intrigue the Editor/Owner of a very influential magazine. Later that evening he told her the stunning news that he was going to marry her someday—a statement quite incredible, since he had a wife and had only met Clare twice.

Clare was thirty-one, and Luce, worth about ten million then, was thirty-six. She left for Europe, never expecting to hear from him, she says, but he followed her and courted her. She fell in love with him, so the story goes, and after securing a divorce

from his wife and settling two million dollars on her and providing for their two sons, Luce was ready to marry Clare. Meanwhile she had written a play called *Abide With Me*, which
opened in New York in 1935. It received terrible reviews and
was Mrs. Brokaw's last public effort under her old name. Three
days after the play opened, Clare married Henry Luce in Old
Greenwich, Connecticut.

Her ability to express herself, her analytical mind, her ambitious nature coupled with Luce's articulateness and their individual egos and lust for power, made them a formidable two-
some. There was seldom a silent moment.

Clare's dreams, however, of being a force on *Time* once she
was the boss's wife, were quickly disappointed. "When it became
clear that there was no place for me, despite the fact that I knew
the magazine business and had made the first dummy for a new
picture magazine, I decided to chart my own course." Luce went
to work readying the new *Life* magazine, which appeared on
November 19, 1936.

Luce now owned *Time*, *Life* and *Fortune*. Clare told me of her
disappointment in not being able to help start what had really
been her idea. "My husband's editors felt, as most businessmen
did, that there was no place for a wife and husband in the same
organization. I thought and still think it's pernicious. So I said to
Harry, 'Well, O.K. I'm going back to what, after all, is my first
love. Not editing, but writing. So I wrote *The Women* in 1936
and it ran for six hundred and fifty-seven performances. I went
on writing plays until the war." *Kiss the Boys Goodbye* and
Margin for Error were among the more successful ones. But *The
Women* had a curious vitality and a life of its own, because it has
since been translated into twenty-six languages and twice made
into a movie, but it never got the publicity that its revival brought
in 1973, which was the reason Clare Luce was in New York. Its
premiere was chronicled by the press, television and all the other
communications media. However, her greatest satisfaction and
rather pussycat grin came when she told me, "In spite of the fact
that I've been sick, this has been a great week. All those years that
I never got into *Time* magazine—except, as they say, in a *Time*
"piece," with rather snide references—but now, at last, they've

devoted a whole page to me and my play." It clearly came as a personal triumph to Clare.

All of Clare's great national accomplishments have been noted and photographed for years—as a correspondent for *Life* maga-ine in Europe and Asia, as a Congresswoman from Connecticut, and as Ambassador to Italy. She has never gone unnoticed. But among these honors and appointments, the death of her only daughter, Ann, by her marriage to George Brokaw in 1944, in an automobile accident, left an otherwise able, responsible, self-willed, woman almost unconsolable. In her grief she turned to religion for solace and became an ardent Catholic, under instruction from Bishop Fulton Sheen. Between 1944 and 1947 tragedy struck again and her mother and brother were killed in accidents too. Her family was then wiped out completely.

Perhaps in her aloneness she became even more determined to become and stay involved in the center of the American political arena. With the power of her husband's publishing empire and ambitions far beyond most women, Clare Luce dared and suc-ceeded. She even attacked the then President in her articles and was heavily criticized. In defense she tried to justify herself. "A lot of what I said about the Roosevelts was exaggerated," she said. "Although it is absolutely true that I said, in a speech in Chicago, that Mr. Roosevelt lied us into war, the last part of that sentence has never been printed. But it is in the records. I did say 'The President lied us into a war,' but they omitted the rest, 'into which he should have led us.' . . . and that's quite a differ-ent feeling. Now, to be sure, in those days, admittedly, using the word 'lie' was in bad taste. It isn't any longer, and every time you pick up the papers somebody is accusing someone else of lying. But I admit it was a strong word then. The press called me an in-terventionist. Now I'd be called an internationalist. But I saw very clearly that we had to get into World War II and, in fact, that we were already involved in it. Roosevelt had soldiers in Norway. He had already made many commitments. So it was obvious."

It must be said that the Luces were Republican, that they cam-paigned and supported Wendell Willkie in his thrust against FDR, in which the latter was re-elected to the presidency. No warm feelings were every known to exist between the Luces and

Roosevelt, whose policies *Time* and *Life* never ceased to attack. "I was very vocal," Clare admitted. "When you're campaigning, like everything else, there are techniques, and in the heat of the battle everyone makes charges, and if your opponent is saying something against your candidate you sling it back, and so it goes. When you get out of politics, as I have been for many years, you write very temperately and judiciously, or you try to at any rate. But I didn't just criticize, I also gave praise where it was due, and one person for whom I have always had the greatest admiration was Eleanor Roosevelt. She was a person who believed in getting out and doing things, and I always said of her, 'She is a woman who comforts the afflicted and afflicts the comfortable.' There were and are so many reasons I would criticize President Roosevelt, although that doesn't mean I didn't think he was a great President, but as for Eleanor, I never had anything but respect for her."

This statement led us rather obviously into a discussion of whom Clare did consider an effective and able President, and she answered my query with her own personal recollection and illustration. "Well, if a house is on fire, who is the most effective person on the premises? It's the person who locates the fire, extinguishes and uses it. So the greatness of the President is always measured by the crisis which he can surmount. Now, I'll tell you an amusing little story." She settled back in her chair, lit up another of her constant cigarettes and began a story which I felt should have had a roomful of listeners to appreciate the intimacy of a glimpse into a brief moment in history that I alone was there to share. Dinner parties rise and fall on public figures holding forth on a general topic of interest, and all of us, as I then, are more than eager to listen.

"Shortly after the Bay of Pigs," she began, "I got a call from the White House saying that President Kennedy would like me to come down to Washington and see him. I really didn't want to go because I was at that moment engaged in writing an article, which was later published in *Life*. The theme concerned the fact that force was going to have to be used to solve the Cuban question because of the guided missiles and various other weapons the Cubans were readying. My article was ready to be published, and I didn't want to argue my position with the President. I mean, I didn't want to argue with him whether I should or shouldn't publish the article. Right or wrong, I'd written it. So I tried to get out of meeting with Kennedy, but getting out of an invitation from the President to lunch with him privately was impossible to do and never should be done, except I was trying to protect myself. I did accept and found myself with President Kennedy alone in his little dining room at the White House.

"I was prepared not to open up the subject of the Cuban crisis and hoped that he would not bring it up. We chatted awhile, and at a certain point he was called out of the room. He came back, having gone to the telephone, and told me with considerable satisfaction that the White House forces had gotten through a certain agricultural bill. I replied innocuously that wasn't that fine and then he turned to me and asked, 'Clare, what's on your mind?' And I answered, 'You mean at this particular moment, Mr. President?' And he said, 'Yes.' And I said, 'You know.' And I told him the truth. 'When a writer wakes up in the morning he sometimes has a thought, or a sentence comes into his mind, that he hopes to use someday. Usually by the time he's had breakfast, he's forgotten it. But because, Mr. President, I was lunching with you, I remembered it.' He said, 'What was the sentence?' 'Well,' I said, 'here it is. A great man is one sentence, and that sentence is characterized by having an active verb in it which describes a unique action. You shouldn't even need to know the man's name, because the action describes him.' He listened for a minute and then said, 'I don't quite follow you, Clare.' 'Well,' I said, trying to explain my thoughts more clearly, 'You and I are both Americans and Catholics, so I'll give you sentences that we both are familiar with: "He died on the cross to save us"; or "He set out to discover an old world and discovered a new one"; or "He rallied the rebel armies and created a new country"; or "He preserved the Union and he freed the slaves"; or "He lifted us out of a great depression and helped to win a World War." 'I don't have to tell you who any of these men are. So if you ask me again, What was I thinking? it's this—I wonder what sentence will be written after your name when you leave the White House. It certainly won't be "He got the agricultural bill passed." ' The President suddenly read my thoughts. 'Oh,' he said, 'you're talking about Cuba.'

"I had to admit I was, and I felt compelled to tell him the sentence that could only apply to him. 'He broke the power of the Soviet Union in the Western Hemisphere; or the reverse—he didn't.' 'So you think it will come to force?' the President asked. I told him I couldn't answer that, but I would stand by my one sentence. As we walked out through the sitting room that overlooks Lincoln's Memorial and the Washington Memorial, he said, 'You know, Clare, you've spoiled this room for me, because every time I look out the window I'll never forget that one sentence.'

"As things turned out, he wrote his sentence. He didn't break the power of the Soviet Union but he certainly blocked it and challenged it. And of course he will be in the history books forever, if for no other reason than being the first Catholic President."

The autobiography that Clare cannot get herself to write would be full of stories, heavy with import. But she doesn't feel she has the motivations to write, for she doesn't need money or further fame. "The older I get the less I think that fame is anything except a passing phenomenon. Posterity . . . I don't have any message. What do I have to say that hasn't been better said by millions of people?" The public would dispute her, for her whole life is a fascinating study, and her attitudes on life and the world and her philosophy cannot but be of great interest.

She contends she never really has had power, although I would consider her varied roles almost as important and thought-controlling as those of any woman of her generation. Her feelings about power are very personal. "For a woman, being young and beautiful is a form of power," she explained, although I was talking about it in a much more manipulative way. She continued, "If you are pretty and then you happen to marry a man who has money and real power, by extension, the woman's power over him gives her some access to his."

Does this describe her life with Luce? One can only wonder. She believes that position and money and the way in which you use it are the true symbols of a woman's power because they give her freedom. "Women like Brooke Aster and Mary Lasker with their foundations enjoy power. Alice Longworth has the power of prestige and tradition plus the added bonus of a good and witty mind. But this power is not with a capital P.

"Women do enjoy power, but at this stage in our development we are no longer interested in just manipulating men to get it. I think most women would like some more direct access to it themselves. Certainly whenever women have in history been put in the position of power, they are as qualified as men. For instance, if you start looking around among monarchs, you can't get away from Elizabeth of England, and then there's Golda Meir and Indira Gandhi. But all too few women have it or seek it, and that's because most women just want to marry, have children and be loved. The ones who try and compete with their husband are like two people riding a horse. One has got to ride in front, and at this point in time, it's the female who's riding behind."

Clare Luce has been, above all, a leading exponent of Women's Lib, and I wondered how she was able to keep a marriage to a very dominating man going and also have a recognized career of her own. There must have been conflicts, I insisted.

"Well, in any kind of marriage something has to give. But in a marriage where there's a woman with a career and a man too, it's almost impossible to keep it together unless two circumstances exist. One is that their interests do not conflict, that they run parallel. Now, my husband Harry was a journalist, primarily interested in politics, international and cultural affairs, and the fact that I was member of Congress and an ambassador and a playwright were careers that didn't threaten, but interested him. The second condition to insure our kind of marriage is that a man must feel sure of his own power and position. If he feels that his wife's fame eclipses his, the going will be tough unless he happens to be the kind of man who's willing to sit back and let his wife run the show. I was very fortunate because my husband not only didn't mind my positions, he was very proud of what I did. I'm proud that I managed to keep our marriage together for thirty-five years, and only his sudden death in 1967 separated us."

There have been so many people associated with the Luces over the years who have quite different opinions and bear strong resentments against both. They would dispute many of Clare's motives and much of what she told me. It is quite clear that anyone as successful, as beautiful, and as opinionated as Clare is

bound to evoke all kinds of responses from others. Time will
have to be the final judge.

On women's roles, Clare is particularly eloquent and has often
expressed herself. "The so-called identity crisis that women are
going through is the feeling that just being a housewife and
mother (and the word "just" is one they put in themselves) does
not really give enough meaning to their lives. For thousands of
years being wives and mothers was entirely necessary and meaningful, and it still is to many women. But that wasn't my way of
life. I've had fascinating jobs and I've had so many hobbies—
masses of needlepoint, raising poodles, bird shooting, and doing
mosaics. I finally even got professional at that and started selling
them. I used to get commissions from churches, but that was
difficult. They would see St. Augustine's nose one way or suggest that I move a halo a little more to the right or left and I'd
have to whack away with my chisel to get it the way they wanted
it. Then I developed eye trouble, so that became too difficult. I've
always loved gardening, and now my latest interest is in raising
tropical fish in my home in Honolulu. I have two hundred and
fifty gallons of every species, and I also raise birds and train
them. My only plan for the years ahead is to survive in reason-
ably good health.

"As for sex . . . no, that doesn't enter my mind at all. All my
life I've enjoyed the companionship of men, but now my best
friends are all women—not because they're women but because
they're intelligent, and they and I have the time to give to each
other. A sexual male-female relationship at this time in my life
seems unthinkable. It wasn't, perhaps, a few years back—now it
is. At my age an old heart, like an old tree, puts down very few
roots, and if transplanted it's amazing how fast it dies, you see. I
simply couldn't begin with a man all over again. I'd have to take a
deep interest in his business and certainly his children and grandchildren. I couldn't take on a new family life. Many of my wid-
owed friends of a certain age have what they call ' a gentleman
in residence.' Not necessarily a lover, but a companion and a
manager of the household. I confess I'd love the idea, but I
haven't found the 'gentleman.' You see the curious thing is that
we still live in a male-dominated world. If you marry, the man is
going to expect you to take care of him. If I should fall ill, he

would get me a nurse. Well, I can well afford a nurse myself. So I'd say that I'm enjoying widowhood, and probably in many ways I'm happier than I've ever been in my life.

"I have complete freedom, almost to the point of freedom being a burden. When you're utterly free you then have to ask yourself, 'What do I really want to do?' Why, there's so much. I can travel anywhere and, within reason, have anything material I want. But this is difficult for anyone in my position, because the rich can no longer get what they can afford to have. And that means service. It's easy for me to travel around the world, but it's almost impossible for me to find a maid who will go with me. It ruins so much. I'd far prefer to feel secure about my cook and staff than I ever would about my sexual life. I know it sounds like the spoiled rich woman, but if I have any regrets it's that I never learned to cook. I don't care about it for myself. I have a boiled egg if I'm alone. But if I could whip up a dinner for six or eight friends just once a month, or just on the spur of the moment say, 'Come home, I'll fix you a little dinner,' I tell you, I'd be as happy as a bug. Now I flee to hotels and live on room service."

We were nearing the end of three hours. There was a rainstorm beating on the picture windows of the room in the Towers where we were sitting. Clare showed no signs of wanting to stop talking, so I took advantage of the moment and asked her some very personal questions about her husband and their celebrated marriage. She really hadn't brought it up at all on her own.

"Yes, Harry was a very difficult man. But to understand how I managed to work it out, you must go back, as we did earlier, to my childhood. Somewhere along the line, one of my desires was to get married and to stick it out. First, because I feel that a lifetime is not enough time to learn all about another person. Even after twenty-five years of marriage, a woman often discovers that her husband is a mystery to her, and vice-versa. So I feel that growing together with someone is a very great ideal and I wanted to stick it out. Many times when my husband and I would start to have a quarrel, I'd say, 'Are we, do we, really mean we're in this for good?' 'Yeah.' 'O.K., Why quarrel?' Secondly, I couldn't see how any other kind of marriage was going to be much better for him or me. And as I got older, the idea of great new beginnings, great new loves, became kind of silly, you know. And so there he was, and what kept my marriage and his together was that I don't think either of us really bored one another. Because I think boredom is the worst enemy of marriage, in many ways.

"Sometimes people ask me for my definition of love and I say, 'It's lust with friendship.' Well, of those two things, friendship is the far more endurable commodity. And to stay friends with a man whom you have loved, sexually and deeply, in other words the friendship that's been well-rooted in the soil, so to speak, of your body and flesh, is a marvelous accomplishment. Whenever I was in any kind of trouble, most of them being of my own making, in politics or whatever, I only wanted to turn to my husband. And he too, when he wanted help, I was there. I was his friend. Even when he was in trouble about me, or with me, we'd always wind up saying, 'Well, who better than you and I have, or who more than you and I desires, the good of the other.'"

The hard, brittle side of Clare Luce, the legends of a scheming, ambitious woman who was calculating and insensitive to people are, if true, part of the past.

Musing, she said "If I had my life to live over again, I would have been"—and then she paused thoughtfully—"a good deal kinder, I think. But then, in those past days, one operated only in the lights you had at the moment. There's one thing about getting old—you look back on the callous acts you did. I don't think I meant to be unkind; it was just that at a certain time of my life my imagination didn't encompass the sufferings or the problems that other people were having. I now go to the other extreme, perhaps to make up for it. I mean, a friend in trouble gets immediate attention from me—sort of a way of making up for the ones I was too busy to do anything for. I still remember when I was eighteen and a school classmate of mine developed a brain tumor. But what did that mean to me at that age? I just knew she was sick. I didn't see it as imminent death, and her mother called me up two or three times and would ask me to come and see her daughter, and I never went. Well, that still haunts me, and even in my marriage I could have done so much better. I could have avoided a lot of unnecessary quarrels. I know I might have been much more appreciative of the many things people did for me. I have very little remorse about my life. But regrets . . . yes . . . What I've just told you, and also I wish I'd never learned to smoke, and I wish I'd kept a diary. That would have been fantastic. But, you know, looking back, I was just too tired at the end of a day. It was too late at night and too much had happened to set down on paper."

Someday Clare Luce will open that trunk, I hope, where she has carefully kept her life in the form of scripts and clippings and letters. The ribbons that tie them together may be a bit faded, but the lady who created the ideas will never cease to fascinate and volley thoughts. With her it's an involuntary action.

Louise Nevelson

Louise Nevelson, American sculptor emeritus, was officially born in 1899 in Kiev, but that date is about the only event in her life that she had no power over. Since early childhood when her Russian-Jewish immigrant parents moved to Rockland, Maine, Louise has had her own brand of incredible individualism and personality and ESP. Sensing her artistic bent as a child, she has never ceased trying to gain the total experience of life in order to fulfill her artistic creativity, and anything today that she feels is necessary to further her esthetic sensibility is a valid and necessary reason for her actions. She seems to know herself intimately and is comfortable.

"When I began going to school I found right off certain traits in myself. I knew I was going to be an artist," she told me, seated at a bare table in her five-story house on Mott Street in New York City. We were on the third floor and she had stuck her head out of the window when I rang the bell and said (yelled), "I'll be right down." The neighborhood is seedy and her building has graffiti on the walls. This is the house and studio where Louise Nevelson lives and creates. Like her sculptures, there are many rooms, but an absence of furniture. Her black sculptured boxes cover the walls from ceiling to floor; even the stairs to the five different floors are black. "Black," she announced, "is a presence, my perfection."

She has not had time to assemble herself for our morning appointment and apologizes. Her strong face has no makeup, her head is covered by a scarf, her only clothing is a heavy textured robe which is tied at the waist. Her only companion is a black Siamese cat, who keeps bumping my tape recorder. For the first half hour the telephone rang and she got up three times to answer it. After a while she decided to let it ring in order to give me her memories and philosophies of a life that has had many rough periods. She is America's foremost living sculptor—not sculptress, as she corrects me. Her neat, obsessively tidy and glorious wooden art forms, fitted together like a jigsaw puzzle, mock expensive equipment in the simplicity of the raw material. They are simple wooden pieces brought extraordinarily to life in all their intricacy and stature by this talented woman. How she and her artistry have grown and are now world-recognized is a story that she enjoys reliving, and the listener—in this case, me—can only remain spellbound.

"Some people are ready-made, like contained in an egg. Others are never formed. Of course, maybe, like in metaphysics, they may be Old Souls and others Young. All right," she said definitely, as though the lesson was now about to begin, "I've talked to people who never knew what they wanted on earth. On the other hand, I knew *exactly* what I wanted, and the interesting thing is that I wasn't a dreamer."

Louise and her sisters went to grammar school and high school in Rockland, Maine, population 8,000 in those days ("And it still is the same today, so you can see its growth!"). Louise was an active child and loved athletics as well as art. "I wasn't a brilliant student but I got A+ from the first day until I graduated. When I got to high school I elected to take art. I related to it like a duck takes to water and I also had *fortissimo* and *pianissimo*—I had both the light touch (if you've seen my drawings) and the stronger feeling. Art class is something I will never forget. The art teacher used to come once a week, and she held up a sunflower one particular time. It made such an impression on me, even to this day—the flower was so vital. I remember she held it up and the center was brown and the petals were yellow, and of course the leaves were green. She said that our assignment was to paint it. Well, I don't know what made me do it but I made a great *big* brown center, *small* yellow leaves and added more of my own ideas. When she came by my easel she held up my picture and said, 'Now, class, this is original. This is not what I told her to do. Nevertheless, this creates the whole thing.' I was thrilled because I wasn't the kind of student to have had things held up too often. When I was a little older, I remember going to the school library, and upon seeing a statue I said, 'I've decided I want to be a sculptor. I don't want color to help me.' I heard myself saying this but it frightened me, so I ran home, wondering where in hell I had gotten *that* idea. But art became my life in school. The winters in Maine are cold, and I hate the cold. I'd feel cold in other classrooms and then I'd walk into art class. I loved the room. It was always warm to me, and I never realized until years later why I was warm there. It was because I was happy. The room itself was the same temperature as all the others, it was just that I felt excitement working."

Louise Nevelson is a composite of ideas and a physical apparition in clothes. Her early years were the springboard for her later personal assemblage of herself. She remembers her favorite art teacher. "She always had a flair for clothes. She was an old maid of maybe sixty and I noticed that she had a purple hat and a purple coat. Well, that was quite unique in Rockland. I said, 'Oh, Miss Cleveland, that's a lovely outfit' (or something like that). And she said, 'Well, I bought the hat because I liked it and then I bought the coat to go with it.' I was quite struck with that fact, since most women do quite the reverse." Many of Nevelson's costumes now are a fashion collage. She has a cape with chinchilla fur inside, a black riding hat, and peers out from long false eyelashes. She seems to be making a punctuation point of herself, now finally abandoning all hated convention of the early years with an unhappy mother and father.

"Father was exciting but too exciting—dashing around and very gregarious. But with Mother there wasn't a day she was happy. She was beautiful. He was beautiful too. But that doesn't necessarily make for a happy marriage or home. She couldn't adjust to her life, and in those days one didn't get a divorce. She was bitter and morose and she'd have the doctor over every day. There were even three doctors until they got bored being called constantly, and she'd then go to Boston and stay in the hospital, or New York. Sometimes she'd stay in bed for five or six weeks. No one could touch her and she was obviously psychotic. If she ever went out, which was rare, it would be to go downtown and it would take her ever so long. She'd get all dressed up in fancy city clothes, which women in small towns in

Maine never wear, and she'd rouge her cheeks, and of course she'd look totally out of place. She loved pretty clothes, and I felt so sorry for her because she was the kind of woman who should have lived in a palace and had all the trimmings."

As children, Louise and her sisters and brothers didn't have much discipline, but they never noticed the lack of it. Louise liked school and there was so much activity—basketball, glee club and music—that there wasn't any time to get into trouble. She became self-disciplined and self-motivated.

"Studied, why, I never stopped studying—voice, dramatics, comparative religion, dancing, singing, so many things. My parents believed that if you come to a new country every child should be educated. My father's two businesses were real estate and lumber, and he was successful and busy. In those days we even had charge accounts because Mother felt that we three girls should have the best of everything. We looked like city girls out of place in a country setting, and because of this I always felt very self-conscious, even at fourteen. I felt so silly, but Mother wanted us to look our best; that was her art, her pride and job. She learned about keeping house and how things should look from watching others. The lawn would always be clipped in a straight line. The house was spotless, the curtains just right. She was meticulous to a fault."

Her daughter's precise eye was obviously influenced by her mother's love of beauty and perfection. But Louise, too, felt the stigma of being different. Jewish people were unheard of in Rockland. Louise claims the town would probably have preferred blacks to her foreign family with an unpronounceable name like Berliawsky. "Dressed in karakul coats and big hats, we were an obvious group and prominent in appearance. Being bright, too, we were a threat on every count, so it wasn't easy."

But the fact is that the stifling small-town life in Maine didn't suppress Louise Nevelson. It served to encourage and broaden her horizons.

"You see, I've always had a blueprint of my life. There's not a surprise in the package," she told me quite solemnly, almost mystically. Except, as I reminded her, her marriage, which did not come out as planned.

"That wasn't a surprise, really. It could never have worked, but I wanted to get out of Maine, come to New York where the opportunities for study were greater. My ex-husband and his family were small men, but refined socially. The Nevelsons had a shipping company called the Polish-American Navigation Company. I never really wanted to get married. I'd told my mother that my one aim was to be an artist. I'd met Charles Nevelson's brother and he was pretty nice. And one day I got a phone call that Charles was coming to town and wanted me to go down to the shipyards and look at a boat. I took my mother into the living room and said, 'Mother, Charles Nevelson's coming to spend some time here and he's going to propose and I'm going to accept.' My mother, who didn't know what the hell I was talking about, didn't say anything. Sure enough, after one date and having listened to his older brother, who liked me, he asked me to marry him. I accepted but I knew I shouldn't have. He certainly was gentle and nice and I obviously recognized that he had quality, which no one else in Rockland had. I didn't know anything about sex but I wasn't really curious about it then (only after in my life), but I thought marriage would be better than an unhappy family situation, so we went out together for two years and were married in 1920."

Neither her brother nor sister made good marriages either, but Louise's marriage to Nevelson did last ten years.

"I had told my husband before we were married (I was eighteen and he was thirty) that I was going to be an artist. See, I put my cards on the table and I figured, since he was an older man, he would respect my career and would give me certain freedoms. I probably gave him more credit than he deserved for really being an intellectual. Instead, I found that he loved living the Social life in New York, which I didn't. I wasn't looking to improve my Social position, dear. If I had wanted that, I would have chosen a man from the top. Nevelson was, I would say, upper middle class and extremely jealous. He'd have detectives following me. I had no freedom. He'd phone twenty or thirty times a day. Once, I had a maid who said to him, 'Mr. Nevelson, please stop calling so often. I can't get my work finished.' All of this made me terribly nervous. We had a son after two years of marriage, and that's why I stuck it out so long. I was also very shy and, realizing that ladies didn't do certain things, I couldn't conceive of my son not having both parents together. All of my family were having problems. My mother had become quite sickly and thought she was dying. My sister left her husband, my brother wasn't married, and my younger sister stayed with her husband out of sheer despair."

Louise feels that the disappointment she and her siblings felt in their marriages was definitely traceable to her parents' example. Too, it was the First World War and then the Depression of 1929, but Louise still wanted to study art. Her mother, ill though she was, volunteered to take Louise's son Mike to live with her. Louise knew that she never could fit the pattern of a New York Society woman and the limitations and responsibilities of marriage, and her mother knew that Louise was very unhappy. In 1931 the Nevelsons separated and Louise's mother took her grandson to Maine, while her daughter went to Munich to study with Hans Hofmann, the greatest teacher of cubism in the art world. It was only nine months, but leaving her son with his grandmother enabled her to fulfill her artistic yearning. However, she realized that there was a great price to pay for her freedom. What that price was Louise only alluded to. Her son never had security passing from school to school, and without his mother life was difficult. So in her own search for identity and freedom she abrogated her responsibility as a mother.

"Yes," she repeated, "you pay your price. I wanted to commit suicide for forty years. I ran to everything available. I began drinking and doing all sorts of strange things. I knew I was gifted but I was without direction. I couldn't be appeased. I was in such a state that I was getting boils and abscesses and even sciatica. I was constantly ill. I knew I was nervous. I knew I didn't have enough money to really execute my concepts. I didn't even want to go to work for anyone, because slavery is slavery, whether you work for a dollar or a million dollars, so I learned how to sustain myself. My family helped me a bit. I pawned the jewelry I had and worked on my art."

In return for financial assistance, her sisters took (were given) some of Louise's sculptures in the early days. She didn't really live. "In those days I just existed. It was during the thirties and the forties. I never lived in any place longer than a year. War was at hand. I was frustrated that I couldn't get hold of any metals. If I had money, maybe. But I had to satisfy my inner urge or kill myself. I had to find some material that I could work with, so I said, 'To hell with searching any longer. I'm going to use what's available.' So I began picking up old pieces of wood anywhere I could find them." Someone once asked Nevelson why she used such cheap material as wood. It wasn't an artist that asked her. She makes the distinction that it was an ordinary (insensitive) person. She was angry and answered cynically, "I was told that wood was gold, and anything that you found on the streets of America was gold."

"People are a little more advanced now, but in those days I made up my mind that, if it took until doomsday, I was going to get people who thought wood wasn't material for an artist and make them buy my work, and, furthermore, spend a lot of their money on it. The public was going to take old wood and like it and was going to consider it art because *I* was putting *life* into it."

She went unrecognized until the fifties, rarely showing but experimenting with all kinds of crates and boxes, creating three-dimensional effects and working in black. The chronology of her shows starts with group shows from 1933 to 1934; then in 1941 at the Nierendorf Gallery, her first one-woman show; later, in 1943, a stunning *avant garde* show called "Circus" at the Norlyst Gallery, and in 1959 her friend Dorothy Miller offered her participation in a group show at the Museum of Modern Art. Alfred Barr was the Director then, and Louise never quite forgave him for not recognizing her talent earlier. "After all, museum directors are paid to search out new talent. That's their business. It's easy to buy a recognized artist like Picasso or Matisse.

"Who do you think really discovered me? Europeans. Artists from Europe would come to my house and buy my pieces. Dorothy Miller actually heard about my reputation in Paris. That's why she called me up, and I told her that I would create an all-white show."

It took until the 1950s for the public to recognize this remarkable woman who had gone through personal hell for years. Her gratitude has remained undimmed for one man who supported her creativity and had the vision to recognize her artistry —Karl Nierendorf, an import dealer in New York. He gave her

her first one-woman show in 1941. "When I was struggling, he was nice to me. He was a very cultivated man and I needed money badly, to work and to fix up my house on Thirtieth Street. I found I had to have more money. You know, you always have to have a little more—this time I figured a couple of thousand dollars. I also needed a show. I got up my courage and went to see Mr. Nierendorf. Now, he was a rather stingy man. For example, if he took you to lunch he took you to some sandwich place and you couldn't possibly order a drink. This didn't stop me from asking him for some money. He looked at me and then he turned to his secretary and said, 'Miss Prentiss, give Mrs. Nevelson two thousand dollars.' I nearly died! When I left his office I was so thrilled, I showed the check to every artist. All artists were broke then, but I had to show it to my friends before I put it in the bank. I also had the audacity to ask him for a show. He had seen my 'Circus' at Norlyst, which was quite revolutionary—pre-pop art. But I wanted Nierendorf to give me a drawing show. He said, 'Why didn't you ask me earlier. Just look at my calendar.' I was shy, but persisted. 'I must have a show in April.' Surprisingly enough, he relented and said, 'All right,' but, more importantly, he looked at me and said, 'You know, Nevelson, you're going to have every wish in art fulfilled.' And I looked at him (this was 1941) and I was amazed, you know. And I said, 'What makes you say that?' and he said, 'I know Picasso. I know Matisse. And you've got the quality of them and you can make every wish of yours come true.' That's why I've always called him my spiritual godfather."

Nevelson's art, like her being, is an extremely personal statement. She is totally aware of this, totally attuned to it. She has been known to work twenty-four hours at a stretch without sleep, possessed by an expressive urge.

"You see, what I do is very individualistic. I have things that are different, that belong to me." Pointing to her head, she continued, "Like these eyes—they belong to only me. I don't create masterpieces. I hate even words like that. (I hate words. I think they destroy people.) All I want to do is to make something live. These sculptures of mine are all reflections of me. We all have bodies and blood streams, but they function differently. What sets me apart is that I have an awareness of what I can do. I want what I'm doing. I've never asked anyone in my life what they think of my work." As though addressing the room, she said, quite flatly, "Who am I going to ask? If I don't know or can't judge my own work, how can anyone else? I'm a compulsive worker and I've never stopped."

To have stopped trying to appease her insatiable appetite to fulfill herself would have been to stop living. And part of her living, although marriage was not a life style for her, are continuing relationships with men. "I happen to be very feminine," Mrs. Nevelson confided, "and I love men. Age hasn't changed that. Sex is just as great at seventy, but these days I'm free-lancing, dear, in that department, so I ask nothing from any man and they ask nothing from me—no demands. This is the first time in my life where I command my own time. A man has to take whatever time I have left over. My work comes first. I don't want to get married and I don't want to sleep in the same bed and see the same person every morning when I wake up. I can pick and choose and do what I wish."

Permanency of any male-female relationship bothers Nevelson. She feels she couldn't sustain it for long. "I've gone to bed for weeks at a time during a love affair. But the same man for a couple of years? Oh, dear! I have lots of ambivalent feelings. A psychiatrist said to me once, 'Please remember the word *ambivalent*.' When I get clogged up, I do think of that word."

Louise Nevelson's philosophy is contained in her Mott Street house. She has created an environment. She has achieved the confidence and gained the respect and public acclaim due one of America's greatest sculptors. It took decades, a personal development and a life style totally without pretention or artificiality. Way ahead of her time, a worldwide exhibitor now, she can comfortably handle the fame that took so long in coming. A dramatic figure, her own strength of character beams through her black walls and sculptures, and her own integrity is strength in its purest form.

Lila Acheson Wallace

ONLY ONE WOMAN in a million could be co-founder and co-editor and co-owner of a magazine whose circulation is the largest in the world—*Reader's Digest*—and that one woman is Lila Bell Acheson Wallace. She has, strangely enough, received relatively little publicity, and her name is relatively unfamiliar in this country and elsewhere. Yet her story is the plot of the American dream, and Mrs. Wallace at eighty-five is still active on the magazine and one of the most unheralded philanthropists in America. Her life has been as interesting as the magazine she and her husband, DeWitt, created. But more than that, her philosophy, meticulously carried out over the years, is indeed at the heart of her success.

In her job she has always had enormous power, but she has always used it widely and not blatantly, carefully but with strength. Moreover she has made the most difficult achievement seem perfectly natural. She has made a success of being a partner with her husband in marriage as well as in the business life they share, and, as everyone knows, few men and women are adept at both.

But Lila had a good and warmly secure childhood. Even her birth in Manitoba, Canada, was heralded by the bright blue ball (ornament) falling off the tree on a happy occasion—Christmas Day, 1889.

"Lila Bell has just been born," her Presbyterian minister father announced to the family.

Later, Lila was to recall the next birth. "My brother Barclay and I were very close. We did everything together. One night he woke me up to tell me our sister was born. I can see us creeping

up the stairs to see her. That was one of the first ways I knew
about sex—the birth of a baby."

When Lila was one year old ("I crawled over the border") the
Achesons moved to the United States, traveling throughout the
North and Middle West—Illinois, Minnesota, North Dakota—
and finally ended up in Tacoma, Washington.

The art of living was and is a specialty of Lila Wallace's. It's
difficult to know how to trace it, for her leadership seems to have
rooted itself in the family setup even as a child.

Meeting Mrs. Wallace is apt to be an experience, because her
life is a living story of how to make the most out of yourself.
Her husband of fifty-three years unabashedly adores her. It is
impossible to know either Wallace, but particularly Lila, alone
without the physical presence of the other. Mr. Wallace is her
alter vocal ego and her greatest supporter, and she his. Being
childless, their love bounces openly from one to the other; there
is no communication problem.

What draws your attention to her delicate-featured face is the
shock of electric-blue eyes heightened by strong blue eye
shadow. Gentian is her favorite flower, and it is not by coincidence that she wears blue, loves turquoise and uses the color
frequently in her decorating schemes. One of her great pleasures
is not only beautifying her own surroundings but those of the
Digest's employees, whose offices all show Lila's personal touch.

Her values and desire to share so generously her good fortune
with others she frankly credits to her parents. When speaking of
them she becomes almost childlike (a strange phenomenon, since
she's eighty-five and definitely wistful). She has never forgotten
the responsibility and lessons in handling money that she learned
from her family, although the figures have changed (greatly)
since her early days. But even though her worth is now in the
millions, the principles of sound judgment have never changed.

Her parents, she told me, would sit down every month at the
dining-room table and hold family meetings with their five children. A discussion of the family budget inevitably told the children how much money was available, how it was to be dis-
tributed, and what each of their allowances and chores were.
Cooking, taking care of the rooms, cleaning and laundry were
all shared by the youngsters. Lila still remembers the warm

framework of home. "Daddy would take us up on his knee over and over again and we'd have long talks. Mummy adored him and was very beautiful and reserved." The atmosphere was easy and parent-child relationships open. "I don't ever remember being told that I couldn't do anything. Daddy would always be willing to listen to a proposal. 'We'll talk it over and I'll tell you what I think,' he'd say, 'Then you tell me what your reaction is and then we'll jointly decide.' "

Responsibility, Lila learned, was a normal and expected part of family life.

"If there was any money left over after the budget had been ascertained, Daddy could have a new book (and that was a big occasion) to add to his library. Once I found out that there wasn't enough money for a new suit for Daddy because Mother admitted she'd spent what there was on *my* school clothes. I was so ashamed I cried for hours." Depriving her beloved father upset her terribly, and happiness was just being near him.

"His study was my favorite place to be. It was a special treat to take a favorite book and sit with him, just reading and watching the fire in the fireplace. You could stay in there as long as you wanted but you had to be quiet."

Public schools, the Ward Belmont College in Nashville, Tennessee, and a degree from the University of Oregon completed Lila's formal education, but she has courted personal knowledge ever since and a working career has never interfered with other interests.

"The summer after I finished at Ward Belmont I tried to convince Daddy to let me work," Lila said. "But he was of the Old School and argued that daughters shouldn't. I gave in and spent one whole summer at home, bored to death, but by fall he agreed to let me teach. I went down and saw the State Superintendent of Schools, and he said, Of course, I could do something and get a certificate too. He excused himself for a moment saying he'd see what jobs were left, since most schools had already opened. When he returned he looked quite bothered and told me he was very sorry but there was only one opening at a school and no one had lasted out a term there. I guess he thought that statement would finish me, but I liked the challenge. 'I'll take it,' I bravely said, and I taught at that Eatonville School for two years."

After a successful stint helping run a local YWCA, the YWCA induced Lila to come East and work for their industrial division. She took a training course and set up a recreational program at the Du Pont plant in Pompton Lakes, New Jersey, and was put in charge of thirty social workers. From there she was sent, after the war, to New Orleans, and then was appointed head of a new social service department begun by the Presbyterian Board of Home Missions. Speaking and fund-raising all over the country, she was borrowed by the Inter-Church World Movement to start a recreational program for migrant families, a day-care setup in Mississippi, New England and New York. It was in Minneapolis–St. Paul, to be exact, that a telegram changed the course of her life.

DeWitt Wallace attended the University of California from 1909 to 1911. While there he met Barclay Acheson, Lila's older brother. Barclay invited DeWitt home for a family Christmas in Tacoma. He was immediately smitten with Lila and proposed to her after a few hours. But Lila didn't take him seriously, and anyway, as she confessed, she was already engaged to another boy (an engagement she subsequently broke). Eight years later, DeWitt ran into Barclay again in St. Paul, where he had published the first trial issue of *The Reader's Digest*. It was called "Getting the Most out of Farming" and the 120 pages were packed with advice, proverbs, self-improvement and useful facts digested from a myriad of farm publications. Still remembering Barclay's sister, he inquired about Lila. Finding, to his delight, that she was still single and working in Bridgeport, Connecticut, he decided to send his now famous telegram: "CONDITIONS AMONG WOMEN WORKERS IN ST. PAUL GHASTLY. URGE IMMEDIATE INVESTIGATION. DEWITT WALLACE."

"I spent every evening with Lila and we had a rather public courtship," Wallace recalled. "Our chief recreation was riding the streetcar back and forth in St. Paul. At least we managed a little privacy because I made sure we had the back seat."

Wallace and Lila were married in October of that year, 1921, in Pleasantville, New York, with Barclay Acheson, now a minister, officiating. Today Wallace proudly proclaims that "Lila has been the most ideal wife any man could ever have. Early in our marriage she was willing to work day and night, and she is the most beautiful example of how to grow old—it's her spirit that counts."

The Wallaces, after their wedding, rented a dingy Greenwich Village basement in New York under a speakeasy. "I remember DeWitt telling me his dream of publishing a digest. 'We're going to do it,' I told him. But he wasn't sure we could make a living out of it."

Lila was undaunted and, as always, determined. "Well, I don't care if you can't support us. I'll support us both if you'll start working on your magazine right now."

And support her husband she did, continuing in the industrial department of the YWCA National Board in New York, a second job with the Presbyterian Home Missions Board and still another job with the U. S. Labor Department among the migrant workers. ("I loved to work.")

Wallace borrowed $1,000 from his father, $500 from his brother and put in $400 from his savings account. Together, he and Lila mailed circulars asking for subscriptions, placed a 5,000-copy order with a Pittsburgh printer, and Volume I, Number I of *The Reader's Digest* appeared in February 1922.

DeWitt Wallace and Lila Bell Acheson were and are the co-founders, co-editors and co-owners. She owns 48 per cent of the stock, he 52 per cent.

In 1922 the venture was successful enough for them to afford a $25-a-month studio apartment over a garage in Pleasantville, New York, with a downstairs bathroom. A little later they paid $10 for a nearby office. The magazine was all subscription until 1929, when it was put on newsstands across the country and publicly sold.

It is as difficult to separate Lila from *The Reader's Digest* as it is to isolate her as an individual from her husband. Many of her beliefs are probably deeply rooted in Presbyterian principles of religion (DeWitt's father was a minister, too) as well as in his drive for the betterment of man. And with a zeal I have never known before, Lila has totally devoted her life to enhancing the lives of others. Whether by moral example or philanthropic clout, she leads in every area of life she has touched. Seemingly unconsciously driven, she nevertheless is at the seat of power, holding it, manipulating it with determination.

"If I want something done, I always get my own way," she told me. And examples loom large to illustrate this.

The Wallaces bought eighty acres of land between Pleasant-ville and Chappaqua in northern Westchester County in 1936. The *Digest* had outgrown the Pleasantville studio and, later, floor space rented above and below the Pleasantville Post Office. More space on three floors of a bank building in town was still not sufficient. Fourteen separate offices scattered around still wouldn't do.

Lila took on the job of supervising a new home for the *Digest*. The red-brick Georgian building which opened in 1939, at a cost of $1,500,000 had 185,000 cubic feet of working space. In the final stages, as the brick was about to be laid, Lila told John Mackenzie, her architect, that she didn't like it. It had the wrong look to it. She toured New York State until she found a brick factory with just the right shade and brought it back and said, "This is what I'd like." Needless to say, you don't argue with the co-owner. He also was about to put spread-eagles on the cupola as the symbol for *The Reader's Digest*. Lila had second thoughts. Somehow eagles didn't seem right, and she told him to wait while she thought of a more appropriate figure.

"Suddenly," she said, "I woke up in the middle of the night and thought of Pegasus, the winged horse. When he stamped his foot he was supposed to have inspired men to write." That was the spirit she was looking for. Mackenzie was informed, four Pegasuses were put in place, and they have been the symbol of *The Reader's Digest* ever since. ("When I'm determined, I don't stop until I get what I want.")

That one woman can be so creative is really astounding, and I suppose it is the reason it is so hard to fault her. All the land-scaping at the *Digest* and the interiors were creations of Lila's. The magnificent collection of impressionist paintings, worth about five million dollars, that hang throughout the *Digest* build-ing and in their home in Mount Kisco were all chosen and bought by her, and fresh flowers at her direction are arranged by an expert twice a week, for all *Digest* employees to enjoy at the office.

Perhaps it is the almost fanatic concern with the daily life of *Digest* employees that makes the operation seem like a Mom-and-

Pop store. The workers have benefits almost unheard of in other companies, for they are really like the children Lila never had. Employees work from eight-thirty to four o'clock, and have all Fridays off in May so they can enjoy the lovely spring countryside. Every room at Pleasantville is furnished with the idea that, should the staff wish, they can copy any decorating ideas for their own homes. Floor plans and decorating information are happily furnished on request.

It is hard to believe that in this country-estate atmosphere originates the most widely read and circulated magazine in the world! But all these personal and homey touches are strangely intentional. The credit probably is due to both the Wallaces, who believe that if life is made easier and more pleasant one's incentive and creative powers thrive, and by leading, they introduce ideas and thought patterns they hope will be copied. Every employee is given $200 to give to his favorite charity. All that is required is to fill out a form and state the name and address of the preferred project or projects. A check is sent in the donor's name from Wallace's private foundation. Over the past years $12,200,000 has been given to employee-designated non-profit organizations. Christmas bonuses every year amount to 15 per cent of the workers' salary. On top of that, on or about April 1 each year (just before taxes are due), employees are very likely to find a little happy surprise in the way of an added bonus to help out with their tax returns. The latest thoughtfulness from the co-editors comes from their interest in broadening the scope of each person's life. To that end, every one of the 70,000 employees with one child per family who wants to go to Europe can have his trip underwritten by the Wallaces for a visit of up to six weeks. The only requirement with respect to editorial policy is that they must support and promote the American way of life.

The Wallaces' faith in the country that gave them a million times over their original investment is constantly being stoked. If you're for America, for God, and for right-wing Republicanism, chances are you're their kind of people.

With a total gross of about $500,000,000 a year from 100,000,-000 monthly readers, *The Reader's Digest*, here and abroad, in thirteen languages and with a braille edition, with books and records, is a powerful and important company, and one of the few with a woman at the helm.

But that a working woman, not a wealthy dilettante, should carve her own niche in other fields such as philanthropy, is very unusual. But more unusual is the enormous financial contributions she has given and her wide range of interests and tastes.

Boscobel, an eighteenth-century mansion at Garrison-on-the-Hudson in New York, was restored totally by her gift of $8,000,000. This was not a mere check donation; she insisted, as elsewhere, in supervising the interior decorations, the flowers and the manor-house gardens.

The Metropolitan Museum has long been a favorite of hers, and she and Thomas Hoving have conferred at length on mutual projects fostered by her, the restoration of the Great Hall, and her personal contribution of the Egyptian Wing. She loves to watch her money translated into visual reality.

"You know, I looked at those beautiful tubs high in the niches in the Main Hall. They must have been there for a century, I guess, and nobody even put a pansy in them until I decided to have fresh flowers daily arranged in perpetuity." And as a result, what really touched her was an incident with a little boy.

"It was one of the sweetest things that ever happened to me." An eleven-year-old boy asked one of the museum guards if the flowers in the tubs were real, and being told they were, asked, "May I smell them?" The guard told him he could if he was able to climb up to the four-foot niche. He did, touched them and came down. "You know, that's the first time that I've touched a real flower," he said. "How does the museum get them? Does some nice lady give them to you?" The guard admitted that indeed he was right. The boy asked if he could have her name and address so he could write to her. Lila will never forget the letter.

"It was on paper with little lines on it, and this eleven-year-old told me in his own words what it means for him to see real flowers for the first time. You can't imagine what it meant to me."

Millions went and still go to special interests of Lila's: $4,000,000 to Lincoln Center and to its Juilliard School; $3,000,000 to the Bronx Zoo for a new building, The World of Birds; $2,000,000 to her alma mater, the University of Oregon; $2,000,000 to the YWCA, where she had once worked; $1,000,000 to the

Bronx Botanical Garden; $1,000,000 to the Sloan-Kettering In-
stitute for Cancer Research; $2,000,000 to the Near East Founda-
tion; $1,000,000 to Northern Westchester Hospital; $1,000,000
to an ancient Egyptian temple called Abu Simbel to help salvage
and rebuild it. (The Wallaces had been to the Nile Temple site in
the 1960s and had never forgotten it.) To the Black A.M.E. Zion
Baptist Church in Mount Kisco, in response to a letter of solicita-
tion for $25, she gave $50,000—with the stipulation that local
businessmen match it.

"They not only matched it, but raised $67,000," Lila proudly
said. "And they bought a new church that three other churches
had bid for. The colored people got it, and that made me very
happy."

She has given to the Mount Kisco Presbyterian Church, refurbishing it, building an addition, adding a parking lot and im-
proving the landscaping, "which I can't help but always do
where and whenever it's needed."

But church doesn't lure Lila often now. "I told Daddy when
he was alive that for the first twenty years of my life I went to
church often enough to take care of me if I live to be a hundred: four times every Sunday, twice during the week, and I'd
play the organ at other times. Fortunately, Daddy didn't get angry. And he needn't have. I prefer the woods for meditation and
prayer, anyway."

A minipark on Lenox Avenue in Harlem, a new building on
the campus of the International College of Lebanon at Beirut, a
rebuilt bridge in Central Park, the Martha Graham Dance Company, a Japanese skating house in Leonard Park, Mount Kisco, a
new six-million-dollar, six-story wing on the American Hospital
in Istanbul, in memory of her favorite brother, Barclay, and un-
derwriting two new productions for the New York Metropolitan
Opera—all finished projects.

"I'm being very careful of my next one because I want it to
be very special."

There's a well-known story that is told on Lila. Asked at the
Juilliard School, after she had given them a multimillion-dollar
contribution, what she had left in her will, she replied without
hesitation.

"I remember exactly," she said. "I've memorized it. Being of sound mind and body, I've spent it all."

This little dainty lady, basically reticent about her accomplishments, is little known to the public. But that is by design. Eschewing interviews, she pursues her job, her interests, silently but with purpose. Giving away millions so that "I hope I can really spend all my money before I die. At least I'm still trying."

Living Legends

BECAUSE THEY DARED to be different and offbeat in an era when conventional behavior was the only accepted way of life, particularly for women, these three ladies were, and still are, trailblazers. Their backgrounds and incomes were totally different, but each individualism and nonconformity combined with a strong will and a natural flair to keep them undimmed in spirit and steadfast in purpose. It is no wonder that they are greatly admired and sought-after women.

The youngest is seventy-one and the oldest is in her mid-nineties. All have tremendous followings, and it is indeed remarkable that their sometimes bizarre and always consciously different behaviors have not worn out their popularity over the years. Feminists all, they ignored the road signs of their generation and traveled on to maturity as arresting trend-setters, oblivious to criticism; if anything, they rather thrived on it and turned it to their advantage.

American pioneer women used their rugged womanpower alongside their men to help build our country. These three women have the same hardiness as their earlier counterparts, along with a strength of conviction, a perception born of self-assurance, plus an attitude of laissez-faire that establishes them forever as a different kind of wildflower. Each woman has boldly set a life style which flourishes in the midst of society's restraints, and neither time nor age can dim their charismas. Their quality of leadership shows in their ability to discard the unnecessary baggage of life in order to hone their personalities to suit themselves.

Diana Vreeland made all American women "fashion conscious" through her clothes-trained eye and publicity know-how. She gained top kudos in an industry which has always looked to leaders who, year after year, could come up with fresh ideas.

Alice Roosevelt Longworth, coming from a family in which individualism was expected (and the crowds were rarely disappointed), has for ninety years provoked shock and excitement by her very presence. Happily reaping the joys of a quick mind and facile wit, she has become a character within a character. Her "lib" began as soon as she could speak, and she has shot from the hip ever since with verbal barrages that would flatten the average person of any generation—yet she is lauded for her honesty and sought after for her company.

Peggy Guggenheim came out fighting, determined to have her own way, oblivious to society's mores. In her field, she has been regarded as a seer in choosing paintings and amassing an art collection that proved to be years ahead of its time.

The others, too, have stayed head and shoulders above the crowd, all on the strength of their personalities and their ability to be comfortable in their own skins.

So many women have the need to be fulfilled but feel grave insecurities when, sometimes, family and jobs only partially satisfy this need, and in every era women have had to fight their way out of this male-dominated paperbag society. Well, to be able to achieve power by dint of character is a trait of remarkable people; that these are women gives them an extra chalk mark. The fact that their sex is far from meaningless but the foundation on which they established and maintained themselves as beacons is a tribute to their bold breed. Like film classics, they will always titillate and fascinate and inspire not only their generation but totally new ones that find themselves irresistibly attracted to opinionated, liberated and intelligent human beings.

These women are particularly and peculiarly famous. That is not to say that the same traits did not or do not exist in other women of their seniority or in women who have not enjoyed such public acclaim. I wish I knew others, but in this instance I have chosen these women because they are special to me. "Livin'" *ain't* so easy, as the Gershwin song suggests, and to have quality and assuredness is admirable; but to be so self-possessed as to proudly come out even in times of adversity requires guts.

Idealism may be fine for some women, but for these it certainly isn't enough.

I happen to like a certain human style which, to me, is best exemplified in these, my living legends.

Diana Vreeland

There has been a Vreeland Cult, Vreeland devotees and graduates of the Vreeland Method.

DIANA VREELAND, at seventy-one, has spent her life dominating beautiful women. In the field of fashion she is a priestess. She has discovered beauty and given girls and women their own identity. Through her work, first at *Harper's Bazaar*, then at *Vogue*, her power of discovery remains unchallenged. With an uncanny and unerring eye, Diana can spot a new fashion star. Girls like Penelope Tree and Verushka were her creations. Women like Marella Agnelli, now considered one of the world's greatest beauties, were unrecognized until Diana's imagination saw fabulous possibilities in their striking, patrician features. She can take these nonclassical beauties, mold them, dress them, pose them, feature them in the top fashion magazines and, under her tutelage, they become instant trend-setters.

For a woman who is her own best advertisement, Diana has managed to capitalize on her weaknesses. Instead of de-emphasizing a rather large nose, she skins her dyed black hair back from her face, making it the most prominent feature. Her ears, too, which might have remained hidden under a softer hair style, have been purposely left uncovered and heightened by rouging the lobes. Her whole manner is theatrical, her gestures large and grand, almost as if to mask a hidden insecurity.

It has been said that Diana's mother was a beautiful, spoiled, dominating woman. It is quite possible that her daughter was made to feel ugly. Diana's drive and aggressive character surely were rooted in those early days. The desire to prove her worth and dedicate her life to her work were achieved despite lack of money and education. She worked nonstop to get to the top and still puts in a full day. Nothing is gained in low gear, and Diana has operated full-throttle all her life. At the peak of her fashion-magazine career she was offered many more lucrative and less confining jobs. She refused them on the grounds that she would have had to use her connections, her friends, to push "commercial" products.

As Richard Avedon, one of America's top fashion photographers, told me, "Diana is like litmus paper to quality." She would never vulgarize herself and has always been more interested in helping others. She has helped girls to discover themselves and to learn the self-assurance that she has so brilliantly mastered. It is an art.

At *Harper's Bazaar* Diana always worked under an editor-in-chief. She had talent and innate knowledge but never the authoritative voice in the magazine's policies. At *Vogue* she finally achieved that power and had time to concentrate on the business end of the magazine, not just fashion. She created the eccentric, electric personnages of the sixties. Jackie Onassis and Lee Radziwill have known her since their teens, as I have. And they too have benefited from her beauty advice and friendship.

Diana is exaggerated in her entire life style. She doesn't walk, she lopes. She doesn't talk, she trills—in fact, yells and punctuates vocally. She has been known to hit models to make them more alert and learn under her tutelage how to project themselves. She comes on strong and glaring, but her creativity is undeniable. Her fashion sorcery is unique. Emphasis is her trademark, and she is emphatically a polished, self-disciplined pro. How and where this bizarre character had her early origins are facts that Diana has chosen to select and edit mentally. That they may not be the actual facts only adds to the mystique that is Diana Daziel Vreeland.

Factually, her father was English and her mother American. The Daziels chose to live in Paris in the early 1900s, and that is where Diana and her sister were brought up until they came to America in 1914.

"We were never wealthy, but of course life then was so different," she told me, sitting on a rubber ring, conscious of her posture on the banquette in her Park Avenue living room. It was six o'clock and Diana had put in another long day. She had just returned from her job at the Metropolitan Museum. Dressed in an unadorned, yet perfectly cut, black wool pants suit, she had really hardly changed since I first met her in my teens. She wasted no time taking off her coat, going back to her bedroom and then joining me. The ever-present cigarette holder and the theatrics of long, graceful fingers fitting cigarettes into it, were a superb piece of stage business I had almost forgotten.

Life was surely different for Diana in the early days, for her youth was the only carefree time she ever knew.

"Mother and Father always had a car and chauffeur, and we went to Venice or Deauville in the summer or wherever everybody else went. Our parents spent their days having a good time. They never contributed a bloody thing, and they and all their friends lived the life of Riley."

Perhaps this is why Diana developed ambition.

"Felicia, *everyone* should live a full life. I do believe there is so much to learn. One thing that I definitely missed as a child was concentration. I had to learn that later. A spoiled sort of person like my mother was a good example. You only spoil yourself. One must learn discipline, Felicia. Everyone must make their own life."

What influenced Diana were her early childhood years in the Paris of *La Belle Époque*. The color, the excitement, still remain dramatically vivid.

"It was the Edwardian Period of Europe. The era of grand dukes and archdukes. All the money in the *world* was pouring into Paris when we were young. Beautiful people wore beautiful clothes. My parents had a salon of sorts. (They were sort of cooking with something because the place was jumping.) We entertained and were entertained. Nijinsky, Diaghilev, Ida Rubinstein, the Castles. All those marvelous people were in and out of our apartment. It was those kinds of people who really influenced my life and are still influencing the world as we know it. I remember hiding behind the curtains in our drawing room and watching Ida Rubinstein. She was a beautiful, exquisite creature who was a nobody and she came with Lord Guinness. *He* put up the money for the first performance of the Ballet Russe in 1911.

He was in love with her and I'll never forget her. You see she was *demi-monde*, which is the half-world. People in this class had their own hairdressers, their own newspapers, their own *world*.

"Later, when I was in New York in the early twenties, the comparable set went to the Colony Restaurant. When I first dined there every man in town was sitting with his *beautifully* dressed mistress. I remember William K. Vanderbilt and his marvelous girl; I think her name was Helen Springer.

"But, darling, there's always a *demi-monde* in every era. When the men go up the ladder of success, make a fortune, have the power and know the world, their wives are often left behind. So then they look for someone more colorful and a more exciting existence."

This was the stage setting of Diana's youth, high spirits but no formal schooling. When the Daziels remembered, they'd drop their daughters into a school wherever they were in September and pull them out in April.

"I even ended up in Staten Island one winter because my parents were going to Nairobi. They decided they'd have to get me out of New York Society, looked up schools in the newspapers, and found one in Staten Island. (I lasted there less than a year.) In the middle of another winter we were sent to Brearley, but I really had no continuous education."

While Diana's education was spotty, her childhood trips were memorable. In her teens, she and her sister and mother spent most of the war years in Cody, Wyoming.

"Buffalo Bill was the famous Colonel Cody and we used to go on pack trips. We'd be up in the mountains for months at a time. It was a very lonely and frightening life. Except for my sister, who was four years younger, there was no one around. (She and I were never too compatible. We never talked. I only talked to my horse. I'd go off riding for hours and hours and hours, just talking to my little pony.) We usually ate with the wranglers. Mother would be with the Great Spirits of the West. (Father never went to Wyoming. He thought that was for the birds, so he stayed in New York.) We lived at the Irma Hotel, which was named after Buffalo Bill's daughter. Our life was just like a movie Western—saloons along the streets, cowboys shooting it up. Why, it used to take us about a week on the train to get from

New York to Wyoming. And when we'd visit my grandmother in Southampton from New York, it was a *big* trip. Long Island was really country. It would take about eight hours in a car from New York City."

The times in between trips, Diana spent studying dancing with Russian ballet teachers, going to parties and leading quite an independent life. When she met Reed Vreeland she was, as she said, "so intoxicated with him I didn't care what my parents thought. If he'd been *black* and they'd thrown us both out of the house, it would have been O.K. by me."

She was eighteen when they were married, and he was learning banking. I can imagine how he would have appealed to Diana, for when I knew him he was suave and distinguished, European in taste and manner, and always a gentleman—albeit without wealth. Living in London after they were first married put Diana right back in the happy milieu, much like Paris, that she had loved so years earlier. By this time she was old enough to become part of the fashion, and the fashionable world.

"I always adored everything that was amusing and gay. I adored clothes and ornamentation, and I was *jeune fille*, my dear. The great fashion houses, if they liked you, would give you clothes for practically nothing. That was the glory of Europe before World War II. I reveled in it like so many others. My life became *completely* European. I had no interest in anything except educating myself."

This was Diana's period of self-education, making up for lost time, steeping herself in history, reading, going to museums and traveling.

The Vreelands didn't return to America until 1938. By that time they had two sons, who had been educated in England. After they returned to New York the boys went to Groton. However, Reed's job in banking didn't bring in enough money so that they could live the way Diana wanted. She realized, after six months in the States, that in order "to live the *big life* which we both adored (my God, to have fresh flowers, someone to look after your clothes, to pay for food and rent)" she'd have to work!

Carmel Snow's telephone call in 1938 was the beginning of Diana Vreeland's famous tenure at *Harper's Bazaar.*

"We had been at the St. Regis dining and dancing, and Mrs. Snow had apparently been in the same room. We had some mutual friends who gave my number. When she telephoned she said, "I saw you last night. I don't know who you are or where you come from, but you look so European.'

" 'Well,' I answered, 'I've lived there half my life.'

"She asked me to come to the magazine and she offered me a job and I took it, and I was twenty-eight years at *Bazaar* as Fashion Editor. I went in like anyone off the street would go in . . . to learn . . . to learn . . . to learn about journalism. (Fashion I knew. I mean I knew more about fashion than anyone in *this* country.) But I had to learn about how to put a magazine together and the discipline of work. Suddenly I found that *my whole background was my future*. You see, everything has come back to me a million ways. If you work in an office you get the temperature pretty quick. I loved going into the downtown market, the wholesale district. All the people there were of European background. We understood each other despite their thick accents. I adored the fur district and the marvelous cloak and suit world."

After *Bazaar*, Diana moved to *Vogue*, doing the same things for them that she had done earlier at *Bazaar*, spotting trends, traveling to Europe four times a year for the collections, and in general creating a fashion mystique. All have been Diana's life. Also creating the Vreeland Mystique, a role she enjoys almost more than anything else. Her flair, her artistry for the bizarre, follows her like the scent of perfume. Her offbeat tastes are watched, copied and chronicled by everyone in the fashion world. But to copy Diana is never to capture the true essence of an artistic, antennaed woman. She doesn't shock to evoke a response. She truly lives an aura of theatrical awareness. Reed Vreeland went along with her vagaries, always a detached, aloof gentleman, and through her job she always brought the most talented and amusing people into his ken. But she was whom they came to see. Their forty-two-year marriage, her two sons, all fitted into Diana's life but never made demands on her. She was first and foremost, like a trained ballerina, the epitome of fashion. And still is. Among others she was responsible for the thong sandal in America, for women's acceptance in pants, for snoods, for bringing cosmetic surgery to the public's attention.

Her habits are well-known in the trade. She loves to work in her New York City apartment, particularly in the bathroom.

"I love the atmosphere there. I don't think of a bathroom as just a place to take a bath or do your teeth. I like the light and I telephone from my wicker chair. I never work in my bedroom. I never take a phone call there or even read the newspaper in bed. I can't stand being in bed and alive. I use a bed just to sleep in, and, Felicia, I sleep like a brick."

Her bedrooms, in the two apartments she has lived in and in the house in Brewster, have been exclamation points in decorating. She has always had a strident sense of color: violet Porthault sheets with chartreuse borders, red and hot-pink combinations, always three black satin pillows. In the early forties her hair was almost blue. It had so much bluing in it that she had to cover her pillow with a linen towel so that the color wouldn't come off. But despite the wild expressions, everything in her rooms is in almost pathological order. Books are piled on her night table in perfect blocks. The dressing table has at least twenty different little pots, bottles, brushes, all lined up. In the living room are collections of horned boxes, plants and drawings, all in a geometric progression. But this is the distillation of a selective person. Her clothes are linear; no frills, no extra clunks of jewelry adorn her. There is a reason for everything she does. She is the most definite and totally self-confident woman I know. Her vocabulary is expressive and she is articulate and to the point. The most extraordinary quality, however, is her originality—across the board. In her manner, her thinking, her performance, *she* is one of a kind. Even age hasn't marked her. Perhaps, as she says, "it's because I haven't noticed it. I've been too busy."

"If you're totally absorbed in your work, totally interested, you're never lonely. Life has been just a great bowl of cherries. I've lived off the money I've made and, when I'm not making much money, I just can't have or do all the things I'd like."

If anything, age becomes Diana better than youth or the middle years. She feels totally comfortable with it. She slips in and out of social activities and diverse social groups like a chameleon.

When she's with artists, she takes on their coloring; with workers, she becomes one of them.

Looking back on seventy-one admitted years, Diana thinks that her earlier life was a preparation and test for the present. She's learned to appreciate more and had the time to log the experience.

"I'm happy now because I've been on this plateau for a while. I think the agony of youth is *too* ghastly. Just *ghastly!* Each age has gone to building towards the next. But"—and she leans back, drawing in on her cigarette holder, in a reflective mood, pulling out her thoughts—"the twenties and the sixties were the two *great* periods of my life. For me, every other period was an interval. The twenties had the same excitement one found in the sixties. They were both youthquakes. Right after the First World War there was renaissance; music was different, clothes were different, even the minds of boys and girls. The world *moved*, and I wish I hadn't been so young and so ignorant or I would have been more involved. The sixties, when I was at *Vogue*, were extraordinary too, new beauties, new boys and girls, jets, everything came on fast and strong and easy. And *youth!* Youth really came to life for the first time in the sixties. They came out to life without waiting for life to come to them. *Aaaaaaah!*" said Diana, pleased with her discovery, "life was marvelous. *Marvelous!* If you wanted to do something, you *did* it. You didn't wait around. You could see a revolution. (Always look at the clothes, Felicia. They reflect the changes within periods.) There was adventure *then*."

Diana Vreeland is on her own new adventure now. No longer active in the magazine world, she has found a happy setting as Special Consultant to the Costume Institute of the Metropolitan Museum, a perfect job for a woman who has spent all her life in fashion. Now she has added another red-walled room to her previous string of red-walled offices, and the fashion exhibit she planned received rave notices.

She proudly proclaims that the Costume Department "is the most beautiful place I've ever been in my life. I took Babe Paley there. She almost died! I took Cecil Beaton up there. He almost died! The museum has assembled the greatest collection of period clothes, dear, it's absolutely *fantastic!* You put your finger on a drawer and it rolls out on ball bearings, and there . . . *there*"—now comes a theatrical pause pointing up the dénouement—"and *there*," she continues finally, "lying before you is a dress perfectly preserved from 1905. You die. It's too marvelous. And just today"—at this point Diana is really carried away —"*today* my white balsam mannequins arrived from Zurich. *I* died! I just fainted dead away."

If one forgets for a moment and thinks that this is just a campy person, an exhibitionist with the heart of an artist and the gestures of an actress, one is brought about abruptly in one's musing.

"Felicia, you must remember. You must realize what a lot of people forget, that I've been a working woman always. My friends talk about places and exhibits and stores in New York. I've told them that all I've seen of the city is going down to work in a cab in the morning and coming back in another cab in the evening. I never buy clothes here because the shops don't stay open late enough (except maybe Bloomingdale's). I don't have any time to shop here, so I buy everything in Europe. I always have."

What of the future? Diana always has something positive to say.

"I see very little action. People, I think, want to go back to a static life because they don't know what to do with themselves. I think the great adventure in fashion journalism has been made. It was all over ten years ago. Now fashion is more in the hands of stores and merchandise managers and buyers. I don't think there's as much originality. And everything is *too expensive!* If I were starting my life now, I'd like to be a computer expert or learn a modern language such as Chinese or Russian. They're going to be the great languages of the future."

Such Vreelandism's are special little nuggets that only such a positively opinionated person like Diana can make. Not always of great intellectual depth, they certainly are memorable little class notes that could only be told by another doer of this special generation.

"New York has no Social center any more. There is no one woman who pulls the town together and knows how to entertain people, to give them a good time and make them happy. New York is too scattered, too fragmented."

On her coming-out party: "It was the biggest thing you ever *saw!* And naturally it was at the Ritz. Every party was at the Ritz in those days."

On fashion: "My interest began when I was born. In Paris."

On her career: "It began when I'd been in New York for about five months. It was 1938. I was *penniless!* I realized I was spending in a week what I would have spent in three months in London. I knew then I'd have to work."

On Society: "Well, that comes very naturally to me. One likes people and they are very attractive. I've never liked anyone but attractive people."

On her children: "They went to school at nine in Switzerland, which is when European boys go away to school. Then to Groton. Then the war. The boys never lived anywhere near us. So we're all the greatest of pals."

On her grandchildren: "I'm *insane* about the girls and boys. I've got two of each. We're *ver-*ee close. Ter*ri*fically so!"

About Clare Luce: "Oh, that marvelous clipped language of hers. And that extraordinary voice. She's fascinating. Clare has been absolutely consistently, con*sis*tently on the mark."

On power: "I'm very interested in power. It's an intoxicant which comes to you through a sort of glory around you."

On criticism: "I do think that any woman who has risen to anything has never been aware of criticism. It's only those who have been left behind who are bitter. When you're on top, you sweep others with you."

About all the women who at one time or another worked for or with Diana on the magazines: "Do you realize that almost everybody who liked fashion worked with me. Now, suddenly, Ali McGraw turns up in the movies. She was my assistant. Lee Radziwill suddenly turns up in the news. She worked with me. You could hardly mention anyone who didn't. I can't even remember who they all are. They were all so charming. *Adored* them all! Loved them. *Doted* on them!"

Diana Vreeland has been such a power in the fashion world that her approval is eagerly sought. Her disapproval most probably dooms one to oblivion. She has been known to shriek about dull hair as though it were human.

"Brush it. *Brush it!*" (the voice rising) "Make it absolutely *glisten*, darling. You over there . . ." (to a scared model) "you have droopy eyelids. When you're in a taxi, open your eyes wide and look *way* up—*way*—*way* up!"

There have been many Vreeland imitators. Women who have tried to copy her way of dressing, her sense of style. But they are only dull copies. Diana Vreeland in her seventies can be found at the Metropolitan Museum. But more truly, she herself is a museum piece to savor and study, for such originality and creativity does not appear many times in a generation.

Peggy Guggenheim

PEGGY GUGGENHEIM, now seventy-six, lives in her villa in the Palazzo Venier Dei Leoni in Venice, one part of which she has turned into a museum whose collection of art will one day be part of her family's Guggenheim Museum in New York City, the founder of which was her uncle, Solomon R. Guggenheim.

A pleasant-looking, short, gray-haired woman, she hardly exhibits the bohemian life style she once led in company with some of the world's greatest artists. She has made a great contribution to the art world—not just in discovering talent but providing the milieu in which artists could gain public recognition.

She opened her first art gallery in 1938 in England, and her shows included works of her friends—abstract, surrealist and *avant-garde* painters. But the public wasn't ready for what she had to offer, so she closed down Guggenheim Jeune in 1939. Her second gallery was called Art of This Century, which she opened in 1942 in New York City. It consisted of a collection of art bought in Europe and put together by her then artist-husband Max Ernst. At that time, with André Breton, she put together a catalogue, *Art of This Century* which has become one of the important sources of reading for modern art connoisseurs.

Her New York gallery was a success but it became too much of a burden, so she closed it in 1946 and moved to her present home in Venice. In the intervening years her collection has been exhibited in Italy, Holland, Belgium, England, Sweden, Switzerland and the United States. But, in truth, so have many others. What makes Peggy Guggenheim noteworthy is that she dared to be different and an individual when her background and her contemporaries were hamstrung by the mores and social codes of her era.

She was born into the well-known German-Jewish family of "Our Crowd" status, the Seligmans. She was the daughter of Benjamin and Florette Guggenheim, but from the age of five on she seemed headed in a most unconventional direction. Her father was quite a character. She remembers him as always having mistresses and with seeming ease going through a great deal of his smelting fortune. He will best be remembered by her and history for performing a gallant act on the fatal voyage of the *Titanic* in 1912. Refusing, as the ship was sinking, the offer of a life vest by the deck steward, he and his male secretary went to their cabins and dressed in evening clothes so that they would go down with the ship as "gentlemen." In so doing, they gave their places in the lifeboat to a woman and child.

After the death of her father and of her grandfather four years later, Peggy inherited four hundred and fifty thousand dollars in trust, as did her two sisters, one of whom, in her memoirs, she admitted hating. In fact, she says of her childhood that "it was excessively unhappy. I have no pleasant memories of any kind and it seems that it was one long-protracted agony." Her mother and she never got along and she was bored with her "*haute* Jewish bourgeoisie friends." Indeed Florette was an extremely odd woman and had many strange habits. One was always repreating a phrase three times. She also carried three coats at all times and was constantly changing them. On the hottest day she would wear two silver foxes and then carry a fan to cool herself. She had three watches; one she wore around her neck on a chain, the second on her wrist, and the third was part of her lorgnette. She hated spending money but did put money in trust for her daughters and gave Peggy a fur coat or a car every year. She was, however, a secret gambler and a miserly tipper.

In 1918, Peggy had taken a desk job helping young officers buy uniforms at a discount. She had no sense of direction. It was wartime and she became engaged to a flyer. He subsequently dropped her. His name, she recalls, was Harold Wessel. Having nothing better to do in 1920, she had her nose fixed by a surgeon who was a specialist in making women beautiful. It was done under a local anesthetic and was hideously painful. "But

I came out with something resembling a tip-tilted nose like a flower."

From this point on, for twenty-one years, Peggy Guggenheim starred in a series of self-admitted romances. First, there was Lawrence Vail, who was twenty-nine when they first met in New York. He was an "incurable neurotic" but had some strange fascination for Peggy. She moved to Paris, not to return to the United States for twenty-one years. She was twenty-three and, as she frankly states in her autobiography, lost her virginity to Vail in a hotel room in Paris on the Rue de Verneuil. This was the beginning of a Bohemian way of life for Peggy. She and Vail were married and remained in stormy relationship for seven years. Her only two children were born of this union. They were divorced in 1930. In 1939, her mother died, leaving her another four hundred and fifty thousand dollars. John Holms was her second husband, to whom she claims she was never legally married. He seemed to have taught her a great deal about life in the five years they lived together and totally dominated her. He had an answer to everything, and other people bored him. Gradually he became unhappy, started to drink, and in 1934 died on the operating table under anaesthetic for a minor operation.

After his death, Peggy, still searching for love, went to live with a friend of John's whom she had met while still married. He was married too and they started having an affair. When he became a Communist, three years later, she left him and went to live in London. It was here that her interest in art began and another series of lovers took over: a young surrealist poet called Mittens; a strange man called Oblomov; a frustrated writer; a young surrealist painter; another artist, Yves Tanguy (he was married); an English sculptor called Llewellyn (also married) by whom she became pregnant, then had an abortion at a nursing home; a hairdresser; an old fisherman; a shipper of paintings. And then she met Max Ernst, the painter, when he was fifty and living in Marseilles. He had been married twice before. They lived together across two continents for a long time and finally were married in Virginia. Marriage became unbearable. He had girl friends. She took a lover called Luigi, took drugs to sleep, and nearly went crazy. At this point in her unhappy life a British Intelligence Service worker, effete and extravagant, discovered

Peggy. He was in his thirties and they took an apartment together. This was really a spiritual relationship and not a physical
one. By this time, Peggy had developed her own philosophy.
"One lives and learns, or maybe one lives too much to learn.
Somehow I have always found husbands much more satisfactory
after marriage than during."

Peggy Guggenheim wrote of her free-swinging life in two
autobiographies, one in 1946 and one in 1960. She frankly admits
to leading a wildly romantic, uninhibited life. But she also admits
that it was not a preset plan and that she never set out to be an
enfant terrible. "I just *was* one." She has no regrets about that
period of her life; for her it seemed the natural way to live at
that time.

What has changed her in the last twenty-five years? Many fac-
tors. "My daughter Pegeen was a wonderfully talented painter.
She died six years ago and nobody knows why. She was just
found dead. We were terribly close to one another and her death
has left me quite bankrupt. Her loss and my becoming older have
caused me to quiet down considerably. I am more indifferent to
everything than formerly, and if you call that inner peace,
maybe you're right. My life is no longer turbulent in any sense
of the word, and I intend to live in Venice always. But if I were
asked by young people for my advice on how to lead their lives,
I would answer—to the fullest."

So, for a restless, unbridled spirit, time has settled happenings
for her which were shocking to that generation. But in her early
gropings she added immeasurably to the art of collecting for the
public to now enjoy. And she will always be remembered for
her aid to so many painters as well as to little-known American
artists. Her early recognition of Jackson Pollock was perhaps
one of her greatest achievements. So, nearing the end of an un-
structured, free life, now Venice has proved the haven she
sought unconsciously for so many years. Here she can enjoy the
treasures that her keen artistic sense discovered, and the public
will have the benefit of her interesting selections.

Alice Roosevelt Longworth

THE GREATEST, GRANDEST DAME in America is ninety-one years old, and Alice Roosevelt Longworth is still going strong. She enjoys bright, intelligent people and in her musty, mementoed house in Washington, D.C., she has entertained the greats of the world. Certainly an invitation to be with her at teatime, a daily ritual, is a mind-honing experience. No one is spared her tea and cookies and her delicious verbal barbs. The ambiance of the old house has remained unchanged for decades, and all the old furniture is covered with crumpled plastic "so cat won't get at it." The rooms defy traditional-decorating buffs, and it is part of her humor to allow poison ivy to grow around the entrance to her door. She, not the house or the contents, is the star attraction, and her popularity is such that, were she physically able—but more important, socially eager—she would be at every event in the nation's capital. She is, however, as selective about whom she wishes to see as in the invitations she accepts, and she is bemused and amused at the continued interest in her activities by the public and the press. Her storied hats, and her acid and witty remarks, never pass unobserved.

Fame is really her trademark, and she bears it and bears herself regally and with patrician patience. Age certainly has not dimmed her perspicacity, plucked freshly from a fertile mind, and she has an insatiable appetite for reading and keeping up with news and world events.

Her memory is staggering, and without hesitation she instantly recalls her childhood.

We were sitting at her tea table and I was balancing questions and a teacup at the same time. Her cousin, Joseph Alsop, the columnist, had brought me to meet her and discreetly withdrew when we began talking.

"My mother died as a result of my birth," she remembered. "She was my father's, Teddy Roosevelt's, first wife, and apparently very fetching and feminine when he met her while attending Harvard. Her death was a great shock to him, and he had said that life was over for him and he could never love again. But I was three when he remarried Edith Carew, a woman whom he had known for years," Alice continued, "and Father saying life was over was just so much nonsense. It was just one of those silly Victorian theories.

"Why, I even remember their wedding in 1887. I was frightfully pleased with myself standing in my Auntie Bye's house, all dressed up, holding a large bunch of flowers at the top of the stairs—very happy about everything, waiting for my new mama. I can see myself now, slowly walking down the staircase, and I was only three." And then, in her typical immodest fashion, she added, "I was rather sweet, if I do say so myself."

Alice fortunately took to her new mother immediately. "I really wanted to call my parents Mama and Papa but the emphasis in our family was politics and America and these titles sounded too British, so we all called them Mother and Father. My own mother was never discussed—ever."

Her childhood years were happy and carefree with added half-brothers and sisters, all of whom, surrounded by Roosevelt cousins, would make a built-in community at Sagamore Hill. Mischievous, willful and independent, she set her own pace, growing as an adolescent with the image that her future was to be a wife and mother. Accounts state that she was her father's favorite. Protesting, she set the record straight. "I wasn't. I just wasn't Father's favorite. He was a terribly nice man and I was devoted to him, but I often defied him."

Owen Wister, a friend of her father's, asked him once if he couldn't somehow control his willful daughter. T.R. replied, "I can either run the country or control Alice. Not both."

Her defiance was always amusing and spirited. She acquired a pet snake which she called Emily Spinach (Emily "after a friend," Spinach "because he was green"). She would take great delight bringing him to a friend's house for the weekend, where on one occasion the hostess opened the bedroom door and, to her horror, found Emily asleep on the bed with her recently shed skin next to her. Quincy Shaw, Alice's cousin, also gave her a ferret, which, with the snake, evoked all kinds of shock. She adored smoking cigarettes in open defiance of her family and the social traditions of the era. "Father had said I was never to smoke under his roof, but I remember," she said very pleased with herself, "circumventing that rule by kneeling by the fireplace and puffing up the chimney. I also sat on the roof of the White House smoking, and I was one of the first girls to drink in public. Yes, I was very bad," she brazenly admitted. "That's why I have a great sympathy with the young. I only cared about having fun in my early years. I was amused by life. I never took a serious interest in anything that nice young girls were supposed to. I never even really thought of marriage. I do remember, though, being a bridesmaid at Eleanor and Franklin's wedding. That was 1905. Yes, because I was married the next year. Eleanor couldn't come to my wedding because she was pregnant with Anna. Isn't it idiotic? I don't think it was because of her pregnancy, but, my dear," she said in a mincing high voice reminiscent of Eleanor's, "it just wasn't considered quite nice, something like unchic."

When it comes to sentiment and memories about her husband, Alice Longworth is rather purposely forgetful, and the subject of her marriage is not one of her favorite topics. "Where did I first meet my husband?" She sat back and toyed with the answer to my question. "In Washington. He was in Congress, I suppose. I really can't remember. Except my father did say, 'There's a new Congressman coming and you might find him useful. He's Harvard and Porcellian.'" One supposes that Alice got married at twenty-two because that was the accepted route for a young lady to take. She gives no reason for the alliance and one can only presume that she agreed to marry Longworth, who was pursuing her because no other opportunity presented itself. They became engaged and, since Alice hated any show of feelings, she waited to tell the news to her stepmother while she was brushing her teeth. "It was the only practical way of telling her because I didn't want any sentimentality . . . any of those dramatics . . . lowering the voice." (Alice lowered hers accordingly.) "My father didn't have anything particular to say about us because, I suppose, they realized something was going on, and besides . . . they knew me. I wouldn't have stood for any dramatics." As to whether the marriage was a happy one, her only answer is, "I suppose so." She candidly told me that she had no particular feelings about her husband. With definiteness she said, "No. None. Absolutely none." For obscure reaons, she waited eighteen years before having her first and only child. "Yes, it was a tidy age," she admitted. "It was just something that happened and the publicity was a nuisance, so I kept it in the dark—more or less." She named her first child Paulina, who, when she grew up, married a man called Alexander Sturm. They had one child, Joanna, but Sturm at thirty-one, died tragically under mysterious circumstances. The cause of death was attributed to the effects of taking non-narcotic drugs. Whatever the reason, her mother has chosen not to think or speak of it. "No, I don't feed on tragedies. I've disciplined myself." Her granddaughter, Joanna, in her mid-twenties, lives with her, and the rapport between the two, despite the age gap, is remarkable. She keeps Alice up to date on the woman's movement and the outside world, and her youthfulness invigorates her grandmother. A headstrong young woman, she seems to have great control and influence over her famous relative, and, in turn, Alice accepts her attitudes, brusqueness and lack of manners without visible pain. She has the willfulness of her grandmother, but not the wit or amusing charm.

Alice Longworth is a study in ambivalence. She has the remarkable quality of self-restraint and inner calm, yet a total lack of respect for convention and emotion. When her husband was defeated for Congress, he was definitely upset. "Well," his widow said, unsympathetically and quite frankly, "he behaved rather badly." This remark made me believe he had done something quite terrible. Indeed, in her eyes, he had. "Imagine," she told me, "he cried, the stupid fool. I told him that it wasn't an attractive thing to do. A defeat isn't that terrible. I told him it was perfect nonsense to take it that way. 'You'll come back,' I assured him, and of course he did . . . as Speaker of the House." Her chief objections was that he allowed his emotions to show. The difference with me, you see, is that all my life I've learned to shrug my shoulders naturally."

Being brought up with politics and politicians for as long as she can remember, she developed a toughness. She even says about her famous father, "I can certainly see why people used to dislike my father, loathed my father—a horrid man, great big teeth, bouncing around, throwing his weight around. Those cartoons—those cartoons—marvelous—'Bad Little Teddy' and 'Oh, Mercy Hannah.'"

"Oh, everyone asks me about my cousin Eleanor. She was a dear, but she was not particularly interesting for me. She was an amazing do-gooder but for me not exciting. I knew she had a miserable life as a child—just a wretched family life. Imagine being called 'Granny' as a child. It was really vicious. Later in life of course she turned very pious and kindly in her reminiscences, but I did enjoy doing take-offs on her high voice and her gestures, but then I even did them for Eleanor and the children upstairs in one of the rooms of the White House. I think she was even amused. But it was Franklin whom I really enjoyed. We could have had much more fun had we seen more of each other. I really liked him. We had lovely, silly times together, and we enjoyed laughing at the same things."

At ninety-one now, most of the old friends, admirers and family are gone. "I have only friends of my own age left, and age has certainly put a cramp in my physical style." She is very thin and no longer walks with assurance. "I'm not nearly as useful as I was. I still stride a bit. I don't eat much. I have," she said sadly, "in my old age lost my greed. Lost my greed. I once weighed a hundred and fifty. Now I'm too thin. But I guess it's better to shrivel than to swell. I used to smoke. *It* gave *me* up. Never cared for drinking except good wine. As a debutante I'd drink champagne and my parents would say, 'We think it would be better if you didn't, because you're naturally high-spirited and people will think you are drunk if they see you with a drink.' So I only did it a little."

Despite the infirmities, two mastectomies ("I'm the topless wonder of Massachusetts Avenue"), and less activity, in Washington a visit with Alice Longworth is as much sought after as a visit with any figure in government. And getting to see her is no

easy task, since she doesn't believe in answering any correspondence and leads no particularly organized day. When she isn't at
a dinner party (and she goes out less and less), she's either reading or sleeping. "I'm like a polyp—take a nap, go to sleep—and
to keep me from being lonely and bored I have my books. I'm
really too old to travel. I'd be a nuisance and a terrible responsibility. Although I'd really love to go to China again. Chou
En-lai is the only person in the world now that I'd like to meet. I
haven't been to China since 1905, but now I'd like to go back
and take a look at the Great Wall again," she mused.

The dose of publicity that accompanies her every utterance
and appearance doesn't seem to disturb her. She's annoyed that
the newspapers said that she's known every President since
Benjamin Harrison and has been to every presidential inauguration since she was old enough to stand up. "I missed the Nixon
second inauguration because I was ill. Actually, it's the first one
I should have remembered going to. The Nixons are old friends,
that's why I would have gone, but normally I never go. Those
occasions are such bores. I remember hearing my father sworn
in as Vice-president when I was little, but so many stories I hear
about me are such tripe."

Her entertaining is sporadic but her guests are always interesting, although she claims the dinners just happen and are totally
unplanned. She is a great admirer of Henry Kissinger and likes all
kinds of talented people, young and old, but they must be able
to parry with her intellectually. Joseph Alsop, her devoted and
brilliant cousin, comes by to needle and amuse and give his in-
terpretation on world affairs. She is still close to her sister Ethel
and her brother Archie. Her contact with present-day politicians
has dwindled. She knew the Kennedys and liked the President
and his sister Eunice very much. She admires Rose Kennedy—
"delightful, sharp, has all sorts of qualities. She's been extraordinary with all those children and the tragedies. She's so effi-
cient. She can go take a walk, hop into church, have a little talk
with God, feel the better for it and then go on."

Alice hasn't the same religious feeling, although her own
daughter became a Catholic and Joanna's godmother is Clare
Boothe Luce. As far as Alice's religious background is concerned,
she hasn't changed. As a child she refused to be confirmed

"because, to me, it was perfectly useless nonsense if you didn't have faith. God, no, I've never been to church," and she seems not to feel the urge to be comforted.

The stories still swirl around Alice Longworth. In her book *Crowded Hours*, written in 1933, she made all sorts of outrageous statements. She didn't like to dance, she wrote, because men didn't know about deodorants then and they smelled. She supported her father's running in 1912 on the Bull Moose ticket, although her husband, Nicholas, was running for re-election to Congress on the Republican ticket. She did everything possible to attract attention and somehow, living out what must be dreary days compared to the past, the old, tacky, worn-out furniture comes alive because of the lady who dwells within these walls and whose mind and tongue transcend age and politics. A visit is merely appetite-whetting to learn about another time, to listen to the acrid, but certainly refreshing, wit of an honest observer of nine decades of history who's towering, unsmothered, outspoken spirit (in the words of this generation) "says it like it is."

Epilogue

It is clear that life is not over for women past seventy. Given the precious gift of reasonable health and the desire to continue the pursuits of a lifetime, there are still the unused years ahead. Certainly they have the advantage of experience, which youth does not, and surely, despite mistakes in judgment, they have developed a deeper sense of responsibility and a special method of communication with people that is more sensitive than that of those of us who are younger.

I find that these special older women developed keener sense of their environment and an appreciation grown of respect. They are genuinely interested in other people and their lives, of new advances in varied fields of current happenings. They take greater advantage of time and are grateful and uncomplaining of their lives.

Acceptance and the sheer joy of living characterize this group far more than succeeding generations. Joy of family, pleasure in their work, pride in their creations make them exciting to be with and a never-ending source of enjoyment to share their total of human experience.

Except perhaps for Jacqueline Onassis, Alice Longworth at ninety-one is America's most revered and delightful lady. No one who is interested in history hesitates to seek her out and benefit from her stellar personality, undimmed by age or events. So too with the other doers and dowagers whom we respect and honor while they are still part of our lifetime! The century is drawing to a close and with it many of the mores, life styles and legends of the past.

My children and I have found a great affinity and a security in knowing many of these celebrated women, who will, as will we all, pass from sight. While these chapters are certainly not in-depth portraits, I hope they give some inspiration, some hope and creativity for all of us as we grow older and, with maturity and generosity of spirit, share ourselves with all who wish to have been our friends.